SERGE

FOR
THE
LOVE
OF
GOOD
FOOD

SERGE DANSEREAU:
A 20-year journey through
the Australian food scene

ABC
Books

CONTENTS

ACKNOWLEDGMENTS

I WAS VERY RELUCTANT TO WRITE THIS BOOK, NEVER THINKING that my story could have much attraction for the public. So the credit for this book goes to Jane Ogilvie, my agent, as her persistence convinced me to do it in the end.

I thank Cath Proctor, my editor, who made my words seem far more polished than my original text was. Her constant reminder that she loved my stories and tribulations in my various kitchens gave me the renewed confidence to pursue my writing.

My impossible deadline was just another challenge to rise to. The credit for making the deadline should go to Kristy, my assistant at The Bathers' Pavilion, for not only typing a great amount of text, but also for prodding me when I slipped behind.

I obviously have a great deal of gratitude for Yvette, my wife, who again put up with me being never being at home due to my work commitments. She also endured my spiritual absence between my return from work, late at night, and my waking her up when I finally made it to bed in the wee hours of the morning, after I finished my writing.

There are many people who I have worked with since my arrival in Australia in the early 80s who have made most of my achievements possible. This list includes all the chefs that I worked with or who worked for me, including Ron, Andreas, Xavier, Terence, Udo, José, Phil, Ross, Birk, Lucy and so many others.

I would also like to acknowledge the friendship I received from all the other chefs around Australia. They welcomed me and gave me the chance to see so many personal approaches to innovative cooking.

But, most importantly, I have to thank all the small producers, merchants, fishermen, suppliers and growers who came to me with their great products. They made my menus so much more interesting and have, in the process, helped make the food we offer in Australia so much more vibrant, fresh and on par with some of the best the world has to offer.

1

MY FATHER'S GARDEN

I T WAS 5AM AND I WAS ALREADY WIDE-AWAKE WITH THE excitement of starting my first paid job. I had heard that a friend of my father was looking for pickers to collect his bean crops. His field was on the Boucherville Island, in the Saint Lawrence River, and it had been traditionally used for decades as market gardens. From the edge of the river as young boys, my friends and I could distinguish cornfields and we had often dreamed of building a raft to cross the river and land on the mysterious islands. Now I was to make the journey across on a barge that carried the pickers and an old truck to load the crops that we picked. I felt very grown up, even though I was only 12 years old.

The sun was just rising as I caught the ferry over to the island. By the time I reached the fields the sky was stunning, softly illuminating the low green bean plants that were neatly set in rows of beautiful black soil. Each of us was given a few jute bags and our instructions, then we were all dropped by truck into different groups. Once we had filled a jute bag we were to just leave it in the row and start filling the next one. The truck would eventually follow to pick up the bags.

After an hour or two I realised just how hard this work really was. We worked all morning until lunchtime, when it got too hot to work the field. By lunchtime I had filled several bags, and while this was nowhere near as many as the experienced pickers I still felt great satisfaction. We got paid 0.02c a pound and I think I made $5.00 on my first day. I was dirty, thirsty and tired, but I was also thrilled to be working.

From that point on I always worked: having a newspaper run, painting the church, and just helping here and there. I enjoyed the responsibilities of work. Despite the fact that my first paid job was with food, I did not realise at the time that my long-term future rested with food and cooking.

I come from a food family, though we did not really think of ourselves as such. Ever since I can remember my father worked in his garden. My father's garden was a large plot covering nearly the whole backyard of our home. We were a family of five children so the produce was very important as money was always sparse.

Not only did my father grow the common and expected garden vegetables like potatoes, beans, peas, carrots, tomatoes, beetroot and onions, but he also grew some of the more exotic varieties for the time like rhubarb, raspberries, strawberries, plum, asparagus and fresh herbs. Some years he had a bigger variety then others, but it was always diverse and plentiful. He even grew the new and exciting zucchini, which my mother used in many different dishes, including relish, jam, cakes, soups and chutney. My mother was always preserving fruit and vegetables. A huge freezer was one of her prized possessions and she used it to freeze the summer fruits, as well as the pies she prepared. She also canned other garden goodies and made jam from fresh blueberries that we had picked on our camping trips. My parents loved using the produce that they grew, collected, fished or hunted for. They did this more for the love of cooking than for any real sense of necessity, even if it all came in handy.

My mother did the everyday cooking, while my father cooked mostly on camping trips and when we went fishing. The real cook in our family however was my grandmother. She was a natural and a tireless worker. She used to work for lumberjack crews, cooking meals for up to twenty men in the Canadian wilderness. The crew would spend the winter chopping trees (usually upriver from a sawmill). The cut logs were dragged by horse to the frozen river and at the end of winter when the ice started melting and the river started flowing again the men would decamp and ride the logs back to the sawmill at the mouth of the river. Logjams were common and hard to clear, so they sometimes used dynamite to unblock the passage. This was really dangerous, as the sudden rush of logs could be fatal if you were in the way. The journey to the sawmill often took a few weeks, and when the logs and their workers arrived at the mill the lumberjacks changed roles and increased the miller work force for the summer.

During the winter my grandmother would live in the cabins with the men, where she cooked for them on her own. At every meal, each man would consume one freshly baked loaf of bread and a stew or large meat pie. The meals were huge but the men were big and they were always hungry from the exhausting work.

In later years my grandfather bought a combined grocery and butcher shop in the east of Montréal. My grandmother would cook for the shop, making beautiful thick apple pies, molasses and raisin pies, cherry pies, meat pies and many other dishes from traditional recipes. My grandfather was an experienced butcher and I always remember with fascination the quarters of beef hanging in his cool room.

Food was always around us in one way or another. One of my uncles owned a dairy farm and in summer we often visited. As young children it was fascinating seeing the cows being milked, and we loved playing with all the cats. At the end of each winter we always got to visit the 'Cabane à Sucre', a maple syrup cabin set in the forest of Québec, where huge vats of collected maple water was boiled down to make the beautiful maple syrup. Every year my father would make wine from imported grapes in the basement of our house. It was a simple upbringing that was rich in experience.

My father and brothers loved fishing and we constantly went on camping and fishing trips. Anything that we caught would end up either in the frying pan or we would take it home to be frozen and used later on. I learnt a lot about survival and self-sufficiency from spending time with my father, he was a strong quiet type who expected you to learn by watching him.

I remember camping once with my father in an incredible national park. We caught a beautiful trout for our dinner, which we cooked on the campfire. He then cooked his famous baked beans in the sand overnight to have them for breakfast the next day. (My father would always cook beans in the sand overnight when we went camping and I still use his recipe to this day.) For lunch the next day we pan-fried frog legs that he had taught me to catch with a fishing line and a touch of red thread wrapped around a hook. The huge frogs went for it every time.

I loved camping; I loved the forest, the lake, the rivers and the wild animals. I felt totally at ease in the wild forest of Canada and I eventually joined the Boy Scouts. There was a time where I wanted to become a forester working for Park Canada; I would have been quite happy doing that. Fishing, on the other hand, was quite literally for me a different kettle of fish. I have always hated fishing; I find it boring and just do not have the patience for it. Unfortunately for me, our family fishing trips were not consigned just to the summer months. To my extreme reluctance my father loved to do this in the winter as well.

How does one fish in the Canadian winter? Well you drive your car on the ice of a frozen lake or river. You find a favourite fishing spot and you dig holes in the ice with a special power drill—sometimes up to one hundred. You install special fishing lines on tilting sticks and you wait until the fish bite. If you are mad about fishing (like my family was) you have also a little cabin that you assemble on the ice semi-permanently. Our cabin even possessed a small wood stove. Those in the family who were old enough used brandy as a form of antifreeze while they waited for the fish to bite. The rest of us just froze. Winter fishing does have its fans but I really was never one of them; I physically could not cope with the cold of Canada. I was always the first of my friends to freeze to the bone on skiing trips. I will always miss the Canadian countryside, but only in summer.

My father was never content to stay still. One year he had planted too many carrots in his garden, so when the first snow came very early we still had a lot of carrots left in the soil. There was at least one foot of snow and the remaining carrots were slowly freezing. He had a very pained expression on his face until he suddenly said to me, 'Serge, go and get the carrots from the garden.'

Not one to question him, I went outside with a wheelbarrow and shovelled all the snow off the carrot patch. I then dug the carrots out of the partially frozen ground, and we took them to the basement of the house where he had his workshop. At that time my father made wine from imported fresh Californian grapes, so he decided to turn the carrots into wine. But how do you make wine out of carrots? My father first juiced all the carrots and then he added sugar, yeast and water.

The orange slurry fermented but it became a type of spirit rather then a wine; it was probably over 70% proof!

This exercise was a good attempt at not wasting the garden bounty but it took a terrible toll on many of my friends, as I became the source of their first encounter with alcohol. Over the next winter and summer I started to siphon away my father's supply. Once I had taken all the bottles from the back row I then emptied the front row bottles and cleverly refilled them with water. My father didn't realise what I was doing; because he thought the wine was a failure he didn't drink it, however my friends loved it.

The effect that potent alcohol has on inexperienced young drinkers is quite staggering! I remember begging some of my friends to get down from the tree they had climbed like monkeys; at times their behaviour was turning dangerous and embarrassing. One night I decided to host a small party for some friends. We proceeded to have a great time with the carrot wine until things got out of control with a couple of my friends. We all ended up in the back of police cars after being picked up for drunkenness. The worst ones were driven directly home to their parents but I was sober enough to salvage our bikes and bring them back home. Suffice to say that nearly every mother of the neighbourhood eventually lectured me for my contribution to the debauchery of their sons. Yes, I loved food, but I was starting to also love wine.

———

My mother began to get slightly concerned about my future when my school results started to falter. I always started the year with great intentions; for the first few months I would be focused and dedicated, often finishing first in many of my subjects. Then boredom would inevitably set in and slowly I would lose interest. We both realised that I needed to think about my future and start getting some work experience to focus my energy.

It is always helpful to use a family contact when trying to get a job at a young age. I had done all the usual paid chores like having a paper run, painting and other casual work, but it was time to find something more regular for the weekend and in the school holidays. My mother decided to phone my uncle at the hotel kitchen where he worked.

My mother's sister was married to one of the most famous chefs of Canada: Jean Merlet, a Frenchman who used to be a traiteur in Paris. Jean Merlet was by then the Executive Chef of the Château Montebello, which was built in 1930 (the same year as The Bathers' Pavilion). When it was built it was the talk of North America, and it was featured in all the newspapers across the continent. It was a giant Swiss-style log cabin, built in from 10,000 huge cedar trees. It had a three-story atrium with a six-sided massive fireplace at its centre.

For the first thirty years the Château Montebello served as a private club for the political elite of the Canadian federal government, before becoming part of a famous chain of hotels that were built and run by one of the oldest railroad companies in Canada. They had a series of incredible hotels, including the Château Frontenac in Québec City (perched on the amazing cliff tops of the city), a stunning hotel at Banff Springs, one in Lake Louise in the Rocky Mountains, and the Empress of India on Vancouver Island.

My aunt asked my uncle to recommend what would be the best way for me to get a job in a hotel. He recommended that I contact Klaus Odermatt, a former colleague of his. Jean and Klaus had worked together at the Château Champlain in Montréal. Klaus was now the Executive Chef at the Holiday Inn Longueuil and he was willing to take me on as a plongeur, or kitchen hand. Klaus Odermatt was to become my future guide and inspiration; it was a turning point in my life.

2

LEARNING IN LONGUEUIL

I STARTED WORK AS A PLONGEUR IN MONSIEUR ODERMATT'S kitchen in Longueuil, where I was washing dishes with a wild bunch of Haitian immigrants. That was in a sense my first contact with a totally different culture and for a naive 16-year-old boy it was a fascinating look into the behaviour of older, independent male adults who were not living at home.

Monsieur Odermatt was certainly the embodiment of all the best qualities you would wish to have in a chef. Hard working to an extreme, talented, precise, silent and with piercing dark eyes that he used for communicating. He was lean, tall, and fit, with a goatee, long before they became popular many decades later. He spoke very little, waiting for me to use my resources and initiative to do whatever work needed to be done.

After finishing school, I would take the bus for thirty minutes to work and work all evening and then come home again. My mother said (I cannot remember this) that sometimes when I arrived back home after completing my evening shift, a message would be waiting

8

for me to see if I could return to do the overnight shift as the intended worker had not shown. I apparently never once hesitated to get on my pushbike and then go back and work until 7am.

I loved working in a big hotel kitchen. The work was hard and fast and extremely demanding, and the sense of camaraderie was excellent. There was a lot of pressure, especially because I mostly worked on weekends, which were their busiest times. As well as having a busy coffee shop and an elegant hotel dining room, the hotel did a staggering amount of trade with functions. The most fascinating aspect of the weekend was the series of weddings, mostly large Italian ones, where ten courses of interesting but traditional Italian food were consumed. It was a whole new world for me and I got the bug big time of working under pressure.

In summer the place was even busier, so I kept my head down, just trying to keep up with the fast-talking and quick-thinking crew. Monsieur Odermatt would often come and help to organise the sorting of all the dirty plates coming in from functions, room service, the coffee shop and the dining room. It was just amazing how many things we needed to wash: plates, glasses, serving trays, butter dishes, flower vases, coffee cups, food platters, pots, pans, roasting trays, food storage containers, display mirrors for the food and multitudes of other items that a large kitchen needed to have. Then there was also the wall, floor and fridges to wash, the garbage to take out and the bins to be washed—it never seemed to end.

I soon realised that these kitchens were very structured and disciplined places that focused on making deadlines everyday on every shift. The pressure was constant, nerves were always raw and the clashes of different personalities made for interesting working conditions. At that time Swiss chefs dominated the kitchen. The Swiss actually controlled the top positions in most hotel kitchens in North America. It was a very closed little world, a community of ex pats who trained in the same country, used the same methods and liked to stick together. Despite the fact that they viewed other nationalities with suspicion I only had admiration for their professionalism, knowledge and work ethic.

There were all types of functions at the hotel, from sit-down business dinners to buffets to pool parties. The buffet was extremely popular for large groups as it offered a wide choice of foods. A few months into my time at the hotel I was asked to come in earlier on the Saturday and prepare tray after tray of bacon for the breakfast buffet. Over the next few years the trays of bacon became one of my regular tasks. One day Monsieur Odermatt asked me to get dressed in a chef's uniform so he could use me to carve the meat on a buffet for a large function. It was one of those jobs that most of the chefs hated to perform, standing with a hat in the function room. That was the first time I had held a knife professionally and it felt great.

—

For the next year I worked in the hotel most weekends. I followed the instructions that the Sous Chefs gave me and I'd alternate between washing dishes, emptying garbage bins, washing pots or washing floors. I became quite good at producing a clean floor using extremely hot water and just the right amount of soap. Often inexperienced plongeurs would not change their water often enough and they would end up with a very greasy floor. The floor was made from a type of extremely slippery terrazzo tile. When it was wet you couldn't tell if it was washed properly, but after 15 minutes the floor would dry and if it hadn't been done properly you could see all the streaky grease marks. Klaus was fanatical about his floor and to this day I feel the same: I like my kitchen floors spotless.

Increasingly I got to do basic food preparation tasks like peeling potatoes in the automatic rotary machine or shredding cabbage in the specially built industrial shredder. I also continued to be assigned to slicing roast beef for the buffet. I had to learn to slice economically as only so many rumps were roasted for a given function. If you ran out then you had to stand there and explain to a hungry crowd why you didn't have any more roast beef. I managed each slice judiciously, by giving just two slices before being told by the customer that they wanted a third one. I knew I had to be careful. Well-done pieces were often requested and the trick was to save the crusty exterior of the rump ready for the inevitable request for well-done meat. To this day I am able to eat any type of meat, from blue to rare, medium rare to well done. I normally prefer medium rare but never make a fuss if I cannot get that. If I ended up with a whole rump unused at the end of a function then Klaus would use it the next day for either sandwiches in the café or cold roast beef on the lunch buffets.

In the middle of the summer, during the school holidays, my tasks changed markedly towards more work in the kitchen. I was washing fewer dishes during the day but still joined my Haitian friends in the evening to help with the bulk of the washing up. I really enjoyed working with them. Most of them had university degrees and they all were so happy despite the fact they could only find work as plongeurs in the hotel kitchen. They felt that there were much better opportunities in Québec than back home. It certainly reinforced in me the need to find a career and I began to realise just how much I enjoyed working in the hotel.

Being able to handle a knife I was gradually allowed to help in the coffee shop section of the kitchen. I became very good at making Club and Reuben sandwiches, which were pastrami and sauerkraut on rye bread. Smoked meat and hot pastrami sandwiches were very popular in Montréal and every coffee shop menu included club sandwiches as well as a big selection of hot smoked meats. In specialised smoked meat restaurants they employed dedicated carvers who earned incredible salaries. Rumour was that they earned more than $700 a week; considering that a qualified chef earned around $250 a week it

11

sounded like an incredible skill to have. I applied myself even more with my roast beef slicing on the buffet and I became quite adept at giving people the impression that they had a large slice when in fact it was quite thin.

My duties as a sandwich maker were challenging. There were only two chefs working for both the coffee shop and the restaurant and their food preparation sections were in the same kitchen. I had to make their mise en place, cut their tomatoes, fetch bags of frozen chips from the freezer, and roast the bacon for the Club sandwiches. I also prepared pickles, sliced onions, cooked the spaghetti, filled containers with the various sauces, and ensured there was enough bread in that section of the kitchen.

When all that was done I had to keep up with the orders, which inevitably come thick and fast because the café was usually full until 11pm. I needed to work fast, be clean and not lose the plot. Within a few weeks I was left on my own to run the coffee shop on some shifts. The menu was predictable for a coffee shop, featuring such North American favourites as barbecued chicken sandwich. This consisted of two slices of white bread, chicken, and piping hot barbecue sauce, served with chips and coleslaw. Actually everything in the coffee shop was served with chips and coleslaw except for the dessert. I loved the sense of responsibility and the fact that I could run that section.

On the other side of the kitchen was Serge Guidit, a French-speaking Swiss Chef Saucier who was responsible for the restaurant cooking. I loved Serge, not because he had the same first name as me but because he was a real chef, as opposed to a coffee shop cook. I first met him when I started cleaning the kitchen in the overnight shift. Serge would normally finish last in the kitchen and then he would take a long shower and groom himself impeccably before he left the hotel. He was a creature of habit, doing the same thing, everyday, at the same time. When I arrived at work and was changing into my work gear he would be finishing his shower and getting dressed. We would always have a small chat. Serge was very lean and fit, with very defined muscles that were developed from years of climbing hills and mountains on foot back in Switzerland. His dream was to earn plenty of money in Montréal and then to return to Switzerland to take over the post office his parents ran in a small mountain village. I could see him delivering mail by foot and being quite happy doing that for decades to come.

Behind the stove Serge was a great chef: fastidious, precise and extremely demanding with the waiters. He did not suffer fools and when it was time to pick up an order for a table the waiters needed to be there or he would go berserk. He was obviously a perfectionist and there was no comparison between his sauces and the ones I served in the coffee shop. Whereas my sauces were made from powder and water, his sauces were made from homemade stock, wine, cognac and cream. It was fascinating to see him cook prime rib of beef, Yorkshire pudding, Sole meunière, langoustines à l'ail, pernod snails, curry prawns and fillet mignon forestière. The idea that you could travel the world by cooking in foreign kitchens was seeded in my brain.

I continued working on the buffet and I was shown how to decorate the meat platters that were so popular at that time. There was paté campagne, salami, pain de viande and every type imaginable of ham, pork and veal loaf. I learned to glaze ham with chaud froid, decorate whole turkeys, poach salmon and giant halibut, and set them on these huge mirrors that enhanced the cold food so well. I learnt how to make salad by the bucket loads and learned how to arrange them in the big wooden bowls that they used on the buffet. I was also shown how to set a buffet table with beer cases as building blocks to create height and how to cover the buffet with tablecloth to cover the table and beer boxes. I was soon able to produce a whole buffet on my own as long as the experienced chef did the hot food and had the whole salmon and halibut pre-cooked for me.

At the end of summer there was a famous competition for professional chefs and somehow Klaus and the other chefs encouraged me to enter it, along with the other chefs. I had no idea what to do so I spoke to Serge and he suggested I do a crown roast of lamb. I had never heard of it so I did some research and found a picture in one of the cookbooks. Klaus gave me an old mirror without a frame that I could use for my presentation and Serge ordered the lamb. I explained to my parents what I was doing and on learning that the mirror did not have a frame, my father came over the next week with one he had made out of cedar, polishing it to a high gloss.

We all experimented with different garnishes and types of presentation during the week. Max, the Sous Chef, suggested that I make some vegetable baskets with a base of yellow turnip and dry spaghetti. I cooked the spaghetti and then deep-fried it to a crisp. It produced quite a realistic-looking woven basket that I filled with glazed vegetables. I cooked some lamb cutlets, glazed them with the chaud froid, and then decorated them with fake black truffles, which I had cut into different shapes, using fancy cutters.

The tension in the kitchen was getting quite palpable as the exhibition day was approaching. A truck was rented to transport all the mirrors to the Windsor Hotel in downtown Montréal. On the morning of the exhibition we polished for one last time our mirrors and set out our cold decorated food on them. Klaus had made a salmon with decorated trout fillets, Max a glazed ham with cornets of jambon filled with a delicate mousse. Jurg, the other Sous Chef, did a halibut with an intricate lattice. My crown roast was quite a disappointment for me: it did not cook as precisely as I had imagined, even with the help of Serge, but at least the little curly paper hat stuck on the end of each bone hid some of the imperfections. My garnish looked better and my mirror frame made my whole work stand out beautifully.

I did not travel with the other chefs on the truck as my work was just a very junior entry, but I went with my parents to the salon when it was open later for the public. All the hotels in Montréal took the competition very seriously as most chefs prided themselves on their buffet and their presentation skills. It was quite an event to win the Best Hotel prize, but it was also quite important to have a good showing from all your chefs. The ratings were excellent, trés grande distinction, grande distinction and distinction. Many of the dishes were left unmarked because they had not reached the high standards that were expected.

I saw Ben's work first (distinction), then Jurg's (no rating) and then Klaus's (grande distinction). Finally I spotted mine, not far away, with a tag. I had won a prize. I was elated! Once I got closer I realised that I had won a trés grande distinction! I was totally stunned and in a sense I also felt ashamed. I had been given so much help and guidance from the other chefs that I did not feel it was fair for me to win one of the best prizes for our hotel. The frame my father made must have been a pivotal reason for my win: it was so beautiful, and the dark mahogany wood went so perfectly with the glazed crown roast of lamb that I was sure it must have fooled the judges. Still, the win gave me so much encouragement, as the great majority of the other competing chefs were Swiss, German or French. It was a small victory for the future.

I gradually developed more confidence in the kitchen and felt quite at home working in that environment, but I still didn't know how to make sauces, as well as the many other dishes (such as terrine, paté, ice-cream and mousses) that the qualified chefs could make. At the end of summer I went back to school with my friends but school just wasn't the same by then.

For grade 12 we had been moved to a new mega school. It was one of the first of its kind in Québec, and it was created to concentrate the educational resources. The teachers had better equipment, the administration had brand new offices and public address systems (where the entire school could be addressed) but the students were the ones that lost out. We became a kind of a commodity to be managed, coerced and guided into a uniform product. There was no room for individuality in an educational system that taught by formula from grades 8 till 12. The whole thing was very impersonal and quite intimidating.

Not surprisingly, many of the students rebelled in various ways. Vandalism started to appear and in response to this more private security officers started to patrol the grounds and the classes. It became a bad social experiment in educating young impressionable souls. The consequence of all of this was the same as what happened in the Columbine school in America, albeit on a smaller scale, but it was more then 30 years earlier. It did not help that the protagonists were two of my best friends. It was time to move on and I decided to leave that school for good.

I did not quite know what to do and after seeing Klaus he told me he would take me full-time at the hotel. I loved the kitchen work, but I also had to do a lot of the menial jobs: bus boy, cleaner, carver or whatever was needed at the time. I now realised the value of an education, so when Monsieur Odermatt mentioned one day that he thought that I should consider going to cooking school, I jumped at the chance. It was a great endorsement from him and my mother was overjoyed. We investigated all the cooking schools and decided to apply to L'institut d'hôtellerie et de tourism du Québec (The Québec Institute of Hotel and Tourism Management). This school was the only one recognised by the major hotels, and it trained chefs, waiters and hotel employees. The course was two years full-time with a working summer break.

We filled in the application form and waited for the reply. The school invited me to come for an interview and a special test to see if I was suitable to work in the food industry. I was very excited by this and I felt ready to take the challenge. I turned up well before the allotted time, brimming with confidence. The interview went very well, but then it was time for the test. I will never forget this test; it was a nightmare!

I was made to smell tiny canisters of an esoteric content and was then asked to pick what it was. To this day that test has baffled me and I'll never know if I picked any of them correctly. Was it orange, rose petal, cinnamon, fennel, sage, or another ingredient? Smell has been always a weak link for me and over time I have realised that in general it is a very underdeveloped sense: given a blind test on smell, most people won't have a clue as to what they smell. I was sure that I had failed the test.

When I finally received my letter from the Institute I was reluctant to open it. I eventually did and was very surprised to discover that I had been accepted. I finally had some clarity in my future and a sense of direction. In those days being a chef was viewed as being well below other trades, such as a plumber, electrician or carpenter, but it felt right for me. I was ready to commit myself to acquire the skills that I needed for my new career.

3

COOKING SCHOOL

I STARTED SCHOOL IN 1974 AND WAS INDUCTED BY A VERY colourful teacher called Jean Brancheau. He was a butcher by trade, a larger than life character who made a huge difference to the school. Jean Brancheau was a teacher who exuded confidence and experience. He taught us a lot and instilled enthusiasm in each of his students.

Our class consisted of a mixture of students from both the city and the country. The boys from the country would most often stay with friends, four or five of them sharing one apartment. Many of the country girls stayed at a catholic hostel run by the nuns. It was always interesting to go and visit them at the hostel, with its off-limit areas and special rooms for meeting male friends. Still, it was cheap, central and safe for them, much safer than with us sleek city boys.

My first year of hotel school was held in a very old building that was filled with character. All the different trades—from cooking to pastry to hotel management—mixed together and the camaraderie was very supportive. In my second year the new school was opened and this closeness disappeared. The students who were training to be managers developed a certain sense of superiority, and this in turn, created a fair amount of resentment from the other students.

In Canada the system for training chefs is very different to and far more intense than the Australian system. We went to school five days a week and we learned theory in the morning and practice in the afternoon. In the first year I learned soup, butchery, stock making, vegetable cooking and the basic sauce making. It was very rewarding, especially because I was still working most weekends back at the hotel, as well as some nights. I was able to observe at work some of the things I was taught at school. My understanding and curiosity were very much sharpened.

Most of our teachers worked part-time at the school and full-time in restaurants or hotels. This produced very capable, informed and dynamic teachers, who were in the thick of it every day of the week in their busy kitchens. In Australia many teachers are full-time teachers who have not cooked in restaurants for years. This often means that their syllabus is outdated. In Sydney there was a great initiative to use the restaurant chefs to teach a new course called 'Australian Contemporary Cuisine', where the likes of Chris Manfield, Steve Manfredi, Matthew Moran, myself and others would go and teach the promising students of the schools. I wished that this course could expand to include all the students in the course, not only the few chosen.

It is interesting to weigh up the various merits of the Canadian system verses the Australian system. Is it better to train young chefs on a full-time basis for two years, or is it better to have the apprenticeship system over four years, with students going to school one day a week? The Canadian system produces great chefs who have a very good understanding of each kitchen task, but with very little practical experience. Many of them leave the industry when they realise the full implication of the hard work it takes to be successful in a commercial kitchen.

The apprenticeship system of Europe and Australia takes double the time to produce a qualified chef, but the main flaw with this system is that it is so undemocratic. So much depends on where you serve your apprenticeship. Some work in a good kitchen where the head chef or the owner is keen to teach the youngster, while others end up working in kitchen that is not committed to training and the chance for the apprentice to learn their trade is quite limited. Obviously you can put five times more students through school in Australia (as they only come to school one day a week) as opposed to Canada. The Australian system is very attractive for governments, as they do not have to build too many cooking schools, thus creating a great saving, as cooking schools are very expensive to run. I think the perfect balance would be to train chefs on a full-time basis, with maybe four months industry placement in the busy summer season.

The next two years were very rewarding and full of great challenges that I lapped up without any fear. The experience I had working in a large hotel kitchen made my task at school much more logical and also much easier. The teachers were amazing, the food was sensational and serious and the environment was extremely creative. It was a great place to learn.

There was a very healthy sense of competition between the groups of students. We would team up and try to finish our assignments faster and better than any other group. As the year progressed the sense of competition increased, and what started as small encounters would lead to more serious ways to get the better of the other group. Our assignments could range from boning perfectly a leg of veal, making a terrine, or producing a perfect béchamel sauce.

After one of competitors borrowed the expertise of a second year student to fillet his salmon—thus beating me in that exam—I decided that I would not lose my next contest. Justin I were great friends but there was also a strong sense of rivalry between us. The next assignment was to produce perfect tomato soup within an hour and it was to be judged by two teachers. The five groups got to work, all trying to produce the best soup possible. After 45 minutes my soup tasted great but unfortunately the colour was pink instead of red.

The tomatoes we were using had come from California because it was winter in Canada. They were hard, pale and lacking in sugar and flavour. I could compensate for flavour with the right amount of herbs, I could compensate for sweetness with sugar, but I realised that the colour of my soup would let me down. I wasn't going to allow Justin to beat me again, so I sneaked into the pastry supplies and took a bottle of red food colouring. After just two drops my soup soon looked great.

Judging time came and I did my best to look pained with my result, making sure my soup pot was covered with a tea towel. I was fourth in the judging circle and while everyone was looking the teachers opened my pot, revealing a smooth, sweet tomato soup with an incredibly deep rich red colour. The look on Justin's face when he saw my soup was priceless, and after looking at his soup it was evident that it was no contest.

The teacher gushed over my soup, explaining to all the students how I had achieved this result. It had to be skill and technique, he said, because we had all started with the same ingredients. Then to my horror he asked me to explain what I had done differently. I had to think quickly, so I said that instead of sautéing the tomatoes in a pot, I had roasted them in the oven to extract more flavour and colour. My teacher was delighted. 'There you have it,' he exclaimed, 'some one who thinks of flavour to achieve a perfect result.' I felt a bit guilty after this, so I then tried to pair myself with weaker students to balance my experience and over competitiveness.

My duel with Justin moved eventually out of the class and on to other pursuits like snooker and chatting up girls from other classes. It was healthy and fun and we ended up at the end of the school year with no clear winner. I hope that Justin and my old teachers never read this book for fear of revealing that secret!

———

Our first year was nearly over and summer was fast approaching, which meant that we all needed to find summer work. It was stipulated that we needed to work one full month over the two-month summer break. I had my job at the hotel to go back to so I didn't need to look for work. One day, however, I got a phone call out of the blue from a person with a deep beautiful voice called Daniel. He explained that he was working with Radio Canada in Winnipeg and that he was opening a restaurant in the French part of the city and was looking for a second in charge. Daniel was a friend of Monsieur Perrault (the father of my best friend) who was himself a classical radio announcer. Monsieur Perrault had recommended me to Daniel, despite that fact that I had got his son drunk on carrot wine many times.

I organised to meet Daniel at the headquarters of Radio Canada. He was very convincing in his pitch; the restaurant was going to be high profile and brand new, with a famous chef in charge and with me as second. I would be paid $250 a week, which was a great sum for those days, and he was also paying for the two-day train ride to Winnipeg. I did not know much about the job, but there was a certain thrill in going away to a different city and province, to a different restaurant and a different way of cooking.

I was very excited but I told him that I needed to talk to my chef and parents before I gave him an answer. Klaus was very gracious and he encouraged me to go, even if in my rush to accept the job I forgot that maybe he would miss a reliable worker. I thought that my mother would have been more apprehensive but she did not show it. By now I was very independent but also very responsible. She was used to not seeing me very often as I was either sleeping at friend's places or working late.

When I caught the train to Winnipeg I was very pleased to be joined by many of my fellow students who were going to Jasper Park Lodge, Bannf Spring or the Château Lake Louise on Lake Louise. These were very popular destinations for a summer job because they were some of the most magnificent hotels of Canada, situated in the Rocky Mountains. Many of my colleagues had succeeded in getting jobs there as cooks, waiters, waitresses, housemaids or receptionists. The jobs were not very well paid but for many of the students it was their first time away from home and the jobs were perfect because they were just for the summer and they also provided accommodation.

Well it certainly made for an interesting two-day trip. It is funny how you can often see people in a totally different light once you are in a new situation. I developed a mutual crush with Melanie, who was a vivacious girl taking the hotel administration course. Due to respect for her higher-rated course I never had tried to approach her before but it suddenly seemed okay for us both once we were out of the context of the school. It was a shame that trains are such uncomfortable and public places. Our capacity for intimacy was limited by the lack of privacy but we did as much as we could do to make ourself comfortable in the airline type chair of the train. It was with a heavy heart that I left her on her way to Lake Louise, however the excitement of the new adventure ahead took over as I alighted the train at Winnipeg, eager to met Daniel and start my new position.

4

LA GRENOUILLIÈRE

I ARRIVED IN WINNIPEG READY FOR MY BIGGEST CHALLENGE yet. True to his word, Daniel met me at the station. He was a supremely confident person, tall and lean, and he carried an air of knowledge that made people respect him. He was well known in all of Winnipeg, but especially so in Saint Boniface, the French-speaking quarter of Winnipeg where the restaurant was situated. Daniel was the number one French-speaking radio announcer, possessing a deep and melodious voice that drew people to his program.

As soon as we sat in his Renault Laguna Sport he said, 'Do you want the good news or the bad news?' I shrugged my shoulders and he continued. 'Well, the bad news is that Enrique Borgas, the Executive Chef, will not be coming to run the restaurant, as he could not leave his present employer.' I did not really know what to make of this, as I was not aware of exactly what I was getting into.

'Do you want the good news now?' he went on. 'Well, you are going to be the Executive Chef.' I was stunned. How could he say this to me? Was he aware of my lack of experience? Didn't he realise that

I was really just a student at a cooking school? And how did he know whether I could cope or not when he didn't know me personally? All of this did not seem to bother Daniel at all, but I didn't know if I was capable of what he was asking me to do.

We arrived at the restaurant as the place was being prepared for its imminent opening. I was introduced to the head waiter, who was setting up tables and folding newly unpacked serviettes. The restaurant was really a coffee shop at the front, facing the street, and a restaurant on one entire side of the building. The small but central kitchen had one side facing the coffee shop and its front facing the dining room. There was also a basement preparation kitchen.

This was clearly an exciting establishment that Daniel had taken over. He had renamed it 'La Grenouillière', which translates as 'The Frogery'. This was a Canadian colloquial term that was used to describe French Canadians, who loved eating frog legs, much to the horror of food shy English Canadians. The name was more then just a clever play on words because we were to have a few dishes on the menu with frog legs.

The first thing that I noticed about the kitchen was that there was no stove or oven. I also couldn't see any of the basic equipment: no pots, pans or pie plates, knives or cutting boards. There was just a fridge and some stainless steel benches. I asked Daniel where all the equipment was and he replied that I had to choose it myself. We got back into his car and he drove me straight to a commercial catering supplier, telling me to just select whatever I needed. I was still in a state of shock and I was certainly lacking confidence. For me to be selecting equipment with no idea or experience was quite frightening. I was very apprehensive and I started to feel a heavy weight on my shoulders at the tender age of 17, as I ordered all the paraphernalia of a commercial kitchen.

Our next stop was for lunch at the most well-known restaurant of the city, called The Carriage. It was set up like an Old World diner within a train, lost in the suburb of Winnipeg. It was simply beautiful with its wood panelled wall, its white crisp linen tablecloths and its waiters dressed in black tie and black coat. The food was superb: classic, but very well executed. I was impressed.

After lunch Daniel took me to an apartment which he said I could use for the next week until I found something myself. Daniel did not live here but he occasionally used the place. He had a house outside the city. It was a stunning apartment with modern paintings on all-white walls. I now had my own place and I was about to run a restaurant myself. I was feeling pretty grown-up.

Over the next few days I received the stove, unpacked all the kitchen equipment, and tried to familiarise myself with the place. Daniel and I visited some of the recommended suppliers like the butcher, baker and pastry shop. The menus had arrived on the previous day and the dining room menu looked great, but its size was a bit daunting.

I was to have just one assistant; an English-speaking red-haired youngster called Patrick, whose only experience was a stint in a coffee shop. The staff were a strange mixture of French and English, with some of the waitress' speaking both languages and some only English, Patrick and the kitchen staff only speaking English, and me and one of the waiters only speaking French. For the whole summer Patrick and I used David, the dining room garçon, as an interpreter. The orders were written in English but my instructions and the food ordering were written and ordered in French. Such is Canada and especially Saint Boniface.

I was told that Enrique would come with his kitchen team for one day to teach me the menu and help with the mise en place. Enrique was the Executive Chef at The Winnipeg Hotel, the oldest and largest hotel of the city. When Enrique and his team arrived I was very surprised to see how old they all were. Enrique looked nearly the same as Don Corleone in The Godfather. He had extremely dark sunglasses that he always kept on, even inside, because he did have a serious problem with light. This made for an eccentric display in the kitchen, because he was dressed in the traditional chef's white uniform with a tall hat and those sunnies on. All Enrique's helpers were also in their fifties and they also worked at the Winnipeg Hotel. Enrique was one of the longest serving chefs in Canada. Despite his strange appearance, Enrique was obviously very talented and experienced, capable of leading large teams of workers. However he was also quite fiery, which is probably why every time I went back to visit him in later years he was at a new place of employment.

Enrique was a master of presentation and traditional dishes. He was a chef's chef, with a wealth of knowledge on how to cook with flavour, albeit in an old-fashioned way. To this day I still have the recipe book he handwrote for me. It is faded and yellowing, but it is lovely, a memory of a past era from a giant of that time. I now understand why he would not come and be the chef at the restaurant—it was probably wishful thinking by Daniel to have such an experienced chef.

Enrique had organised the first food order to arrive the day before the restaurant opened. We had rainbow trout, olive oil, pork hock, veal mince, whole chickens, dry spices and flour, lard for making the piecrust and boxes of vegetables. His team got stuck into the supplies and over the next 12 hours transformed these into completed dishes. Enrique explained to me in detail how to make each dish and then how to present them. I absorbed everything he said and made sure all the recipes were written down. By the end of the night my head was spinning from information overload. It was a high-energy day, spent working with a crack team of professionals but at least now I knew what I would be cooking. The next day I would be on my own.

We opened the restaurant at 8am for breakfast. The menu was in French with English subtitles. The dishes were simple and to the point, classic dishes that would still be enjoyed today. The blueberry pancakes that I now serve at Bathers' were there, as well as my father's baked beans recipe. Breakfast went smoothly and I felt that I pretty well had it under control with Patrick's help. He had previously cooked breakfast so he had an idea of what was expected.

We hit our first lunch order at 11.30 from the coffee shop. The coffee shop menu was typically French Canadian, with the addition of a few American diner favourites. There was the paté and the cretons (a meat spread like rillettes, made with minced pork) on the menu, as well as slow-cooked pork hock, tourtiere (the traditional meat pie) served with my mother's green tomato ketchup. There was a selection of hamburgers and hot dogs called the froggeries, with cute fresh names of different frogs. There were hot and cold sandwiches and a selection of old fashioned pies made from recipes in regional Québec like 'Tarte au sucre et pacane' (sugar and pecan pie), 'tarte a la Ferlouche' (molasses tart) and either cherry or apple pie.

The dining room menu was fairly daunting because of its size. I felt pretty good on that first day knowing the mise en place was fully done. But with a menu with six entrées, two salads, five soups, five traditional dishes, frog legs, no less than 14 choices of vegetables or potato side orders, nine meat and five fish main courses, followed by seven desserts and three cheeses, I was going to be tested. The menu had some traditional dishes, such as casserole of sea snails, garlic snails, noisette of lamb, and beef rib with béarnaise sauce, but there were also some dishes with a more modern twist. We served roast duck with applesauce, stuffed pork cutlets, rolled veal escalope and beef fillet with scampi and grilled shrimps.

The public had been waiting for the opening of the restaurant and we were very busy in our first week. Enrique dropped by on the first few days to make sure I was okay, but then after the first week I did not see him much any more. His job had been to write the menu and train the chef and that was all done. It was now up to me to run the restaurant and I was starting to feel the pressure.

Every day I was starting work earlier and earlier and yet I was starting to run out of mise en place faster than I could replace it. So I started to also push my work hours later and later into the night. I was now starting at 7am and often finishing at 2am. As we got busier it was still not enough and so I started to work even later in the night. One particular night we were nearly out of everything after an especially busy day. At 5am I was still at work, making meat pies, filling veal escallops and making pea soup. I saw that there was no point going home, so I kept on working. By 5pm I could feel my apprehension, as I didn't know if my mind could keep pace with my body, but I made it through the evening service. I was pretty glad to see my bed that night after 40 hours straight at the stove.

The next week I once again had to work through the night to keep up with the volume of food preparation, but this time it was even harder to get through to the end of the shift. Forty hours straight in the kitchen I would not recommend to anyone. The next day Daniel came and saw me and asked me to have a chat with him. He had heard that I worked a few times through the night and he said that this should not happen again. He then gave me a lecture on believing in one's ability, developing confidence and pacing oneself. He felt that I was very capable and should be able to make it if I just believed in my ability to do the work. It was a very uplifting talk and was just what I needed at the time. I had come from working under the supervision of others to having to rely only on myself to run the kitchen and it was a big ask—I was not even eighteen yet. Daniel was the sort of person that gave a lot of trust, maybe too much.

After our talk he said that he thought I had a great future and that he respected the work I was putting in. He doubled my salary to $500 a week, he told me the apartment was mine to stay in and that he was giving me his old MG convertible to use for work. I was just stunned when he gave me the key. Well I was now extremely motivated to perform and stay on top of my job. For some strange reason I got much better at my planning. I guess I was spending less time worrying about whether I was going to make it or not, and more time focusing on doing a few tasks at the same time. I was able to have things cooking in the basement kitchen, like the pea soup, the pork hock and the stock, while I was doing the service. It would only take me an hour after service to finish the mise en place and then I would make my way home for a rest.

I found myself with money I did not know what to do with. I went to the provincial liquor store one morning and got myself a bottle each of scotch, gin, vodka, rum, and bourbon, just to feel like an adult with buying power. I have to say I did admire my bottle collection in the kitchen of the apartment.

Daniel would occasionally stay at the apartment and every time he came he seemed to have one-on-one meetings late at night. After a while I noticed that these meetings were always with men—surely he was not doing research for his radio show? The fact that he liked men slowly dawned on me when I keep seeing his Renault Laguna Sport being driven around town by a young pretty boy with long curly hair. Daniel never initiated any thing with me and I never felt uncomfortable at the apartment. His life was his to live but he was certainly a very flamboyant person in a fairly conservative town.

The restaurant got very busy on Friday and Saturday nights, so Daniel decided to hire some help to get me through. Richard, our restaurant manager, recommended a chef called Michael, who he used to work with at The Carriage. Michael was a funny character, a bearded French Canadian who did not say too much but was obviously a great cook.

He worked during the day and he agreed to work with us on Friday and Saturday nights.

Michael was like a mercenary, a hired gun ready to sell his services to the highest bidder. He had no romance left in him but he obviously knew how to cook. His sauce making was very impressive and I mostly learned my skills from him. He was quick and precise, but as the night progressed his skills would start to fade and his speed suffered. I soon realised what the problem was. On one side of the kitchen, near where Michael worked, the bar was set up. Michael often reached into the bar to top up his glass of orange juice, but I suspected that more than just juice was making it into his glass.

My suspicions were soon confirmed and when he realised that I knew what he was doing he did not even bother to hide it. I was waiting for Richard to say something but he never did and I didn't feel I had any right to tell him to stop. I saw first hand the addiction of alcohol and it is not pretty. If this did not prevent me from drinking, the drinking session I took on my 18th birthday certainly put a stop to any wish to indulge again in whisky in any form. Why I chose to get drunk on Southern Comfort will not be answered but I will never again touch bourbon for the rest of my life.

The end of the summer was fast approaching and I was starting to wonder what was I going to do about returning to school. Before I could resolve what I was going to do, Daniel approached me and told me that he wanted me to stay. I was not totally surprised by his request. He proposed that I keep the apartment, the salary and the car and stay on. I did not know what to do. There was a part of me that said go back to school, but another part of me said this offer is pretty amazing. I had grown to feel comfortable in the job and more importantly I loved the MG and the sense of freedom that I found myself in. I decided to phone

Klaus, my chef in Montréal, and after telling him my predicament he simply said, 'Just come back. It is better that you finish school first.' That was it. I was to go back in two weeks time.

My time in Winnipeg was a truly defining moment in my life. I had been thrown in the deep end and I had survived. I had learnt to believe in myself and I had acquired new skills, but above all I realised what it takes to be self-reliant. To this day I am not afraid of hard work, long hours, taking responsibilities and forging ahead.

5

CHEF ON ICE

I RETURNED TO COOKING SCHOOL A TOTALLY DIFFERENT person. I felt it was impossible to convey to my school colleagues what I had done for my summer work. Most of them were saying how boring their places were, how little they had learnt and how they never got near a stove. Some had only been allowed to prepare vegetables or make sandwiches: it was a truly depressing picture of what summer work was available. I guess most of them had never worked in a commercial kitchen, so it was with some reason that most of them were not trusted to do the critical jobs. When asked what I did I could only reply that I had worked in a small kitchen in Winnipeg. They never would have believed me if I had told them the truth.

In our second year of cooking school the new facilities proved to be amazing. Every thing was new and there was a sense of commitment from the government to make the institute one of the better teaching facilities of North America. The size of the school more than quadrupled, combining many other schools from around Montréal. It now included a training hotel that was fully staffed by students and open to all travelling government workers at very low rate. This hotel gave all students a chance to have on-the-job training, building their confidence and giving them experience in a realistic environment.

I continued working at the hotel on weekends, as well as sometimes after school. It was usual for me to get up at 6am to get ready to take the bus to school. After my 7am track running group I would have a shower and then attend school until 4pm. Then I would take the Montréal metro (it was right under my school) and get out at Longueuil, where the Holiday Inn was. I normally worked until 11pm, and caught the last bus home at 11.10pm. I always worked on weekends at the Holiday Inn because it was busy with functions and the preparations for Sunday brunch. For some time I even took another job on Sunday night in one of the busiest brasseries in the famous Rue St. Denis. To think that one job was not enough as well as school beggars my own belief but here I was on Sunday night dishing up roast quail, baby chicken, skirt steak and onion soup because I was bored if I didn't work Sunday night.

Holiday Inn Canada possessed over seventy hotels, mostly based in Canada but some were in England. The Holiday Inn standard system was one of the most highly regarded systems in the world, especially their reservation system. The Canadians decided to have a much higher quality food operation than their American counterparts and it showed in the delivery of services: it was basic but excellent. Their inspections for the systems of points were quite rigorous and when the inspections happened they created a huge amount of nervous activity in the hotel. Everyone was suddenly asked to clean, polish, wash and bring all the books up to date for the impending review. The report would then rate each hotel and ensure continued affiliation with Holiday Inn and a critical lifeline of business.

The company grew to be huge player in the Canadian market. It was a driven and creative environment with a very capable management that nurtured its staff. Senior staff would often be promoted to another location, thus enabling another internal promotion. When I heard that Klaus, our Executive Chef at the Holiday Inn Longueuil, had been promoted to look after all the kitchens of the district I was sad to see him go, as he was such a strong chef and he had taught me so much. But I was happy to hear that Klaus was to be replaced by Max Benz, Klaus's assistant of many years. Max was Swiss, as were most of the chefs in the company, and he had that tall, striking, Nordic appearance. He was very talented and more approachable than Klaus, but did not quite carry the same authority that Klaus had possessed. Still, I was happy to work with someone that I knew.

———

A few months into Klaus's new role, Max asked if I would be happy to go to Québec City for the weekend to help Klaus down there. It was quite a surprise to be asked, but it was a busy time in Québec City and Klaus needed more hands on deck. After having worked at the Longueuil property for a few years I had reached a certain level of competence with the food preparation and the menu. I could either work on the buffet or basic kitchen preparation and by then I was also extremely competent with the coffee shop menu. I was to take the bus for the 2½ hour drive to Québec City on a Friday afternoon. Once I arrived I would be given a room for the weekend. I checked the bus schedule and saw that I could take the 5am bus back on Monday morning to be able to be back in time for school.

I was still only eighteen at the time, so I nervously made my way after school on Friday to my first out-of-town work with Holiday Inn. I had no idea what was waiting for me at the other end. I felt quite grown-up in my first hotel room; little did I know that the hotel room would become a constant feature of my life. I was finally standing in the foyer of the hotel and I gathered my courage to face the front desk clerk and ask for my room key. He gave me a superior glance, refusing to believe that I actually worked for the company until he found my booking sheet. I could tell that he was thinking what was this young kid doing here? The people who worked for the company normally come from head office and were certainly not from my age group.

After changing into my chef's uniform I made my way down to the kitchen and was amazed at how frantic it was. Québec City was a crazy place, something I was to quickly learn. I am not sure if it was the price of the food that made their buffet, coffee shop and banquet so busy, but it was out-of-control busy. Klaus just said 'Monsieur Dansereau' in a welcoming manner before he turned around and continued working. I knew this was my signal to find out what I needed to do from someone else and get stuck into it.

Québec City was my baptism by fire. The work was frantic and we often worked from 6am till 11pm. There was no time for breakfast, lunch or dinner, but sometimes we'd have a pizza at 2am. Because there was no time for meals, the chefs would instead survive by drinking heavily sweetened coffee all day. It was a kind of precursor to a badly made flat white: in a highball glass you put three to four teaspoons of sugar, and then you would add half North American coffee and half milk. I didn't understand the chemical relationship between coffee and sugar and the energy buzz it gave you, but it certainly was a lethal combination to overdose on. It was the first and last time in my life that I drank coffee. After just a few weeks of drinking coffee all day I was to give it up for the rest of my life. To this days I like the smell of coffee but I would never think of drinking it.

It was while I was working for Klaus that I finally graduated from school. Unfortunately it is quite a hazy recollection as by then I was working so much that I had lost touch with my school friends. I could not go out drinking with them any more and I did not have the time to socialise after school or on the weekends. My working life was now quite different to most of my classmates' school life and I had always been the quiet type, not really belonging to the groups at school.

36

Daniel Blachut was my best friend; at that time he was working at reception but he was clearly on his way up, being trained by the company in all departments. He was an exceptional person who spoke four languages: English, French, Swiss (because of his mother) and Polish (because of his father). Daniel's father was even more exceptional; he spoke seven languages, adding Russian, Spanish and Danish. He was a refugee from Russia, and he became the most important nuclear physicist in Canada, helping develop the indigenous nuclear power industry in Canada. Daniel and I did crazy things together. If by chance I did not work on Sunday we would look at each other and say 'going for a swim?' Nodding to each other we would jump in the car at the end of the shift and drive 13 hours to Provincetown at the end of Cape Cod in the US. We would have a swim, dry ourselves, have breakfast and then drive back in time for work on Monday morning.

At this time there was an official position in the company called 'travelling chef'. There were three travelling chefs and they all had no permanent place of residence: they lived in hotels for a few months at a time wherever they were needed. Usually their tenure was between a head chef leaving (or being fired by the general manager) and his replacement arriving. This usually created a crisis in the kitchen because it would often take months to find a suitable replacement, hence the need for the travelling chef. My job was far worse than theirs. I became a sort of small gap filler, holding the fort for anywhere between a few days to a few weeks, just until the travelling chef arrived. My unofficial title was 'Chef on Ice', because I was skating on the frozen road of Eastern Canada from one hotel to the other, never quite knowing just how long I would stay in any one location. For the moment, though, I was to continue working with Klaus in Québec City.

Québec City is the most beautiful and European city of Canada. A clifftop citadel built by the French, it is an impressive reminder of the war that was the norm between England and France. Nouvelle France (as the French part of America was called at that time) was an important city for the French and the demise of this city sped the retreat of the French from North America. Over decades the French culture overwhelmed the English occupation to create one of the most beautiful cities of this continent. Being in Québec City is like being in Montmarte in Paris. Hundreds of artists ply their trade in tiny streets. You find sculptors, painters, metal forgers and many other artists who base their skills on traditional crafts, as well as many, many restaurants.

It is also a city that is based on the provincial government. In those years there was a great demand for secretaries, as the computer was not yet in widespread use. The effect this had on a city was quite apparent; there were literally dozens of women for each straight man. If you went out at night to a club or a bar you would often ended up chatting with at least three or four women. It was a bit of a revelation for me, especially at my age. I was very conscientious at first and tried to avoid going out at night after a long day's work, but gradually I ended up drinking too much, staying out too late and burning the candle at both ends.

Québec City was also a city of joy. People loved dating and drinking but above all they loved a parade, a carnival, a fête or any occasion to celebrate and have fun. In Québec City the biggest weeks of the year are the carnival weeks. The carnival is an orgy of celebration, like the one in Rio, except ours is held in winter so people needed to be dressed quite warmly. The whole city gets into the spirit, but mostly it's the spirit that eventually takes over!

For the kitchen staff, it was our busiest time. The hotel was full of guests there to enjoy the festivities and we had to try and stay on top of it. We were making salads for the buffet by the bucket full. However it was not a normal bucket, but rather a plastic pail the size of huge garbage bins. I would start in the morning by steaming potatoes in a powerful steamer, then I would shred at least 100kg of white cabbage, clean four boxes of capsicum, peel three boxes of cucumbers, boil 150 dozen eggs, make 20 litres of fresh mayonnaise and turn everything into salads.

We also had to roast three to four full-size legs of beef, a dozen beef rumps, a few legs of lamb and steam a dozen whole salmons ready to be presented cold. It was relentless work. The next day you just started all over again. In those days the buffets were very popular and priced so attractively that we turned over hundreds of people daily. On top of this there was the function room with the choice of more buffets or a set menu. Everything was freshly cooked and the desserts were all made in-house. It was a huge production that required level-headed chefs to meet all the demands at once.

At the end of the night the coffee shop waitresses usually invited us out for a drink. Being so high on the mixture of coffee, sugar and adrenalin it was hard to refuse. Over time this created more problems for me than the workload I faced in the kitchen. A major part of the problem was my room in the hotel, which was a great attraction for some of the girls who lived at home. In those days many of the waitresses worked during the day at government jobs and then also at night in restaurants and hotels to earn cash tips. Men were at a premium: straight men were prized and men not living at home were a rarity, a young man unattached to the city living in a hotel room for a short time was a huge catch.

Most of the girls I went out with were older than me. In fact until I married Yvette (my second wife and mother of my two children) I had only ever dated women older than me. In nearly every encounter I was told that I should not fall in love with them, that it was to be a relationship of mutual convenience. This suited me as well, but it only worked for a while. I was naive to think that I could say yes to every girl and not have any consequence. As soon as another girl muscled in on my room and my bed, jealousy became a major problem. Tension between waitresses ensued, often spilling in the kitchen, and it started to affect my work. It was time to get out of town.

I called Klaus and said it was maybe time for me to move on. I was back to living the life of a hired gun, with no permanent address. On a rare day off I decided to drive from Sherbrooke (where I was working) to Montréal to pick up my pushbike and visit my parents. I then decided to go and see my friends in Cornwall, another city I used to work in, two hours drive away. I arrived at their home very late at night to be told that they crossed the river to the US to drink in Messina, a small town with a great bar and cheap beer that I had been to before when I worked at the Holiday Inn Cornwall.

It is usually quite easy for a Canadian to cross the border into the US. This time I did not have luck on my side. It was very late at night and I travelled with my all possessions: books, knifes, uniform and my bike, which was dismantled on the back seat. I answered as well as I could the usual questions that I knew by heart. Where do you come from? Sherbrooke. Where were you born? Montréal. Where are you going? To see my friends in a pub in Messina. Where do you live? I had a hard time answering that one. Well that kind of did it and they asked me for my identification. Yet again I had lost my license and did not have any proof, so I was refused entry to the US.

I then had to turn back to Canada and face Canadian Customs. I was asked the same questions but by then my answers just did not make any sense. I was asked if the bike belonged to me and was asked for paperwork. Having none I was refused entry to Canada. I was then trapped in no-man's-land between the two countries. I suspect that the Canadian Customs had been warned that this weird kid was trying to come over to the US and that they should have a very good look at him. I eventually pleaded to use the phone and my mother was not too surprised to hear from me needing her to once again look for my lost license. It was then that I resolved to make a home somewhere more permanently.

Klaus asked me to make my way to Ottawa, the capital city of Canada. The company had two hotels there and bizarrely I was told to go to Ottawa Centre (the large 400-room hotel) and get a job there. Get a job there? I thought that this was strange, but I never questioned Klaus and so I made my way to the city for the first time. It was beautiful: very Georgian, very Edwardian, and very English. I booked myself into student accommodation near the University and proceeded to the personnel office of the hotel. It was the first time and last time I ever filled in an employee questionnaire. Eventually, the Executive Sous Chef showed me to the kitchen. It was the biggest kitchen I had ever seen. The chef was in his office with his hat over his eyes, slouching in his chair. We made small talk about where I had worked for the same company but Ottawa was part of another district and really a world away from the Swiss and French Connection; this was Germany in Canada, as most of the senior chefs were German. I was hired and told to start the next day.

I was to work in the huge revolving restaurant topping the 30-storey building. My first day was terrible, one of the worst days of my life. I was to be in charge of the kitchen but I did not speak any English. For staff I had Tony, a young Chinese boy, Lin, an older motherly Vietnamese women, and Meerak, an aged stubborn Turk. The restaurant served over 200 meals at night, sometimes more. It was the heyday of pepper steak, flambé, steak Diane, châteaubriand and crêpe suzette. I was on the grill, Tony was on the garnish, Lin was on the cold service (mostly shrimp cocktail) and Meerak was lost in the service elevator, trying to avoid doing his work.

There were 13 waiters, two hosts, and one assistant Maître d'Hôtel. All of them were Arabic (Egyptian, Lebanese, Moroccan, Algerian, or Tunisian) and the assistant Maître d'Hôtel was Berber. The Maître d'Hôtel, Paolo Bonnati, was a beautiful Italian man with slicked back grey hair, a lean and regal posture, a small well-trimmed moustache and a professional demeanour that came from working in the great palazzos and restaurants of Europe. He was a living embodiment of the perfect Maître d'Hôtel. If you crossed him in the street, out of his uniform, you still would immediately recognise him as a Maître d'Hôtel. He had worked on the great ocean cruisers of the past era when service was defined by a hierarchy of servers, sommelier, bus boy, Chef de Rang, Captain and a crew of helpers.

On that first night all the waiters ganged up on me. Everyone screamed at me, telling me that their customers had waited too long or at least that was what I assumed they were saying, as I couldn't really understand them. I had never faced that situation before and it was quite stressful. I made it through the night but only just. I had to cook all the steaks, around 100 of them, making sure that each one was cooked correctly. At any one time I had at least 30 steaks on the grill, trying to categorise what was supposed to be rare, blue, medium rare, medium, medium well, well done, and a new one for me, charred on the outside but rare inside.

I could have killed someone that night, especially Ibrahim, the big snobbish Egyptian with the gold jewellery on each finger. But I just bit my tongue and absorbed all the verbal blows. On closing Monsieur Bonnati told me not to worry, that I would be fine and not to take the waiters too seriously. But I sensed that he was a bit of a gentleman, not quite up to disciplining his team.

The next day I was ready, my mise en place was ready, my team was ready and my mind was ready. I choose the meanest, most self-important leader of the pack, Ibrahim. On his first pick up I said 'not ready' he gave me a killer look but walked away. He came back for another pick up five minutes later to be told again 'not ready'. I made him wait for a very long time for each and every single one of his orders. He threatened me, he yelled at me, he fetched Monsieur Bonnati but to no avail. By the end of the night he was nearly in tears, and his customers were abusing him for the time it took him to serve them. All the other waiters were stunned into silence for fear that I would do the same to them. I never had any problems from any of them again and Ibrahim became a good friend. We all became a crack team but I think they never again thought of crossing me, there was a sense of self-preservation in their friendship after all.

The chefs (especially the hard-drinking Germans) often went out after work. We would start in a bar in Ottawa and then when it closed at 12pm we would move across the river to the province of Québec. Ottawa was in Ontario, which had a drinking curfew of midnight. Québec, which had more liberal laws, had a curfew of 3am, and this created an exodus of patrons at midnight on the bridges crossing the river. When the last place closed at 3am we would drive back to Ottawa to have late night pizza. We ate huge slabs with plenty of anchovies and dripping with Tobasco sauce, so much so that to this day my stomach cannot handle it any more.

Downstairs in the main kitchen it was a different world. It did not look like a great amount of work was done by the German duo who hired me. When I picked up my food from the butcher I could see them drinking Heineken's from the mini bar fridge in the office. A couple of months into my job I got a phone call from Klaus and he said 'So?' I did not understand exactly what he meant. 'Well, what is happening down there?' Then I got it, I was sent by Klaus to Ottawa to be a spy! Or at least to find out what was happening in the kitchen. I learned later on that the two Ottawa hotels had been added to Klaus' district and there was growing concern with the way that the kitchen was run. He was told to sort it out and I had been the advance party.

The next day the two Germans were summoned to the office never to be seen again. Klaus took over the kitchen shortly after and I had the chance to work with him again. We were back together but he immediately asked me to go down to the main kitchen and take over the Garde Manger. This was the cold section of the kitchen where buffet food, cold appetisers and dressings were prepared for functions of up to 1000 people. I was back making salad, as Klaus needed someone to fulfil that role and appease the General Manager, his flamboyant Director of Food and Beverage and their demand for great flourish on the buffet.

My time in the Garde Manger was not as fulfilling as when I was Chef Saucier in La Ronde at the top of the hotel. I was okay but my heart was not quite in it. I saw Tony and Lin come daily to pick up their supplies and I could see the sadness in their eyes. We had been a good team. I missed them both, as well as the close-knit bond, Tony's efforts to teach me English and Lin's meals that she prepared for us three before service; her prawn fried rice was a staple that I remember to this day.

It was quite interesting that it was in Ottawa that I learned to appreciate ethnic food. Ibrahim showed me how to make a tomato and bread salad with plenty of anchovies, Tabasco and olive oil. Lin made me appreciate the simple home cooking of Vietnamese food. She kept bringing ingredients to work from Asian shops and would cook curries, stir-frys and salads that were fresh and exotic. I also appreciated the simple pasta dishes that Monsieur Bonnati made when he invited me to his place to play chess. He cooked his onions in water to soften them up then added diced tomato and olive oil to make a simple sugo. Its simplicity amazed me, as I had never made any sauce with less then twenty ingredients. At work I learned the cuisine of cooking books and super luxury ingredients and I learned to visit the summer market to shop with Klaus for great fresh ingredients for dinner. In short it was a revelation of culture, language and custom and it made me a very curious person.

Because Ottawa is the capital of Canada we served a lot of ambassadors and royalty. The city is full of embassies, each with the need for catering. Our hotel was central and we had the capacity to hold both large and small functions. As a result I came in contact with luxury produce that was used for functions. In those days each ambassador tried to outdo each other with their offering. It was a very small social circle of diplomatic entertaining with a sprinkling of Ottawa high society.

In the Royal Penthouse of the hotel, the Saudi Arabian ambassador had taken residency. His new house was taking two years to be built and rumours of its opulence were widespread though out the city. His demand for special meals, buffets, cocktail parties, caviar, foie gras, shellfish pyramids and the like kept us busy and interested. The ambassador gave the hotel a regal flair and the money to keep everyone happy and silent on his likes and dislikes. I learned years later that the ambassador never made it to his palatial home, having been recalled on 'rumoured' grounds of overindulgence and excess.

One day there was a very special menu for a large banquet in honour of Queen Elizabeth II. Klaus ordered special produce: lettuces from France, mushrooms from Germany, and cheese from Périgord: the famous Crottin de Chavignol. The banquet was a regal affair with many white-gloved waiters. The hotel managers all congratulated the Functions Manager for his coup in getting the Queen in their Ballroom. I delicately spread Mache lettuce on the plate for the Crottin salad. As I remember, the Queen did not touch any of the food.

I eventually got my hand on a great one-bedroom apartment subsidised by the city for students and young people. It was a brand new high-rise apartment with parquetry floor and a great vegetarian café downstairs. Even though I had no furniture and was sleeping on a beach chair I felt at home. I tried this time to avoid any liaisons with women, however old habits die hard and my new apartment did have the occasional visit from the beautiful Nicole and Martine from Québec City.

Every night that I worked I noticed a tall woman who came and got a refill of coffee from our supply. She worked in the cocktail bar, one floor below the restaurant. It was another world down there; the bar was huge and very popular, staffed by an all-female crew wearing black tops and very short green miniskirts. Every time she came to pick up coffee the waiters would drool over her, try to make small talk, and capture her attention. She just ignored them in an admirably contemptuous manner. I was impressed. It took time for me to make contact, but eventually we did and over the next few months we grew fond of our meeting at the coffee machine.

I was attracted by her maturity. As opposed to all my other relationships this one took a very long time to develop. It was somewhat refreshing for me to have a courtship and a resistance to engage. Linda thought I was too young for her but I was keen. I was sick of short and often meaningless encounters and while I had no regrets I suddenly felt ready for a steady relationship. Our first date was great until it came time to pay for dinner and I realised that I had left my wallet at the apartment. This was not a good impression to give to the ice lady. I excused myself, caught a taxi back to the apartment and made it back without her dumping me. In fact, I married Linda a few years later, when I was 21 and she was 30.

6

REGIONAL CUISINE

SOON AFTER LINDA AND I WERE MARRIED I WAS SENT BACK to the picturesque regional town of Sherbrooke. I was happy to be told by Klaus that I was to going to work there again. Sherbrooke is a beautiful little city set in the Laurentian part of Eastern Canada, full of mountains, lakes and woods. It is a picturesque in the extreme, especially in autumn when all the trees turn red, yellow and gold. There is a lot of tourism from the US because it is quite close to the border. It is also an area where people own chalets on lakes so they can pursue their love of fishing and hunting.

I was sent there to clean up the mess that the previous chef had left and put things on a better culinary footing. At least that is what I assumed I was asked to do. I arrived to find that the chef was gone. It was left to the GM of the hotel to brief me on the situation when I arrived, but he did not tell me the exact reason why the previous chef had left. The GM was a local man who had made it to the top of his industry in his hometown. He was an accountant by trade and did not quite understand the working of a kitchen, but he was smart enough to realise that his previous chef was not the right man for the job.

I don't know what they thought of a 22-year-old chef being sent in to fix the situation, but he seemed to be pleased to see me. After I installed Linda in her room I went to the kitchen to find out what I was facing. There were a couple of obliging chefs and they seemed to have things under control for that day. But when I checked the store, fridges and freezer, I was surprised to see that they were filled up with pre-made produce. I could see every possible type of commercial dressing in huge jars, packets of powered dessert mixes by the case, and incredibly a walk-in freezer fully loaded with Sara Lee cakes, croissants, Danishes and pre-prepared meals. There were tins of powered soup (cauliflower, leek, potato, vichyssoise and carrot) and flavoured consommé. The whole thing was staggering.

I started work immediately and soon realised that everything needed to be rebuilt from scratch, with the major problem being the suppliers. A few weeks later I received an unannounced visit from an older salesman. I soon discovered the reason the previous chef was no longer here and why all the stores were overstocked. He asked me if I needed more cheesecake and I replied that I didn't. After a dozen similar questions, to which my answer was always no, he realised that I was a different type of chef to the previous one. He then told me that this hotel will be getting very busy and that it would be great to do business together. I did not answer.

Finally, in desperation he put his briefcase on my desk, opened it, took an envelope from it, put it under the briefcase and slid it across the desk. I could sense that funny business was about to be proposed, but opened the envelope just to confirm my suspicions. Once I saw the cash inside I knew that it was just a big scam. I gave him back his envelope and told him that we were finished doing business; I did not even give him the chance to reply. As I went back to the kitchen he sheepishly walked out, never to be seen again. All the suppliers had to go, despite the sly monetary incentive that was hinted at if I was to keep them. I now understood fully what the problem was.

I had heard of bribery and kickbacks during economics lectures at cooking school. It was the scourge of many establishments and was quite a prevalent practice in those days. Chefs were actually paid poor money because it was assumed that they would be on the take from their suppliers. We heard that an Executive Chef often received in cash three per cent of the cost of the supplies purchased to ensure loyalty to the suppliers. It was a bad way to do business. It corrupted the taker and it prevented the entry of honest suppliers. This system caused the downfall of Escofier, the father of Modern Cuisine, who was apparently fired by the management of the Ritz Hotel for taking kickbacks. The system was also prevalent in all the large hotels in Asia. I never accepted bribes and was always reluctant to receive Christmas gifts from my suppliers, in most cases passing on the gifts to my staff.

Over the next year I changed the team, re-trained them and most importantly I rewrote the new menu. I was given the freedom to redesign the menus because the ones supplied by the head office just drove people away. They were too international, predictable and uninteresting for the local people. The problem with the dining room was clearly the menu. Sherbrooke was the first hotel where I was able to design my own menu.

Monsieur St-Laurent, the General Manager, took me to every restaurant in the area and we also visited the local food suppliers. The region had a great abundance of fresh water lakes, there were plenty of vegetables and it was famous for its local apples, pumpkins, cheese, maple syrup and game. I made sure most of these local products made it to the menu. I now had new suppliers and I had discovered some local ingredients and products, such as the local fish. This region of

Canada was quite rustic and agricultural, and it was here that I first formed a bond between fresh farm produce and my kitchen.

One day Monsieur St-Laurent told me that the fish would be running that evening. I did understand what he meant, but I agreed to go with him to 'fish in the woods'. We must have looked silly at midnight, crashing through the dark thick woods, carrying empty plastic buckets, with only a torch to guide us. I felt totally lost and doubted that we would catch anything. Suddenly Monsieur St-Laurent stopped, and listened intently. He could hear running water in a small river. Happily he rushed ahead, crashing through the woods like a brown bear. When I finally caught up with him he just smiled at me and said look in the river.

As he shone his torch into the water I stared in amazement. The beam of light revealed thousands of small fish swimming up stream. It was a sight beyond comprehension; I had never seen so many live fish before. They were very small lake fish that were making their way to spawn, an event that only happens on the full moon, one day of the year. Monsieur St-Laurent scooped his first bucket in the river and it collected hundreds of small fish. We filled all of the buckets up; every catch was like the bear standing in the river to catch salmon, but it was even easier. The fish made it to the menu, floured and shallow fried. For me it was the birth of a long-lived passion, the search for fresh and local ingredients.

I also started to research local recipes, talking to suppliers, owners of grocery stores and older chefs who had worked in the region for a long time. I went to the library and got hold of old regional recipe books and I checked newer compilations of recipes in cooking school books. The province of Québec possesses a very rich food culture going back to the colonisation of Nouvelle France by the French in the 17th century. While the English were never good at adapting to the local food environment, preferred to stick to their salted meat and traditional way of eating, the French were adept at using the local ingredients. The French legacy was a wealth of recipes with strong regional tones and I was only too happy to use all of them. I made meat and potato pie with a golden crust, braised rabbit, molasses tart and many dishes based on the local lake fish. Some of the local chefs that I hired often came with one or two local recipes, like fried cheese fondue or steamed apple pudding, which were great to use.

I turned local and regional in a big way and it helped with the popularity of the restaurant. For most seasoned travellers it was a novelty to eat the local produce rather then the typical hotel food and they grew to like the style of food and the link to the area. The hotel was situated at the entrance to the city and was very popular, because it was fairly new and very well maintained.

I loved working in that hotel: it was small and manageable, I had a direct link with great produce, and I had the freedom to create my own menu. So when I received a phone call from Klaus, telling me to head back to Longueuil, I was very disappointed. This was to be the start of a pattern that would repeat itself over the next few years; as soon I was settled and my team was well trained I would have to move on to the next place.

I was very sad to leave Sherbrooke, so remote and picturesque, filled with fresh air and the prettiness of the valley and mountains. I felt comfortable in Sherbrooke, but I had achieved what I had been sent there to do and it was time to move on.

7

MY LAST ROLE IN CANADA

M Y FIRST DAY BACK IN LONGUEUIL WAS ONE OF THE WORST
and most chaotic days of my life. Well, the actual day itself was
not so bad; it was what was coming the next morning that made it an
absolute disaster.

Longueuil held great memories for me. It was where I had first
started in the kitchen, watching Klaus, Ben and Serge Guidit, the Chef
Saucier, perform their work in a super efficient and professional way.
Their kitchen had been a marvel of expertise and experience. But
now there was a problem in Longueuil and I didn't realise that Klaus
was using me as the troubleshooter so he could continue his work
in Ottawa. I was young, enthusiastic and full of energy, and despite
my young age I had a lot of experience in the company's kitchens.
I knew the system, the ordering methods, the local suppliers, and
the executives of the company, but above all I had the support and
confidence of Klaus.

On my last Friday in Sherbrooke I worked a couple of hours in
the morning to tidy up the kitchen and hand over to one of my Sous

Chefs. I went home to finish the packing and organise the removalist, then we got in the car for the two-hour drive back to Longueuil, where I was to start on the Monday. After checking into the hotel with Linda I decided to go and investigate the kitchen. I walked in and to my immediate horror I saw that the entire kitchen was greasy and slippery, with improperly washed floors. Because I used to wash those floors in my first job there I knew just how hard it was to keep them clean. It required very hot water changed about six times to do the entire kitchen. This was a total mess.

I walked over to a very busy chef who looked like he had some authority. To my surprise it was one of my colleagues from cooking school; Michel was the Sous Chef who was holding the place together until my arrival. The previous chef had been fired because was not able to run the kitchen properly. I quickly asked him if he was okay for the evening and he said, 'No, not really.'

Well, there went my plans for dinner with my parents and a rest before starting a new job. I had to jump right into it instead. I quickly changed in the messy chef's office and looked at the function sheet. There were three functions that night: one large one for 260 people and two smaller functions for 75 and 40 people respectively. After checking what was already done I released that it was crisis time as nearly nothing was prepared. No meat platters were ready for the buffet, and the beef rumps were not even in the oven yet. Salads were half prepared, but not set in bowls or decorated, and none of the sauces were made. The kitchen was a mess and to get through the preparation that was required for that evening would require a fair amount of hard work and a great deal of luck.

Rosa was one of the few employees left from the old team and she was a great help; at least she knew what needed to be done. We all worked like demons: chopping, roasting, tossing, setting, and decorating with maximum efficiently and effort. Hams that should really have been decorated were instead scorched and roasted to

53

achieve a quick decorating effect. The Function Manager kept darting nervously in the kitchen to see if we would make it. He did not dare approach me but I could sense his concern. We finally made it just in time and managed to cater for all of the functions.

At the end of the night when I was totally exhausted one of the hotel managers came over to introduce himself. He was Jean-Pierre, another colleague from cooking school, but he had taken the hotel management course. The students from that class had always considered themselves superior to the other students, especially those of us who were taking the waiter's course or chef's course, because the hotel management students were to be our future bosses.

Jean-Pierre was to be the Duty Manager that night. He was to stay until 5am to ensure a management presence in the hotel during the night, a common practise with most hotels. The manager's task was to ensure coordination of the security, handle any guest issues and to walk all the floors of the entire hotel at least twice to ensure that fire doors were closed and fire hazards were under control. At the end of the night Jean-Pierre and I went through the booking sheets of the hotel to see what was on for the rest of the weekend. The hotel was booked to maximum capacity because the Canadian Grand Prix was being held that weekend. I checked Saturday's functions and saw that there was also a wedding for 300 people as well as a few other small functions. There was no way that I could have the weekend off before I started on Monday. I was already totally exhausted and I was going to have to work all weekend. I decided to try and get some sleep and I finally got to bed at around 1am.

At 3am the phone woke me up. I could not understand why anyone would be calling me at that time of night. I was so tired I couldn't understand what the caller was trying to tell me. Eventually I worked out that it was Jean-Pierre. He wanted to tell me that during his duty tour he noticed with concern that the temperature on the large walk in freezer was indicating minus 40°F, when the range indicated it should have been between -10°F and -20°F! I incredulously replied that I had never heard of a freezer that was too cold!

Clearly Jean-Pierre was a bit slow on logic and common sense. I remembered him doing something very odd when we worked together in Ottawa. He was working on the floor of the restaurant and at that time water was served at every table, in fact the water glasses were often preset and filled with water before the customers sat down. Jean-Pierre came to the kitchen to fill the glasses with ice and then he topped them up with water before taking them back to the restaurant. I noticed that he only half-filled the glasses with water on top of the ice. When eventually I asked him why he only half-filled the glass he replied that it was because the ice would melt and fill the glass up! The same lack of understanding of the laws of physics was being displayed to me at 3am. I told him in no uncertain terms to not disturb me again and I tried to go back to sleep.

At 5.30am the phone rang again. The worst scourge in the life of an Executive Chef is to receive that dreaded phone call in the small hours of morning to be told that the Breakfast Chef had not come in. There is no option in cases like this but to get dressed and go straight to work. I was at the end of such a call and I just could not believe it.

I got downstairs as quickly as possible and realised that the kitchen was in a state of total chaos. Not only had the Breakfast Chef not shown up but the kitchen night cleaner had not come in. I knew that job well because it had been my first job in that hotel. It was critical that the chefs coming early in the morning had all the pots, pans, trays and plates ready for their work and that floor was clean and dry. This morning the entire floor was slippery with grease and, even more disturbing, the pot washing section was a mountain of dirty dishes. To compound the problem there was no serious mise en place prepared for breakfast, no bacon trayed up, no sausages blanched and no eggs cracked. I could sense a looming disaster.

The seasoned waitresses were trying to do their bit to help set up by getting the bread trays ready and starting to brew the huge containers of American coffee that was so important to the upcoming guests. I tried to wash as many trays as possible so I could start making the crisp bacon. Soon after I started breaking eggs for the scrambled eggs and then the coffee shop orders started coming in. 'Two eggs, sunny side up, with hash brown, bacon and sausage.' 'One egg over, lightly grilled tomato and mushroom.' 'Cheese omelette with double order of crisp bacon.' 'Two poached eggs on toast with sautéed mushroom.' And that was just the orders for one table.

Over the next five hours there was a relentless barrage of orders. I was doing my best to stay in touch with who had ordered what but it was proving to be an impossible task. The best I could do was to load the flat grill with eggs and then listen to what the waitress told me they needed. Every half-hour or so I ran out of mise en place. By now Rosa had come in to start preparing the buffet for lunch so there was no way she could help me prepare any more breakfast food. Every once in a while I'd scream 'Rosa, eggs!' and she'd go into the cool room and retrieve one more box. Then I'd scream 'Rosa, bacon!' and she'd fetch me another 5lbs of bacon. We went through 15 dozen eggs that morning, in addition to 12 boxes of bacon and five boxes of sausages. One of the Breakfast Chefs finally arrived, and despite not being the best around he could at least supply me with a few clean trays to bake the sausage and bacon.

I never in my entire life faced such a continuous barrage of orders. There was just no choice but to plod on. I wasted loads of eggs and burnt a few trays of bacon but I just carried on. My jacket was totally drenched with sweat and my hands had constant burns from splashing hot oil. I was feeling sleep deprived and exhausted, but I pushed ahead, trying to catch up to those dockets. My Sous Chef had come in at 10am but he needed to start roasting the meat for lunch service so he could not help me either.

MY FATHER, CAMILLE,
FISHING IN THE
CANADIAN LAKES

MY MOTHER, JEANNINE,
AN EXPERT LACE MAKER

CAMPING, MY PARENTS' LOVE

DURING MY YOUNG PROFESSIONAL YEARS

MY FIRST PUBLIC COOKING DEMONSTRATION

WINNING MY TRÉS GRANDE DISTINCTION

DURING MY HOLIDAY INN YEARS WITH
THE PRESIDENT, MR SVENSON

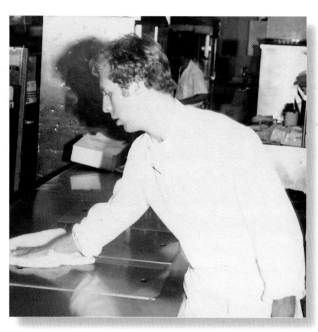

MY LAST JOB IN CANADA, AT THE
HOLIDAY INN POINTE CLAIRE

SOME OF THE KEY PLAYERS AT THE REGENT SYDNEY IN THE LATE EIGHTIES:
(L TO R) MAX DICKENS, THE FINANCIAL CONTROLLER, MYSELF, OVERSEAS
FOOD WRITERS AND TED WRIGHT, THE GENERAL MANAGER

JACKY TERNISIEN AND MYSELF IN THE KABLE'S KITCHEN

MY TEAM AT THE REGENT, SOME OF WHOM
STILL WORK WITH ME NOW

KABLE'S STAFF CELEBRATING RECEIVING OUR
THIRD HAT AWARD FROM
THE SYDNEY MORNING HERALD GOOD FOOD GUIDE

SAMPLING LOCAL DELICACIES IN
TUSCANY WITH ANNIE FÉOLDE

I was breaking eggs in large bowls as fast as I could to make trays of scrambled eggs to replenish the buffet. The buffet in the dining room was open as well as the coffee shop because the hotel was full. In one sense I was glad that the dining room was buffet as I do not think I could have coped with the that many individual orders, but on the other hand people eat so much more at a buffet. So it was less fiddley but certainly more work to produce the bulk of food that was required for a buffet.

At around 11.30am I started to feel the pace slowing and I could see an eventual end to the nightmare. Suddenly there were no more orders; breakfast was finished. I just stood there drenched in sweat and speechless. The leading waitress came in and said, 'Serge, do you realise that you fed over 450 people? It is a record, we have never done so many breakfasts.' To cap everything off Rosa called me into the office to answer the ringing phone that I had ignored all morning; it was Linda, calling to say good morning and happy birthday. I was so busy I had totally forgotten that it was my birthday. I promised myself that things would improve; after all, they certainly couldn't get worse

---

I became obsessed with organisation and cleanliness—I guess that fateful morning would forever mark me. I always try to maintain my kitchen to the best standard possible. I am fastidious with stores, fridges and general kitchen order. I hate food coming near any sticky and dirty surface. I feel if you provide a clean environment the staff will work faster and more efficiently.

Over the next two years I developed one of the closest teams I ever had the privilege to work with. Bruno, my loyal Sous Chef, was French; in those days most chefs were mostly European. The lowly positions were occupied by Southern Mediterraneans (Greek and Spanish) and a few French Canadians. It took a good amount of ability to get the best out of them all, to get them to trust me and to get them to work as a team. We became a superb team, totally bound together and there was nothing that we could not handle.

Once more I received the dreaded phone call from Klaus, asking me to move on. I was going to lose my best team and my kitchen: the kitchen that first formed me, the one I felt totally comfortable in. I had to uproot myself again, give up my nice comfortable apartment, give up the proximity of my parents and family and move.

Klaus warned me that Benito Mugliorati, the General Manager of our other property in Montréal, had asked for me to be moved to his larger hotel in the Western part of the city. I had heard of the hotel, but most importantly I had heard of Monsieur Mugliorati. He was one of those larger-than-life people, a person full of ideas, who wants action and success. He had a reputation of burning people out very quickly. I had been afraid that I would one day be asked to move to his hotel. I was going to a place where I was to face the demands of a difficult genius, one who set impossible goals. As a manager he chewed up people who did not perform to his exacting standards and spat them back in the galleys of mediocrity. Such was my loyalty to Klaus that I agreed to go, but it was with great reluctance.

Monsieur Mugliorati's hotel was one of the busiest in the company. His restaurant was packed, his bar was the place to be seen, and his function centre was one of the busiest in that part of the city. I knew the chef there; he was German, a nice person but he was a nervous wreck. I arrived at the hotel to find the place in a slightly better state then when I last visited. The last time I was there the kitchen was dirty and disorganised and the quality of food was not to my taste. The food costing was impossible to achieve and it showed in the quality of the food served. The same applied to the labour costs: they were set too low and the staff had to cut too many corners to get their job done. To Monsieur Mugliorati's credit he realised that he needed to be a bit more realistic with me coming as I was not going to try to achieve the impossible at the expense of quality. Before I arrived he also hired a company to totally clean the kitchen because he knew that I couldn't work in a dirty kitchen.

The big success of this hotel was its Sunday brunch. It became an institution, with three to four hundred people served in four hours from a large buffet. I never really liked buffets, but that place was enough to turn anyone away from them, especially if you had to produce them. The variety of food that needed to be produced for Sunday brunch was just staggering: frittata, roast beef, merguez sausages, egg dishes, poached salmon, a variety of salads, bacon, soups, breads, brioches, foccacia, jellies, mousses, cakes, French pastries, Danishes, and more. Monsieur Mugliorati tried to encourage me to expand the range even though I was trying to cut back. I worked out that it was better to say yes and do what was possible with the available quality. It was a good challenge for me even though I did not feel attached to the hotel or the job.

One person who kept me motivated and eventually became one of my best friends in Canada, was the Food and Beverage Manager of the hotel. To this day I have the greatest respect for Daniel Rivière. He was born in Rouen, in northern France, and was passionate about the best things that life has to offer. He loved good coffee, drinking it to excess, big Cuban cigars, good food, great wine and beautiful women. He was not a typical company man. The company wanted people with soft personalities, people who dedicated their efforts to achieving better financial results, people who kept quiet and blended in the environment. Only Monsieur Mugliorati was able to get away with his flamboyance and rule breaking. As long as his hotel continued to make money the powers that be would tolerate him.

Daniel educated me on the finer things in life. I learnt to appreciate simple great food; he would talk to me with such passion about a great croissant that it was contagious. He knew little restaurants, bistros, suppliers and shops that offered the best of unique products. I will always remember the meal his mother cooked for us at his home. She served fresh leeks from her garden, which were boiled and dressed with a beautiful Dijon mustard vinaigrette, and pomme dauphinoise (gratin of potato with a hint of garlic and made with heavy cream and Gruyère cheese). It was so delicious and made with flavour and rusticity; I have never encountered such a good one ever again.

Unfortunately Daniel was just not a practical man. His love of the good things in life, his search for quality, his hope for a perfect world made him too much of an idealist for a company that wanted hard men. With his cigar and bow tie he was probably seen as a dreamer, but he was an inspiration to me. I wanted to work for a company that was committed to quality. I was reaching a stage in my life where I was not happy just producing average food for profit. I wanted to devote myself to what Daniel dreamt about.

Daniel's wife, Lola, was one of the most dynamic and impressive women I had ever met. Like Daniel she worked as a director of food and beverage, but in her case it was for a large Sheraton hotel downtown. The hotel was due to close soon because of its advanced years: the rooms were too small, it was getting too expensive to operate and the work force had reached the end of its usefulness. When Lola mentioned to me that a new Sheraton was being built I was very interested.

I resolved to apply for a position in their new kitchen just a couple of months before opening. They were looking for an Executive Sous Chef and I felt that would be an ideal move for me. I had reached a certain limit with the food I could cook and I did not think that the opportunity for me to develop my skills lay with the company that I had worked for since I was 16.

This was a much larger hotel, a company committed to quality, and a role where I could learn more and take a set back from running the kitchen myself. I knew that Klaus understood that times were changing and that the time was right for me to seek a change of direction. The Director of Food and Beverage was Monsieur Garoupe, who was in the same role when I had worked in Québec City. My interview with him went well and he felt I would be an ideal candidate for the role. My next interview was with the Executive Chef, who was an older French man. Our interview was quite good, but at the end of it he said that as much as he would love to take me he felt that I was over qualified for the job. I was stunned. I was only 25 years old—how could I be over qualified?

This was a very depressing time for me. I had felt that this was my chance to contribute to the opening of a brand new quality hotel but it was not to be. In hindsight I can see that maybe the Executive Chef was afraid I was too close to M. Garoupe. In hotels there is often a strange sense of competition between the two key people of the hotel operation. However, I will never know the real reason why I didn't get that job.

Daniel could sense my disappointment. I started to dream about working somewhere overseas, such as America. My mother was born in Detroit, USA, so maybe there was a way that I could claim residency down there. I decided to explore this option; San Diego was floating in my mind as an attractive destination for no other reason then it sounded exotic and inviting.

In the meantime I had kept a link with my old cooking school and went there on a few occasions to judge competitions. This gave me the chance to meet other hotel chefs. I met one very nice man, Claude Boudoux, who worked for a company called The Regent Montréal, to me an unknown hotel. We struck a very good rapport together; he was older but I felt comfortable with him. A few months later our paths were to cross again.

I was in the process of cleaning a large cool room as I was not that busy and felt that it was better to do this one myself. My hands were immersed in soapy hot water when Daniel came and invited me for lunch. I did not really do lunch, but Daniel persisted, saying, 'Serge, please come, it could be good for your future.' I was intrigued. We were to go to The Regent Montréal to meet a former colleague who he had worked with at the very prestigious Four Seasons Montréal. It was Claude Boudoux; he was now the Executive Chef of that new hotel.

Our lunch was amazing, it was a total revolution for me. The food was exquisite, sophisticated and very advanced. The Four Seasons had a reputation for great food but this was a quality that I never experienced before. The Regent Montréal was certainly committed to excellence. Daniel took me to the kitchen and I met Claude once again. He explained to us that the President of Regent International had asked him to be their Corporate Chef, which was a highly-prized job. Most of their hotels were in great locations, such as New York, Chicago, Hong Kong, Manilla and Bangkok, as well as many other exotic locations. It was a small hotel company that was big on service and quality. I was very impressed.

Over the next six months I continued thinking about a way to change jobs and travel overseas for work, when I received a phone call from Claude Boudoux. He was in the process of opening a large new hotel and he needed an Executive Sous Chef for that hotel. The role was to be very important as the new chef had never been an Executive Chef prior to his appointment. The role would be to manage the staff and the kitchen process. The chef would need to be talented and a very good cook, but he would also need to run the kitchen properly. Would this be of interest to me? I asked where the hotel was and he replied Sydney, Australia!

Well that was not the answer that I was expecting. I asked him to send me a brochure and the proposal for the term of employment. Sydney? Australia? I had excelled in history and geography at school: I could name the capital of 100 countries around the world, I knew most mountain ranges, oceans and important lakes, but Australia? Not many people in North America knew about the country; New Zealand was certainly more known. Apart from the fact that kangaroos come from there, not much else was known about Australia.

I went to the library and found an amazing book on Sydney. The cover was an aerial photo of Sydney Harbour with its many bays, coves and inlets, and peninsulas filled with red-tiled roofs. It looked like an amazing city, but even more impressive was the content of the book. Page after page depicted the Sydney lifestyle, with bronzed swimmers, race horses lead around racecourses, parks, sail boats, historical buildings, amazing houses and cars that looked like they came from a different planet. This was not the country town I had expected, with Kangaroos running down the main street.

I received the hotel brochure and I was stupefied by the size, architecture and plushness of the hotel. This was a five-star quality that did not yet exist in North America. I was sold on the idea to relocate to Sydney. It was, as the cliché says, 'a dream come true'. All my friends could not believe how lucky I was to get another great job.

There were a few nervous moments when I needed to provide a police check on my character (maybe they would find out about my excessive driving speed and many tickets) and a medical certificate (could there be some thing wrong with me?) but eventually everything was cleared. For good measure at the same time the Australian band Men at Work had a huge hit that made number one all over the world: 'I Come From the Land Down Under'. Everyone knew the song and suddenly Australia was put on the map of the world. The year was 1982 and that song was a perfect omen for me to immigrate to that mysterious land with unlimited potential.

8

THE REGENT SYDNEY

I T WAS HARD TO COME TO TERMS WITH SUCH A QUICK change of season. When Linda and I left Montréal in February 1983 it was -30°C and snowing. After an interminable flight of 37 hours we arrived in Sydney in 30°C+ degree weather. It was, to say the least, a shock to our systems.

Within a week we were living in an apartment overlooking Bondi. Those red-tiled roofs just amazed me as much as the warm weather. The first beach that I saw was Tamarama, the nearest beach from our home. It was an amazing place, with a sandstone cliff carved by the wind over thousands of years, amazingly fine white sand and warm emerald green water. I had always loved water and swimming, but I had never seen a beach like this before. I sat down on the sand and took in the whole place. It was an amazing sight: the boys were surfing like super athletes, the girls were nearly naked, and everyone was toned, bronzed and bold. It was paradise. The climate and the topography of Sydney left me stunned and completely overjoyed at being in such a great country and city. Little did I know that Australia was to become my permanent home for my long-term future.

Jacky Ternisien, the Executive Chef of The Regent, had picked us up from the airport. He was happy to finally see me arrive as I just missed the grand opening of the hotel. I was late because it had taken so long to get my residency papers; the immigration offices did not know that I was coming on a permanent residency. I was supposed to apply at the consulate, not the Embassy, so in the end we probably wasted three months being processed in the wrong department. That was the way government bodies worked in those days, slow and laid back. Still, I was finally in Sydney and very glad to be here.

I knew Jacky wanted me to arrive sooner but it was to no avail. The General Manager's Executive Secretary (who handled the visa) had warned me not to push immigration. The first Executive Chef had created a lot of bad blood for the hotel with the scene he had made in Toronto Canada regarding the slowness in processing of his visa. He had obviously pushed the Australian officials too hard, and as a result a lot of appeasing moves had to be done to get him accepted in Australia.

In those days it was pretty much tradition to hire experienced Executive Chefs from recruitment agencies that provided the bulk of a new hotel's core staff. These days it would be pretty hard to understand the need to seek candidates from overseas. The depth of experience in the hotel industry is so much broader now than it was in 1982.

Roland, the first Executive Chef, was made to stop over on his way to Australia at one of the flagship hotels, The Regent Hong Kong. What Roland saw there was an amazing operation. Over 190 chefs, butchers, bakers, three chocolatiers, and multitudes of kitchen staff. The harbour side café served over 1000 people a day and the flagship restaurant, Plume, was one of Hong Kong's best. The Regent's Chinese restaurant was eventually voted 'Best Chinese restaurant in the world'. The hotel banquet operation was phenomenal, catering for 12 courses, with banks of searing woks, and rows of Chinese choppers carving and cutting boiled chicken, fried pigeon and barbecued duck for up to 1000 people.

No wonder Roland was let down by his kitchen in Sydney. The people in Asia dined at hotels; it was part of their custom due to the high quality of food and services offered by these reputed palaces. That was yet to be built in Sydney. Each hotel markets to its local place. Roland needed to create the product to attract the people and I do not think he was prepared to put the hard work in. The Regent Sydney had to set the standard for quality in order to create the demand in the local market.

On the opening day of the hotel, when thousands of guests included people such as travel agents, politicians and the Sydney social set, Roland did his block with the GM, Ted Wright. Roland ranted about the incompetence of the staff, the size of the kitchens and basically everyone else's shortcomings, as he perceived them. Ted was very direct in his reply. He said, 'Roland, we obviously will not be able to work together. Consequently, this is your last workday in the hotel.' That was the end of a turbulent few months and that was the reason I came to Australia.

—

I went to work nervously on my second day in Sydney. Because I had arrived after the grand opening of the hotel I felt that I had missed a lot of what was involved in managing the opening. The unpacking of container after container of pots and pans, cutlery, glasses and everything a huge hotel required would have been exciting. The testing of new dishes, the creation of a new menu, the set up of systems to operate a kitchen would have been so rewarding. Jacky was in the thick of it, with Claude Boudoux as the Corporate Executive Chef, helping and guiding.

My first task was to learn the names of everyone: nearly 100 kitchen staff, 40 kitchen stewards, the storeman, the purchasing team, the security team, the department heads and their assistants, the food and beverage managers of all the food outlets and the names of the critical suppliers. It was a mammoth task but one I needed to absorb quickly if I was to make a difference in the kitchen.

My brief came from Claude Boudoux. I was to put systems in place to make the kitchen run smartly and liberate Jacky from the administration of the kitchen. I soon realised that to do this I would have to reorganise all the rosters for all the kitchens. It was a task and a half. The chefs always had particular demands for special days off which I had to allow for. Then there was a real mix of kitchen staff—some good, some average and some very mediocre—so I had to balance the shifts in each kitchen to ensure the right mix of chefs. But my biggest task was to stop them complaining and instead make them focus on the same goals.

The Regent was a very impressive set up, with a lot of French, English and Australian chefs. Each kitchen possessed very strong Sous Chefs running their own section, managing their menus and their staff. The most impressive Sous Chef was Cheong Tsé, who was running Kable's. Kable's was already developing a formidable reputation for the unique quality of its tableware, for its unrivalled service and for the quality of the food. Behind Kable's was a huge organisation committed to make this restaurant one of the best in the country. There was an unspoken rule that we all had to do whatever it took to cook, serve and offer the best of everything. I have never come across such an uncompromising commitment to offer the customer the best. It was a quasi religious focus that was to define the hotel and its place on Australia.

The sheer scale of The Regent, with each area equipped with the best and most exotic materials possible, made this a once in a lifetime chance. There was the best quality silverware everywhere: cutlery, platters, serving bowls, lemon squeezers, tea strainers, and ice-cream thermoses. About three people were employed just to polish each piece of silver twice a week in a special silver polishing room. The kitchen pots, pans, trays and utensils came from the best pot maker in the world, WMF, based in Switzerland. There were carving trolleys that were never to be used as well as hundreds of silver trays and casseroles of all different sizes that were to be used in banqueting for full silver service functions of up to 500 people. Now I understood the meaning of silver service.

That quality reached every corner of the operation and it was more than stunning to see and work with that fabulous equipment. The wineglasses for Kable's were gorgeous, but subject to easy breakage if not handled with extreme care. I did have concerns about the amount of breakages that we were suffering, especially with all the beautiful Wedgwood plates all the restaurants were equipped with. There is no more sickening noise than a huge crash of plates or glasses and it was happening far too often. The cost of these breakages was tabled at meetings and efforts were always underway to reduce these, but with so many young and inexperienced waiters it was inevitable that breakages would happen. One day in banqueting a whole table stacked high with glasses collapsed due to the leg not being clamped properly. That particular crash cost over $3000 and it wasn't the last one!

Still, within four months of opening the hotel was humming to its dedicated purpose: serve stylish locals and houseguests with the best food we could devise. There were over nine outlets where food was served and most of them were full most of the time. The sheer scope and range of all the menus meant that we had to carry nearly every conceivable ingredient. The Regent often feed more than 2000 guests a day, as well as nearly 700 staff. Both guests and staff came from many different cultural and ethnic backgrounds, which meant we had to have a broad selection of dishes to cover all these sensibilities.

The stores were a buzz of activity as well as the loading dock. As soon as food would arrive it would be examined, counted and dispatched to its right store. The hotel was a veritable mini city with its own emergency power generator, laundry and valet services occupying an entire floor. There was also a security department, nurse, human resources department, commissionaire, team of concierges, an in-house florist, and teams of painters, tilers, plumbers, upholsterers, cabinetmakers, and French polishers. There were drivers for the Rolls Royce that the hotel owned, telephonists, pool attendants, masseuses and every type of cleaner you could think of.

The Regent became known for its commitment to training and was a leading example in the set up of training programs for all the hotel trades. It even had a training manager with an assistant. The hotel indenture was a full day of induction in the training room that eventually grew to a mind-altering three days of information overload. The whole hotel was very well structured, led by Ted Wright the General Manager. He proved to be an ideal leader and a sophisticated host to all the hotel guests.

I do not think Sydney was quite prepared for a place like The Regent. Financial critics predicted it would become a white elephant within a year of opening. Unfortunately it opened during a global recession so the room component of the hotel operation took a while to take off, but eventually it did. There was no such problem with the food and beverage operation; it was busy from day one.

The Regent Hotel had a huge impact on Sydney and for that matter on Australia as a whole. We were working for a pioneer company with a visionary leader. The company was seen as a new standard bearer for hotels across the world. It was in the process of establishing its vision, and the reputation of its operation was critical for its future. So it was an unique situation to be working for a company that needed to be seen to have the best service and the best food. It was a creative time and very exiting and motivating to work for such an outfit.

The Regent was the first true five-star hotel to come to Sydney, offering a level of service unseen and I believe unequalled ever since. The same level of service and quality was also found in its many restaurants and bars. There was a fanatical approach to offering the best and there was constant pressure to revise, review and improve our menus, wine lists and bar menus.

Every little detail was ruthlessly perfected and we all needed to ensure that superb quality was delivered. The sheer amount of business going through the restaurants and the rooms made our task quite surreal. There was no place for complacency anywhere. The high standards were based on the years of experience the company acquired while running other hotels in Asia. Usually these high standards were always maintained, but there were some situations where even the most highly-trained staff fell down.

One such incident happened in Kable's one night, with a very drunk client. The man was quite rude when he asked for his table, but the staff were quite used to this. They just accepted that some customers would be demanding and difficult, and their training ensured that they handled any situation with as much grace as possible. Once he was seated it was noticed that his companion was 'a lady of the night'.

As the night wore on, the gentleman drank too much, made constant demands and took his temper out on his companion. The security department was advised of his behaviour, just as a precaution, in case things got out of hand. I knew about him because they came into the kitchen to observe the man's table. But they didn't have to worry as the man fell asleep in his chair and his companion left the table discreetly.

When he eventually woke up none of the waiters were in his vicinity and he was spotted descending the stairs of the hotel foyer. The restaurant manager immediately called security to advise them that he had left without settling the bill.

They caught up with him before he had the chance to leave the hotel and when the single security man asked him to attend the security office he took a huge swing and unexpectedly flattened the security guard. The security guards quickly phoned the police, attended the embarrassed security victim and set off in hot pursuit of our dining guest and amateur boxer.

They reached him in the street and dragged him back to The Regent, with a few well-placed punches to diminish his resistance, where he was unceremoniously dumped into the luggage room. We could all see how proud the security department was at having captured their man while still waiting for the police to arrive.

As I went down to the front desk to get an update of the drama I could hear Jill, our assistant manager, saying to the restaurant manager, 'Let me get this right, you are saying that the man left money on the table? So he has actually paid his bill?'

Well I do not know what happened after, but despite the fact that the man had punched the security guard I imagine that profuse apologies would have been extended and repatriation would have been offered to avoid any possible litigation. I could see the resigned look of Jill when the full implication of the events had sunk in. Such was the work of the assistant manager of a large hotel: they mostly deal with incidents, accidents and angry guests.

One area that was always a big risk was the hotel garage. Cars sometimes were stolen from there (including a $240,000 Porsche) and it became evident that keys could not be left in the ignition of every car, especially the Mercedes, Ferraris and expensive BMWs. Garage attendants running a top-of-the-line Porsche into the wall of the garage made for a costly event, especially as it happened more than once!

The Regent had a policy of assisting disabled people by employing them to work in the garage. One such employee was Anthony, who had a near-genius memory for car models, years and license numbers. Being assigned to wash cars was right up his alley.

One day, when he had become an expert at washing cars, he was assigned to wash a brand new BMW, one of only a few in the entire country. Whatever made Anthony decide to use steel wool to scrub the whole vehicle will never be fully understood, but the cry of despair from the owner of the car I am sure still haunts the entire garage staff.

In 1983 (the year I started at The Regent) we were at a crossroads of food style. Australians to that point expected 'meat and three veg' when they went to a restaurant. Nouvelle cuisine was in full flight and all French-born chefs felt compelled to follow the mother country style. There was a define clash of cultures on the way here: a big portion verses tiny refined portions on a large white plate. It did not take long before adjustments were necessary to satisfy the restaurant guests: portion sizes needed to be increased and vegetables and a starch needed to be provided with the main meal. Because a lot of The Regent staff and management had worked in Asia it was inevitable that an Asian influence was to creep into The Regent's food.

Quite exceptional people staffed the kitchen brigade team. Jacky was to eventually become the Director of Food and Beverage after what seemed to be a short period at the helm of the kitchen. I really enjoyed my time working with Jacky. He had a great sense of humour but he also had a totally uncompromising attitude towards quality. He consistently checked all his soups, sauces, and special dishes before service—something I never quite managed to achieve. He would make his rounds like clockwork to ensure all was in place before service; he always tasted the soup and consommé in the café, the stew in the pub, the salad in the Garde Manger (cold section) and the sauces at Kable's.

Coming from France, Jacky had great classic training, but he had also worked in Canada, which made him good at operating a large kitchen. We became one of the best teams I ever worked with and each of our skills complimented each other perfectly. He had more culinary experience but I was more capable of managing the staff, and the costing and administration systems of the kitchen. Jacky concentrated on producing great menus and dealt with the senior management of the hotel. I ensured these menus were correctly produced and ran the day-to-day workings of the kitchen.

The mix of nationalities in the kitchen provided a great breadth of experience to tap into. The Germans were great at handling the huge production; the English made good soup, consommé and sauce; the French were good at working a la carte; and the Aussies did a good job in the cold section of the kitchen. But most importantly we needed great Sous Chefs to run each kitchen.

Yiu Cheong Tsé was the first Kable's Sous Chef. Cheong trained at the Mandarin in Hong Kong, where he was born. Because he showed so much potential he was sent to the Dorchester in London to learn the European ways. He did this under the tutelage of Anton Mossiman, a giant of European food. Cheong was one of the most talented chefs I ever worked with. Because of Cheong's experience the food at Kable's from day one possessed an Asian influence that was hardly in use in Australia at that time. He was the one at the coalface of the kitchen, teaching, devising cooking techniques and managing the process of putting all the dishes on the menu.

Cheong was trained in both Western food and traditional Chinese food, and he blended both cooking techniques to produce incredible dishes that were intriguing, balanced and delicious. This was done well before the concept of blending the two food cultures was accepted or understood. Cheong was the perfect chef to blend the two cultures, as he had enormous depth of experience and knowledge in that style of cooking. Cheong's style of refined and inspiring dishes, with great depth of flavour, stunning presentation and authenticity, was quite novel and the success of Kable's as a restaurant was as much to do with him, even though my name is most associated with its success. The combination of these skills with the great local produce gave us an inkling of the potential to produce great food in Australia.

Cheong became eventually my second and after leaving The Regent years later became the Executive Chef for Qantas. He was as important as any players of the 80s were, but because he never ran his own restaurant the culinary establishment didn't rate him. So it would not be fair to say that he wasn't recognised as a pioneer in Australia, he was just not recognised by the food press. Hotels like The Regent and their key players have a tendency to be written off by the modern day revisionists when it comes to understanding the achievement they made in raising the standards of good food in Australia.

9

INFLUENCE OF THE LEADERS

THERE ARE SOME LEADERS YOU FEAR, THERE ARE SOME YOU never respect and then there are some who just make no difference. But there are also some leaders who make a huge difference to your workplace and maybe to your life. Ted Wright, the General Manager of The Regent, was in the last category; he was a natural leader, a man loved, respected, listened to, and one that inspired everyone. He was a pioneer in the hotel industry in Australia.

Imagine having to create a new city from scratch with all new staff. And you were only allowed to hire young, good looking, inexperienced staff, albeit with great attitudes. Having all services (garbage pick up, communication centres, and power and water services) fully functional, and with brand-new restaurants, hair salon, gym, parking station, bars, laundry and florist opening without experience all on the same day. That is what Ted needed to manage and he did this with a strength of character that made him part of a select few leaders that had both the capacity for vision as well as for practical achievement.

Ted Wright never failed to instil vision and a drive to excel, even if he often set the bar way higher than was possibly achievable. He was an expert motivator, one who made everyone think that their role was important and critical to the success of the hotel, no matter how lowly their job was. Some people felt that he asked too much of them, demanding extreme work hours and adherence to unachievable goals that he would set. If you were not prepared to try to reach his demands then your future career at The Regent was finished.

Ted was a highly educated man. He completed a B.A. in psychology at the University of Nebraska, where he also played Varsity Football (hence his enormous calf muscles, his athletic figure and his stamina). He then did an Associate of Art at the New Mexico Military Institute, where he probably got his drive and his 'take no prisoner' approach to delivering quality, and he studied Business Administration at the Harvard University Graduate School of Business in Boston. He never stopped believing in education and he eventually became the Chairman of the Board of Directors for Tourism Training Australia.

To this day his achievements in businesses and the perception of his accomplishment by governments is quite impressive. He was recognised as one of the twelve great innovators of Australia by BRW magazine. He received an Award of Excellence from the New South Wales State Government for contributions to the state and the nation; this award is usually awarded to only one person annually and is considered the highest state award. He was awarded life membership in the Tourism Task Force and he chaired 10 Sydney Convention Visitors Bureau annual general meetings. He made it his mission to change the way service was delivered in Australia and he did have a profound effect on the many industries in Australia that see customer service as an essential tool in their business. He received The Order of Australia 'AM' in the Queens Birthday Honours Awards in June 1999 'For Service to Tourism, the Arts and the Community'. It all says a lot about Ted Wright.

His early career found him in Hawaii working to provide great service for the officers on their R&R time during the Vietnam years. It is there that he was noticed by Bob Burns, the founding partner of Regent International Hotels. Ted followed the classic route of an eventual General Manager by working various postings throughout the Asia Pacific area, firstly as a Food and Beverage Manager, and then as an Executive Assistant Manager. He eventually became a GM, before been assigned with the mammoth task of opening The Regent, Sydney. He built that hotel to a rating of number one in the world, as judged by a Michael Carlton (an important syndicated US travel writer) in 1987. The Regent was consistently voted one of the top ten hotels in the world by the 'bible' of hotel rating, the *Institutional Investor*.

Ted always possessed great sophistication, a suave air and an engaging personality. He was a model hotelier, in the European style. He knew how to make the hotel guests feel important, wanted and respected. He spent a lot of time with people and it showed in the effect he had on the staff and customers. The customers or guests of the hotel were always treated in the way that we ourselves would like to be treated in a similar situation.

To run a new hotel of the calibre of The Regent you need the experience that you can only possess if you have worked in several countries with countless different cultures. Knowing how to handle Thai, Vietnamese, Fijian, Chinese, Arabic, North Americans, Germans, Italian, French or Singaporean guests is very useful. To negotiate with English, Japanese or American Financiers and know their customs and peculiarities is a bonus. Ted had worked in Hawaii, Guam, the Philippines, Vanuatu (when it was formerly the New Hebrides), Fiji, Panama, Malaysia and Thailand before he came to Australia. He was an expert diplomat who had the experience and wisdom to deal with the many owners, staff and guess of different nationalities that walk through a hotel every day.

At the end of the day Ted ran the hotel pretty much on his own as The Regent chain virtually imbued its general managers with total independence. Ted relied on his experience to guide him through all the situations that he confronted daily in his job. He would handle all the competing demands with patience, foresight and decisiveness. He was an ideal person to either have as a boss, a person to manage your hotel or as the leader of a great service team.

—

Like most Americans Ted was a mixture of flair and brashness. He loved to exaggerate the positive, and his hyperbole often overtook the reality. Many times he told me that something was 'the best dish he had ever eaten', and it could apply to something from one of our restaurants or a meal he had consumed in France, America or another restaurant in Sydney. The American in him loved big tastes and flamboyant presentation: meals that were different and unique, like the tomato dessert that was a speciality of Arpège in Paris. He was always driving me to create food that would make a lasting impression on people. I tried to tailor some of my dishes to have a bit of theatre about them, even though my culinary nature is conservative, leaning towards understated elegance.

Every week all the managers would meet for the communication meeting. This was the chance for Ted to review the week's operations, to announce major policies and to sermonise us again on the need to be totally diligent about only serving quality. Ted was never one to air dirty laundry in public; that was kept for one-on-one, so these meetings always concluded on a positive tone. But the best support and guidance that I received was ironically in my office on his daily visit. There he would chat about food and new ideas and these pep talk sessions re-energised me with clear goals.

Ted made us all keep pretty brutal hours; everyone was too afraid to sneak out of work before he went home. This was a new hotel and the presence of everyone was required at all times of the day and evening. Most nights Ted would come back to the hotel to have dinner so it was always hard to miss an evening of work. Considering that my workday started around 7am, working double shifts nearly every day took its toll by the end of the week.

The pressure that Ted imposed on all the managers was quite oppressive. He always worked six days a week, being in the office Saturday mornings and expecting all other managers to do the same thing. As much as Ted was a great inspiration he could be ruthless in his demands to give away your family life for the love of your job. Being in that industry is not very conducive for a family life. I was glad my working hours were never an issue. In any case, I was always there very early and needed to be there late to serve all big functions and check the restaurant.

Ted became one of the most sought-after guests at social functions, fundraisers, product launches, parties, gala balls, and anything that required the 'A-list' of the Sydney social set. In the early years his focus on work was such that he rarely ventured out, but once the hotel was established he started to accept the important invitations because it was essential for networking to be seen to contribute to the social life of Sydney.

Slowly but surely his photo started to creep into newspapers and magazines. It was always good to see him well dressed and at the right function. Later on as the economy picked up and the parties got more outrageous, Sydney took on an air of Berlin in the pre-war years, such was the extent that each group went to outdo each other in shock value and excess. Fancy-dress parties were common and you could see many people losing their inhibitions; Ted often wore daring costumes. The staff could glance at his outfit in the social pages but they also saw him in the flesh at the hotel as many of the A-list parties and functions were held at The Regent. Ted always believed that we were on stage once we crossed the door that lead to the foyer of hotel or the door from the kitchen to the restaurants, so it was quite fitting that he could act the part.

Ted was also a Francophile at heart. He did not speak French but he dreamed that he did. He loved Paris, French food, French chefs, French perfume, French haute couture, French soap—basically anything that came from France. Ted could not say no to a good French proposal. We often did promotions in the hotel, and in all honesty, some of them were done simply because Ted was not able to say no when he should have. We had a string of French chefs on gastronomic visits, which for me was always professionally rewarding and challenging to have the opportunity to met and learn from French stars.

Through the years the hotel hit some fabulous highs and some very stressful lows. At all times Ted never wavered on his commitment to quality and I gave him all the respect I could muster. He became like a second father to me and to this day I adored the time I spent working under him.

—

Bob Burns, the American founder of The Regent, was another extraordinary leader. Bob had worked for Hilton International as one of the more progressive hotel men. He developed the world famous Kahala Hilton in Hawaii and made that hotel the new world standard. Tired of the restrictions of the Hilton he left to create his own hotel chain and Regent International Hotels was born to achieve greatness. Almost everything that the Hilton had done, he would do the opposite. There was no garish neon sign on the roof of his hotel, no piped music, no plastic flowers, no buffet, ice carving or imitation theme restaurants. He set amazing standards and was the father of many innovations in hotel services.

The construction of his new hotels was always eagerly anticipated. He rebuilt old classic hotels (like the Halekulani in Hawaii and the Beverly Wilshire in LA), as well as new hotels that were way ahead of their time (like The Regent New York and The Regent Bali, renamed Four Seasons Hotel). The Regent New York cost one billion US dollars to finish and it has the highest average room rate in New York, around $800US per night. The Regent Bali was one of the first hotels to build each guest villa its own pool; there are 147 rooms in the resort and 155 pools. Bob was the one who created the concept of the opulent hotel bathroom, now seen in all aspiring five-star hotels.

In short, Bob was a pioneer that the hotel industry has never seen again. To him it was all about luxury and services and in the late 70s and early 80s Asia was a perfect place to start a new five-star hotel company. Asia's low-cost labour permitted each hotel to double or even triple the staff ratio that was normally seen in North America. For someone unused to this many staff it was a revelation and a dream to work within such an organisation.

I was not long in the job when I first suffered Bob Burn's wrath. One morning, during one of his infrequent visits, he came down to the kitchen after his breakfast with Ted Wright. Bob pronounced that the orange juice was way off the mark; orange juice was always his test and he literally became obsessed with the quality of it wherever he went. I didn't understand what could be wrong with it. The juice had been made to order from fresh oranges, as I knew he insisted on freshly-squeezed juice for every guest. The logistics of producing that juice was quite daunting because everyone that stayed in The Regent for the night received breakfast and the majority of the guests ordered orange juice. Most people had breakfast between 7am and 8am, so with up to 1000 people staying in house the sheer volume of juice to be squeezed on order was virtually an impossible task. We obviously had to squeeze some juice ahead of time to keep up with the orders but the consequence of that was what Bob Burns had tasted.

His assessment of the problem was that we were using Navel oranges, which when the little navel area was squeezed it released a small amount of bitter oil. It was fresh juice, but one that he felt was corrupted. The solution was to use Valencia oranges. He pointed out that if Valencia oranges were out of season in Australia, then I should pick up the phone, order from California and organised staggered delivery of containers with the right oranges.

The next day I was on the phone seeking to import fresh Valencia oranges from California, but due to import restrictions and the bureaucratic nature of the Australian customs, it was not that simple. After much searching I found a grower who grew late season and early season Valencias and with proper storage I was eventually able to close the gap in my supply of perfect oranges for juicing. In every hotel that Bob Burns visited he terrorised the general manger and the chef with his demands for a perfect orange juice; it certainly made his visits both colourful and daunting.

Bob Burns was certainly a unique person with an incredible eye for detail. This could often be annoying and frustrating, but it was also a persuasive way of checking on our capacity to deliver on our own promise of service and quality. The Regent was able to set and maintain its high standards because of Bob and Ted's unwavering commitment to excellence.

10

EXECUTIVE CHEF

A YEAR AND A BIT AFTER I ARRIVED, CLAUDE BOUDOUX (THE thoughtful chef who brought me to Sydney) came to town. He just completed the opening of a new hotel: The Regent Halekulani, a new incredible addition to the chain. A year earlier he had opened The Regent Auckland, a much smaller hotel than Sydney. The news from there was that the Executive Chef was a very temperamental Frenchman who made things quite difficult for all working for him; he was Monsieur Boudoux's assistant when he was Executive Chef in Montréal.

That month it was announced that the Food & Beverage Manager of The Regent Sydney was to leave and join Cathay Pacific as their new Director of Food & Beverage. This was an amazing job in any sense of the industry. Claude spent a couple of days with me in the kitchen and eventually asked me if I had heard that Jacky was to take over his role. I said that I had also heard the rumour. He then asked me if I would be interested in becoming Executive Chef in Auckland! My heart kind of sank. I had fallen in love with Sydney, I loved my team, I loved the hotel and I just did not expect to have to move so soon, especially to a lesser hotel. I did not have to commit myself yet, but he asked me to reflect on it overnight. What could I say? He had brought me to Australia, he deserved all my loyalty and I made peace with myself during the evening over the fact that I was to move.

Events overtook me in the morning. I was called to Ted Wright's office to formally be asked if I wished to take on the Executive Chef role in Sydney—what a turn around! I imagine that the idea of getting a cranky and difficult French chef did not appeal to Ted and I also knew that he preferred to work with people he knew. Nevertheless, I was honoured by his confidence in my ability to grow in the job and I spent the next 15 years working for The Regent to try to repay him and show him that his judgement of me had been correct.

I went back to the kitchen and suddenly the weight on my shoulders felt enormous. Everyone seemed older than me and more experienced, and every manager seemed more decisive and embedded in their role. Where should I go from here, what do I do now and what needs to change?

I was already pretty much in full charge of the staff but the major change was that I suddenly had to do all the menus and the food ordering as well. We had what we called a market list, with three columns: what was in store that morning, what was coming on the day, and the column that I suddenly needed to fill was what to order for the next day. The quantities were staggering: four boxes of green beans in store, six coming, what for tomorrow; 1½ tins of Sevruga caviar in store, time for a new tin to cover the weekend; 38 whole ducks, next kill on Monday, how many needed, 60 or 72? The biggest variable was the functions. Three functions for 400 people in a row (two of them with prawn entrees) meant that 80 or 90 kilos of prawns were needed, plus enough to cover room service, Kable's, the café, the pool and the mezzanine (where we served prawn sandwiches), so let's say 120 kilos in total. It was a huge responsibility estimating every line of that market list. The food needed to be fresh and it was critical to get this right, without running out of produce or creating wastage from unused food.

Making sure the store was well provisioned for all the chefs was another of my most important tasks. If my order was out then this could create a real cascading effect on the various kitchens. If banquets needed eight boxes of mushrooms, Kable's three and the café two, but only eight came in, it would create tension between the chefs and cause problems for their menus. There was always the possibility of getting more stock in, but it may not arrive until the afternoon.

The seafood ordering was even more difficult. I wanted the fish to be in prime condition and I always tried to have just enough stock to last the day. I wrote the menus in the morning according to what fish I could have from the market. I was constantly on the phone with my fish supplier, George, to adjust, increase or select another type of fish if the one I ordered the previous day was not available. I often spoke five or six times a day with him just to stay ahead and ensure I had enough fish. Having a lunch in the function room for 400 people with John Dory would create all sorts of panic as trying to get 100 kilos of that rare fish at the right size was a daunting task. Often we needed to fly fish in from New Zealand and it was delivered directly from the airport to the hotel.

Luckily I had one of the absolute best fishmongers on my staff to handle the arrival of the fish and its raw preparation. José Chaves was Portuguese; at that time he had lived in Australia for over 30 years but his continental accent was still so strong that new staff could never understand what he was saying. José had been a kitchen steward at the Wentworth Hotel for many years and he went on to become one of the most valuable people The Regent ever possessed. To this day he still works there (even though it is no longer The Regent) which is a sign of his loyalty to the hotel.

José would help me estimate the qualities of regular stock that needed to be ordered. A typical weekday list from José would include 120 dozen oysters; 26kg of white, roe-less scallops; 32 boxes of smoked salmon; 12kg blue eye cod; 8kg crab meat; 60 blue swimmer crabs; 44kg black mussels; 36 whole live lobsters; 12kg squid; 8kg cuttlefish; 10kg pippies; 60 whole sand whiting and 40kg of whole snapper. The list would get longer throughout the week until Friday, when the order was just amazing. José handled all the fish himself: he received it, checked the weight against the charge from the invoice and checked the freshness. If he was in doubt he would call me and together we would decide if it needed to be replaced. He then would take his first arrival of the day on a pallet trolley (maybe 200 to 300 kilos of white fish and fresh shellfish) to his dissecting section. There he would sort all his fish into new tubs and he would start scaling, filleting and portioning all the seafood according to the request list from the various restaurants.

His task was enormous, literally tons of fish on a weekly basis. The Regent was by far the biggest customer of any wholesaler at the market. Our account with George, our fish supplier, was protected like a most important franchise one could acquire. There was no way he was letting another supplier muscle in on his territory, so valuable was The Regent business. José never ever compromised on the quality we would receive and he also always insisted on receiving whole fresh fish, not fillets. It was his job to fillet all the fish to ensure the highest quality possible. At that time, when a lot of the other hotels were ordering frozen fish fillets for practical and price reasons, we never wavered on our demand for whole fresh fish. That gave us a reputation that was to become unequalled at the market. No wonder when either José or myself went on our frequent visits to the fish market we were given the glance of respect that big bidders would get. Not only did we make buying decisions for one of the biggest accounts, but we also paid top price within seven days and our level of demand never wavered.

Our fish buying, handling and filleting set up always fascinated people who visited our kitchens. When Neil Perry had just opened Rockpool he visited our kitchens and openly admired the quality of our operation and the unique skill José possessed. I have no doubt that The Regent's set-up inspired many other chefs to treat fish with an ever growing respect and professional manner, making the most of one of our best local food resources.

If you can purchase, handle and cook fish skilfully then you deserve to be viewed as one of the top food outfits in the city. Until the arrival of Neil Perry at Rockpool and Greg Doyle at The Pier there weren't many restaurants that could ensure the best fish would reach the customer. There is a lot of folklore surrounding line-caught fish, but I knew that the quality of the fish we purchased relied on much more that this catchy phrase. For twenty years we were able to have the freshest fish possible due mostly to the quality operation and fishermen that care about their catch. Today we have seen an overall improvement in the way fish is handled, even if some of the bad habits are still present in the industry.

If my role was massive and complex on the seafood aspect of my purchasing then the meat side of the equation was going to absorb me to a new degree. One of the biggest problems we faced in the kitchen was the quality and consistency of the meat we were getting. For a country the size of Australia with such a big meat industry the state of that industry was in total disarray; the lack of standards of the beef, pork, lamb and veal totally astonished me. The meat was not only generally inconsistent, but it often was unsuitable for a place like us. It did not seem to matter which company we used, as none of them could supply us with meat of a consistently high quality.

At The Regent we ordered hundreds of kilos of seafood per week, but the quantity of meat was much greater. People in Australia, especially in the early days of The Regent, tended to order oysters or shellfish for entrée, then meat for mains. We ordered thousands of kilos of meat and used tons of scotch fillets, strip loin or tenderloin. We ordered racks of lamb by the thousands and veal fillets by the hundreds of kilos. In the early days the solution to ensure consistency was to return to the supplier anything that was not acceptable. So every box of meat was opened in the loading dock, carefully inspected by my butchers, sorted, and any substandard pieces were rejected. Often we were returning as much as a third of the order. It was incomprehensible that we could be in that sort of situation. How could a supplier just not get it? Why keep sending us inferior quality? It took me a long time to understand the situation and the cause and effect of decisions the government in Australia never made.

Meat in Australia was a commodity that was governed by the export trade. The domestic side was seen as an add-on, a small, scattered market with difficult players who had a poor record of paying and unpredictable ordering patterns. Whereas a restaurant or hotel could easily decide not to purchase from one day to the next, the overseas contracts were secured by competitive bidding. This made most suppliers direct their energy towards the export market, instead of the local domestic one. Through experience, they didn't feel it was worth addressing the issue of consistency for the sake of the local sales.

I needed to understand why our local market had evolved like this. In North America the whole industry was like a well-oiled machine, working as a total market with much less emphasis on export. Most of the trade is divided between domestic buying and the restaurant and hotel trade. There were two critical aspects of the set up in North America that made it able to produce quality. The first one was a Federal Classification system, which demands that each beef or veal carcass be graded, based on its perceived and judged quality. There are very strict guidelines to evaluate the carcasses and these evaluations are made by Federal Officers with huge amounts of experience, who are posted in every abattoir in the country. Interestingly enough we have meat inspectors in our abattoirs but they do not grade carcasses because they are there to ensure that the meat is fit for human consumption and to safeguard the integrity of the meat supply for overseas export. That they are not there to also grade the meat is a shame and a missed opportunity.

The second telling difference between the two markets is the way we purchase the cuts of meat in restaurants. On a beef carcass (which by far is the most popular meat) you have two main sections: the hindquarter (which contains the front of the animal) and the forequarter (which contains the lesser cuts like the brisket, chuck and blade). The hindquarter is mostly used domestically and is mainly sold in butcher shops and shopping centres in North America. The butchers are very inventive in presenting and selling these lesser cuts, which are much cheaper than the hindquarter, and therefore more attractive for domestic use.

The hindquarter contains mostly the prime cuts, like the strip loin where New York steaks are derived, tenderloin for fillet mignon, scotch fillet for rib eye or prime rib of beef, and rump, which is perfect for hotel roasts. Other lesser parts are also produced out of the hindquarter, like topside and skirt steak, but in general all of the production of the hindquarters end up in hotel restaurants or steak houses. The fact that these cuts receive a great premium from these places means that the forequarter is acutely subsidised by the restaurants that wish to serve these prime cuts. It is rare you see New York steak, tenderloin of prime rib in butcher shops; in general you go out to steak houses to sample these cuts.

In Australia, however, that dual market does not exist. Our dual market consists of domestic or export and this is why we have a problem with maintaining consistently high standards in the meat produced for the domestic market. I tried to understand the lack of federal standards but could never get a straight answer from either the suppliers or the people who I assumed would have known. It became a bit of a fascination for me to try to understand what made this the way it was.

Because I had made a conscious decision when I came to Australia not to have a television I read a lot of books instead. I could not afford to purchase too many books so I went to the library. One day in the beautiful Woollahra Library I came across a book on meat, which gave an historical overview of the industry in Australia. It was a fascinating insight into the reasons why the Australian market had evolved in the way that it had. It explained that the great majority of the meat produced in Australia had been exported for decades. Most of that export demand was for the North American market, which needed huge quantities of beef for hamburgers. Because the beef in America is quite costly to produce (being a grain-feed superior product that attracts a premium price for the producers) there was a huge gap in the market to supply bulk meat for fast food outlets. Australian and Argentine beef filled the gap, with shiploads of beef being exported to America as boneless beef. The whole carcass was boned, packed, frozen and shipped to that insatiable market.

Huge abattoirs were created to fulfil these monster contracts. Australians by the thousands were employed as boners, and entire cities lived off these huge boning plants. Farmers, mostly in Queensland, NSW and the NT, ran enormous cattle ranges. Quality was not a possibility or a consideration and because the climate was so arid and the weather so uncompromising the beef produced was always going to be inferior. The cattle on these huge ranches needed to be mustered and driven thousands of miles to the abattoir. Grain-fed beef that one saw in North America did not exist in Australia at that time. Cattle was run on poor land with only a few head per acres, but the acreages were so vast that it was possible to have not only an economy of scale but ultimately a huge volume of beef.

This vast export demand made the national inspectors concentrate of the 'fit for human consumption' inspections, as most of the beef never reached the southern markets of Sydney or Melbourne that demanded a superior quality. To this day we still do not have a national beef or veal grading system. There are many private label classifications, there is branding and there is an occasional attempt at changing our ways, but nothing that could ever compare to the North American model. Now that beef exports are slowing, due to the fall in beef consumption all over the world, attempts are again being made to brand and improve the image of our beef. This is mostly achieved by private companies setting standards for export and doing this without the help of a federal classification system, which is still greatly needed.

The other way that this can be achieved is through set-ups like Rockdale in Victoria, where there is a huge modern abattoir that was built to supply the Japanese market. They own their land, they own their cattle, they have their own fields to grow their feed and they have their own fleet of trucks to move the beasts around. They employ their totally Australian workforce to produce an outcome of quality that is far superior to what we can find in our markets. Even with our export product, in general we still do not produce high quality grain-fed beef that produces the marble product necessary for flavour and tenderness. Still, there is a realisation that to attract premium price we need a premium, consistent product and some key players are out there trying to fulfil these niche markets.

I was at a loss as to what I could do about this frustrating situation, when my solution walked in one day to the Purchasing Office at The Regent Hotel in Sydney. I had gone to purchasing to complain about the oranges I was getting. I was not happy about the quality or the size, as they were clogging my new machine that produced my orange juice in a more efficient manner. Squeezing oranges by hand for my staff had proved to be a real health hazard. By the time you've squeezed 30 or 40 boxes of oranges daily by hand the acid in the juice eventually saturates the skin and causes sore hands unable to stand contact with citrus juice. I was experimenting with an automatic squeezing machine that required precise orange calibration to ensure the machine did not struggle. If the oranges did not match the exact size of the machine then a breakdown would ensue and six of us would end up squeezing oranges early in the morning to prepare for the breakfast orders.

Aldo, a meat salesman, happened to be in the Purchasing Office ready to make his pitch to sell his meat. After he heard me ranting and raving about the importance of two millimetres in the size of the oranges we were supplied, he started his sales pitch about his meat. Once he explained to me what he could do I told him, 'I do not think you understand what type of standards I expect'. He replied that judging from the orange problem he clearly understood that I was one who would not tolerate an inferior product and that he knew he could help me.

Aldo came from Canada and had always worked in the wholesale meat business. He used to travel to Australia to purchase supplies for his Canadian factory. He eventually decided that there was a real business opportunity in Australia and he moved his whole extended family to the shores of this Promised Land. Aldo established himself in Melbourne where the better pastures of Victoria would allow a superior range of beef to be produced. He associated himself with a quality abattoir and through his business acumen convinced the abattoir operator to let him select his carcasses out of the thousands being churned to the process, by offering them a premium on their price. That arrangement was the key reason for his success. It gave him access to consistent products, being able to select only the premium cuts needed for his restaurant and hotel customers. His packaging and standards he told me would be far superior to what I would received so far. I was certainly intrigued and hopeful that finely I had found a meat supplier who knew what I needed.

I certainly was tired of ordering prime rib of beef and getting one end the size of a grapefruit and the other end the size of a watermelon. When you tried to cook it one end would be totally well done while the other end would be blue. It just did not work any more for me. Striploin was worst: in a bag of four, two would be acceptable, one would be black (like you see from cow meat), and the other one would be totally skinny, more fat than meat. It was just a mess, fighting daily with the butcher to try to make him understand that what he was supplying was just not acceptable.

When I received Aldo's first delivery I knew he was more action than talk, even though he was a good talker. Finally, there was someone who understood exactly what I needed. He eventually became the sole supplier of The Regent Sydney, then The Regent Melbourne, then Bangkok, Singapore, Fiji and many other hotels and restaurants. To this day I still use Aldo; even though his supply comes from Melbourne, it gives me a far superior product than I am able to find in Sydney.

Slowly, I started to add my personal touches to the kitchen operation. I gradually gained confidence but was never totally at ease with my performance. I was racked by uncertainty; I felt that I did not have a strong belief in myself like Ted Wright or Jacky had. I was giving the answers that people wanted to hear, rather than the ones that I believed in, doing what the hotel wanted me to do, rather than asserting myself for what was right for the food. I was more of a peacemaker than a leader, trying to get along with and please every one, from human resources, to security, to the accounting department to Ted himself. Most people who know me now would never believe that I could have been like this, but that is the way that I was then.

The hotel was full of strong personalities and it was hard for me, the youngest member of the management, to impose my wishes or demands. I remember thinking about this and wondering when I should become more assertive. My chance arose around the time when Jacky's tenure as the Director of Food and Beverage came to an end. Jacky had decided that there was a better future in a different company and he was attracted by offers from Hilton International to open a new hotel in Monaco. It was a loss for the hotel and me, even if his relationship with Ted was not as good as the one I had with him. Unfortunately his choice did not produce the result he expected. The hotel in Monaco opened months behind schedule, which caused great problems for him, and a year later he returned to the company in a similar role at The Regent Singapore. Jacky and I had worked together as a great team, one that was solid and self-supporting. With his departure it was now my time to become more assertive and to shape my future by introducing more of my personal beliefs about the type of food I cooked and to find the producers I needed to achieve my culinary goals.

One of the instructions I received from Ted was to make sure I understood what was happening at the other Sydney restaurants and hotels. The most successful hotel up to that point had been the Hilton Hotel on George Street. There is no question that the Hilton Sydney was a hugely successful hotel, especially in the last decade before The Regent had opened. The opening of The Regent would have been a huge disruption to their captive market, however it was time to have a different product that represented an updated version of a five-star hotel.

Our two hotels could not have been more different: the Hilton was uptown, away from the harbour, with a business based on huge functions and a restaurant that was clearly anchored in the past. The San Francisco Grill offered caesar salad made at the table, many flambé dishes, a bread trolley and crêpes suzette. It was the anathema of what

Bob Burns wanted to offer. If the Hilton was all black-tie waiters then The Regent had waiters in white coats and white ties. If the service was more American at the Hilton then The Regent was more Asian or European. The food at the Hilton was classic and predictable (and a lot of people love that), but the food at The Regent was more progressive and tried to surprise your palate.

I developed a friendship with the Hilton chef and we both respected each other for what we produced without trying to pretend one or the other was better. Even though we were situated on the same street in Sydney, we were just worlds apart in terms of our vision for food and style of service. I was growing in confidence both personally and professionally and I finally began to make my mark as Executive Chef of The Regent.

11

CALIFORNIA DREAMING

T ED WRIGHT INFORMED JACKY AND I THAT WE WERE ALL GOING
to California. The idea was to visit all the leading restaurants of
California, San Francisco and the Napa Valley. The bookings were
made by Patrick Terrail, the nephew of Claude Terrail, who owned the
La Tour D'Argent, a famous restaurant in Paris. Patrick left France at
a late age to establish himself in California, where he was the founder
of 'Ma Maison'.

Ma Maison was considered for quite a long time to be 'the restaurant'
of LA. It was a restaurant that changed all the rules of the time. The
attractions were great food, great service and great looking people, but
above all it established Patrick as the host with personality, a sort of
Pope of Gastronomy and a confidant to everyone. To be recognised by
Patrick was a great plus, to be told that he was going to look after you
was very much sought after, but above all, he was the one that could
get you a table when the place was full, as it was most nights. He was
the restaurateur par excellence, but also a kind of chef concierge in LA,

having contacts for everyone everywhere; he knew all the key players of the leading industries and could open doors to money.

We arrived in LA in the afternoon; we were booked at the Hilton Hotel, as The Regent Beverly Wiltshire was not yet ready to open its doors. Our first destination was dinner at Ma Maison. The food had acquired quite an exalted reputation under their recently departed chef, Wolfgang Puck. Wolfgang certainly made his culinary reputation there and because he knew most of the customers it helped him establish his new restaurant, Spago. Stars also loved being recognised by the chef and Patrick was probably one of the best known food personalities to make a big mark in California.

When we arrived at Ma Maison it appeared that we were on a different planet. The restaurant looked like a glorified marquee. The chairs were basic white moulded plastic from China and the floor could have been Astroturf; our perception of what a successful restaurant should look like was totally challenged by this place. We soon realised that how the furniture looked was really of no consequence because the real attraction was sitting in the chairs. The crowd was electric, but it was the women who were truly amazing. We did not need any reminder that we were in Hollywood because the place was full of actresses: established actresses, aspiring actresses, and wannabe pretend actresses.

The menu was also not quite what I expected. By the time of our visit Wolfgang Puck had departed Monsieur Terrail's kitchen and a new chef was in place; Monsieur Jean Pierre (so French—he later became a good friend). His menu was classic French, based on cream and butter sauces, and dishes like Wellington, pauppiette, terrine, cassoulet and pavé. This was a throw back to the past, but I imagine that was the whole point.

Ma Maison was really a California bistro with practical furniture and a lot of character, which mainly due to Patrick. Patrick was probably the most suave, educated, accomplished host one could ever wish to be recognised by when arriving at a restaurant. He had total authority with his waiters and charm with his guests. I am sure that if he gave you the worst table in the room he could make you believe that it was the best because a star had used it to ensure privacy! He could sell you any thing on the menu that the chef would need to sell and he dictated the style of the menu. He had a very clear idea of how to make every guest feel special so that they returned time and time again.

Patrick gave us a table in the middle of the room and he really looked after us. He knew that in the culinary world it pays to help a colleague for reasons often held in the future. Our choice of food was made easy with the notation on the menu of '* *', indicating the personal favourites of Patrick Terrail. This was a real lesson on how to be visible, known, revered and respected; it was the start of the cult of restaurateur and chef as personality and nothing like that existed in Australia yet.

I still remember to this day the spelling mistake on the menu, which was strange at this level of restaurant. It was either the result of a French chef writing an English menu badly or an American secretary typing bad French, but either way I noticed that people notice. This was another lesson for me and to this day I always try to have two other people proofread every menu I write. I always doubt my own spelling and constantly check it with several dictionaries in my office.

We eventually settled down to the food, realising that most of the action was not on the plate but around the room. At the table next to us there was a young lady with a distinguished gentleman; he was perfectly dressed with a superb suit, pink shirt and impressive tie. She, by contrast, was wearing a sheer gauze of a shirt that left nothing to the imagination, exposing her perfect breasts just above her smoked salmon mousse. The man was amazing in his denial of her charms for what I presume was a pitch for a part in a movie. Later in the evening Patrick asked two young women from another table to join us and one of the girls was wearing only a thin strip of material over her enormous breasts. I then realised that such was the scene in Hollywood; the food attracts the crowds, but the crowd set the scene. Welcome to California.

—

Before we had departed to LA we all had made a promise to meet at 7am every morning and run for a few kilometres, regardless of how much we ate or drank the night before. Now I was not in the best shape and apart from swimming, I did not do any regular exercise. On the contrary, Ted exercised every day and he had the build of an American footballer (which he used to be). Jacky was tall and skinny but he professed every day at work how good the run up the hills in Mosman were.

Two months before the trip I told myself that I had better start training and get in some sort of shape so that I wouldn't embarrass myself with these two health and fitness fanatics. One month out and I still hadn't started yet. A further two weeks and I made some further promises to myself, until finally the day came and I found myself outside the Hilton at 7am, jet-lagged, with a bit of a headache from the wine at Ma Maison and totally unprepared. I wisely decided to let them lead the run.

Immediately my heart was pounding and I dammed myself over and over for not training before I left. I struggled to stay with them but pride made me do it. After what seemed an eternity, my old cross-country training from school kicked in and I started to breathe easier. I remembered that my race technique at school had been to always to run second for the whole race and in the last circuit of the race, pass the leader and sprint to the end. I started to feel that we were approaching the hotel, as we passed the amazingly picturesque back streets of Beverly Hills. To reach the Beverly Wiltshire Boulevard was a struggle, but the closer we got to the hotel the more confident I became.

I pushed and pushed myself, finishing well ahead of the others, with a surprising amount of energy left. I didn't lose a single race in the next two weeks. They accused me of tricking them into believing that I had not trained—I swore I hadn't, but they never believed me.

After our early morning torture of a run we made our way to the Bel Air Hotel for breakfast. The breakfast was good without being overly memorable, but what stuck in my memory was the air of exclusivity that permeated the walls of this world-class hotel in the boutique LA suburb, Bel Air. To check out the competition we ended up having lunch at another hotel. This one was certainly more like a giant pink Californian bungalow than a high-rise hotel. The low-rise structure lent itself to courtyard eating alfresco, which was perfectly suited to this beautiful climate. The highlight of the lunch was a traditional cob salad: an unusual but pleasant mixture of diced beetroot, bacon, cheese, tomato, lettuce and chicken. This strange combination of ingredients produced a fun taste sensation that could become quite addictive. To think that Marilyn Monroe, Katherine Hepburn and Humphrey Bogart had all dined here gave the place an air of stardom.

— ⁓ —

The idea of a style of cooking that uses new ingredients and the serving of people with personal flair was in a broad sense what was meant by the new term 'California Cuisine' and its various interpretations. We were going to visit some of the pioneers of California Cuisine, but before we got to these trendsetting restaurants we visited some of the classics of the sunny state, such as 'Gladstone for Fish'.

This restaurant was on the Pacific Coast Highway at the end of Sunset Boulevard. It was right on the beach, which was a local hang-out place for beach boys and girls, but the real place to be seen hanging out was outside Gladstone for Fish, waiting to get in. They only take a few reservations and it was not unusual to wait a couple of hours before you got in, which was a clever strategy. Getting people to wait at the bar, despite their reservation, served the establishment well as it created 'the atmosphere', sold more drinks and made the food seem even better then it was.

Because Patrick Terrail had recommended us we only waited for 45 minutes. It was just enough to get a buzz from our drinks, and put an edge on our appetite. Once inside the enthusiasm to eat was very contagious, I imagine even more so if you had waited two hours. The General Manager introduced himself and selected dishes for us from the menu. A giant platter of mixed seafood arrived, accompanied by lettuce, tomato, boiled egg, and four kinds of commercial sauces. Still, we all loved it. We followed this with crab soup with brandy. We knew exactly what was coming next as we could see the kitchen through a large glass panel that served as one of the walls. Huge tables were stacked about a metre high with large cos lettuce leaves topped with coleslaw to be served with each main course. It was very American but we loved it.

The fish and shellfish were either served cold, steamed or charcoal broiled. It was really just a giant fish 'n' chip shop, an American version of Doyles on the Beach at Watson's Bay. Our visit to Gladstone for Fish was certainly a cultural experience. It was a revelation on how to churn people through the door with a winning formula of low-price food and loads of atmosphere.

—

We were told that there were two people who were leading the big Californian revolution in food: one in LA and the other in San Francisco. Wolfgang Puck at the newly opened Spago was redefining California Cuisine and the other leader was Alice Waters at Chez Panisse in Berkley, which we were meant to visit in a few days time. But first we were to visit Spago.

Wolfgang Puck, like Arnold Schwarzenegger, is Austrian, and there are many more similarities between the two men. Just as Arnold conquered America (via Europe) through hard work to eventually become a public hero, Wolfgang's work took him through the training grounds of Europe to California, where through sheer talent and commitment he made himself even more famous than the stars that his restaurant serves. He was the original celebrity chef: the one who brought a breath of fresh air in the stuffy dining rooms of the past and the one who made the public realise that a restaurant could be lead by the chef, as opposed to the owner. Once the chef is directly answerable to the public I feel the food improves dramatically because there is no more hiding behind a restaurant owner or Maître d'Hôtel.

We arrived on time for our dinner at Spago only to realise that in California this meant absolutely nothing. We were slowly turning into alcoholics, constantly challenging our limit with a new cocktail every night as we waited for our table. The vibe at Spago was one of urgency, as the trendy crowd packed into the bar, everyone trying to impress upon the restaurant manager why they should be seated next. When this did not work, threats would sometimes follow and Wolfgang often came out of the kitchen to cool tempers and assure every one that he loved them and that tables would be available soon. Once he had made a fuss over them the tension would ease and everyone would prance around with a new sense of self-importance that came from Wolfgang getting them seated.

This was pure Hollywood, with the big names hanging out at the bar, sweating on their predicament of not getting straight to a table. These were the perils of having 150 seats but doing 350 covers every night, there is no perfect science to managing bookings at that level. These days you see places like London and New York taking bookings for both arrival and departure times! That is, in my view, the day that a restaurant will start losing their clientele, after the initial visit of all the foodies people will refuse this unwelcoming and unfriendly system.

Even though there was a wait to be seated no-one was going to complain about being surrounded at the bar by Jacklyn Smith, George Hamilton, Sally Kellerman (Hot Lips from M.A.S.H) and many other stars and starlets. Needless to say that most of the room—including Jeff Goldblum, who was sitting at the next table—had a quizzical look on their faces when Wolfgang came and introduced himself to us, and then came back constantly through the night to check on our table. He also took us to the kitchen to show us through his new way of doing things. We were very impressed; this was a man who knew exactly what he was doing.

We gave Spago a rating of 19½ out of 20 for atmosphere, the highest of all restaurants we visited. But for me, the real revelation of the night was Wolfgang's Chef de Cuisine: a young, blonde, extremely beautiful young woman, no more than 23. She was running the kitchen and seemed extremely poised and focused, quite capable of serving over 300 meals every shift. The staff were all young, dedicated, keen to learn and they performed to an incredibly high standard. My whole way of thinking about having a leader manage the kitchen with toughness and drive was shattered that night. Instead of trying to put down the staff (which is the norm in a heavily testosterone-charged kitchen) this seemed a much better way to mould and guide a kitchen. This was a lesson in kitchen management that would stay with me forever.

We started with a crisp pizza, topped with smoked salmon, goat cheese, chives and dill. This dish was a great teaser to start the meal with. Wolfgang's Californian pizza has now become a worldwide phenomenon, seen on menus everywhere, and varying incredibly in quality according to the skill of the chef. At that time, however, Wolfgang had totally redefined a simple classic dish that had been completely ruined by American mass production. Wolfgang's version had light, fresh, seasonal toppings on a thin crispy base, as apposed to the heavy, doughy, meat-laden pizzas that were available at the time.

For the next course we had a raw tuna dish with avocado and marinated onion, and then a superb duck ravioli with baby yellow squash and a glace de viande. The main course was baby lamb ribs with blanched garlic, grilled eggplant, baby zucchini and carrots; all the vegetables were beautiful and freshly exciting, of a type and size I had never seen before. We finished with a sample plate of mini desserts that again set the trend for many chefs and restaurants.

Spago was so incredibly successful because Wolfgang had a rare combination of talents; he was a true chef, a pioneer, a people leader, a role model and a successful businessman. He is an icon in the mind of the new generation of chefs who have seen the transformation of the chefs from hidden worker to becoming the integral element that gives credibility to the food of a restaurant and to the success of the business. Wolfgang eventually opened a succession of restaurants state wide, then in Las Vegas and many other international cities. Most became franchised restaurants where Wolfgang would lend his name and initial expertise and his wife Barbara Lazaroff organised the décor.

We left Los Angeles and moved on to the culinary fields of San Francisco. What a destination; to me it was more exciting than LA. Since I was a teenager I had always dreamed that I would leave Montréal and end up in working in America, and my city of choice was either San Diego or San Francisco. It does not surprise me that I have ended up living in a warm climate. Montréal is a great city with a clear sense of its place in history and a great food culture, but it also has terrible winters that seemed to go on forever, causing an attachment to traditional food that can be very restricting. So the idea of working in a warm climate where fresh produce is grown year round, in a dynamic society that went out to eat and were ready to support new approaches to food, appealed to me enormously.

San Francisco was a discovery. We did not play tourist, but we did get a sense of excitement about restaurant and food innovation in a city that is steeped in great food tradition. We were staying at Campton Place, a brand new hotel that set new levels of personalised service and was focused on providing great food. The young chef, Bradley Odgen, had already built a reputation for regionalism and a different and personal approach to hotel food. His approach was fresh and unformulated and certainly the furthest possible from a predictable hotel dining room menu.

Bradley developed into a pioneer of California Cuisine. He had a strong link to his produce sources and a commitment to cook the kind of great food that you would find in a small restaurant. When you have total belief in your produce you cook in a way to highlight its flavour, even if it means that a dish might sound too simple. However if the chef has passion for the dish then your staff will convey to the customers the same desire to taste and savour your star ingredients. At Bradley's restaurant I tasted a baked Maui onion with balsamic vinaigrette. Now this could be a hard dish to sell in an expensive restaurant, but that onion was something special to start with, it was cooked long enough to release all of its sweetness, and the vinaigrette did not overpower the onion. In short, it was something magic, and it was typical of the type of food that I found on Bradley's menu.

After Bradley showed us around his kitchen and I saw the range and quantity of produce available to him it made me feel that we were missing something essential in Australia. We had to start growing for flavours, not quality or size, and we had to pick produce at its ideal ripeness to provided maximum flavour. I started to understand what could be done in Australia.

The person who made the biggest impact with the use of quality ingredients in California had to be Alice Waters, with her restaurant Chez Panisse. She is part legend, part visionary, part ecologist and, in a sense, part dreamer for a better world all around. I admire her commitment to only serve organic food in her restaurant: food that has pedigree, food that is nurtured by committed growers. The fish is caught in the wild and the meat has never seen the mass feedlot enclosures. Her food has purity and a pared down style that lets the ingredients shine. It is, when delivered as she intended, quite delicious and flavoursome.

Chez Panisse became a cult restaurant, and a magnet for lost souls who wanted to become chefs. Alice was always keen to hire anyone who displayed devotion to great food and share her vision for simplicity and flavours. I am always surprised by how many people have worked at Chez Panisse; some of them became great chefs, people like Jeremiah Tower and Ken Hom, as well as many others.

I ate many times at Chez Panisse over the years, especially because Ken Hom became a great friend and he happened to live a few streets away from the restaurant. Every time I visited San Francisco I would dine on at least one occasion with Ken at Chez Panisse. The food proved to always be a highlight of my visit, especially in the bistro, where simple salads using great ingredients like yellow beetroot, goat cheese and pickled onion, shone with freshness. The restaurant part was very well patronised, with people from around the world booking to eat there on their visit to San Francisco. They have two seatings of around 45 people. This is fine for America, as many guests like to eat early, but I'm not sure if we could pull that off in Australia.

Many people contributed to the menu at Chez Panisse. Jeremiah Tower told me that it was his idea to have theme dinners at the restaurant: regardless of whose idea it was, these dinners became a feature and a fixture of the restaurant. Alice created a certain liberty about the kitchen and allowed the chef the freedom to write a seasonal menu. These were based on relevant seasons like 'a white truffle menu', 'winter menu', 'garlic menu' or 'fall menu of the Napa Valley'. Many other menus were based on eminent food or wine person's visits, and there were also more predictable menus like 'Provençal menu', 'Tuscan menu' or 'Valentine's Day menu'.

One night we were dragged away from our customary pre-dinner drink at the back of the upstairs bistro to be taken to the temple of boutique food one level below. The theme was a seasonal summer menu, and the food lived up to our expectations, with a chilled cucumber soup with wildflowers, grilled paillard of beef with black cabbage, a garden salad and poached white peaches with crème anglaise. Most of the food was classic, pared down and well cooked, but on that night the service lacked to a point of distraction, the kitchen was open for all to see, with a casualness bordering on 'laisser-faire'.

The floor staff were uninterested in our desire to learn more about the food served, and most of the kitchen team were too busy exchanging wine and food to satisfy their own culinary requirements to make us feel welcome. They actually made us feel like we were spoiling their evening and some of the staff had quite a religious attitude that seems to go with serving food with a conscience. A sense of discipline always needs to embrace the whole team when service time starts, however on that night no one was there to remind the 'brigade and garçons de la salle' that their focus needed to shift from themselves to their guests. A balance between military precision and giving freedom to express everyone's skills needs to be achieved, but respect for who pays the bills should never be forgotten. This was another important lesson for me.

One of the founders of California Cuisine, by his own admission, is a great friend of mine who lived in Australia as a teenager: Jeremiah Tower. Jeremiah had a critical influence in changing the way people ate in California and what was served in restaurants. In the early days at Chez Panisse he moulded the restaurant from a French influenced one to a more liberal place, taking inspiration from the produce of the West Coast.

Jeremiah was born in the United States, educated at the King's College in England and he was a graduate of the Harvard School of Design. He fell into cooking at Chez Panisse in the 70s, where he eventually became the head chef and a partner in the business. Jeremiah's appreciation of the beautiful, tasty and rare, and his mixture of formal and informal manners made him an intriguing and much-loved character. He was reserved one minute with people he did not yet know and at the other extreme he was full of exuberance with people that he felt comfortable with and were on the same level of thought.

We came to respect each other over the years and we had many encounters together. Jeremiah, in the 80s came to The Regent to hold one of the promotions the hotel was known for and he made a huge impact on Sydney, its chefs and the style of food that we were starting to cook. Jeremiah was also a loner and a thinker and he was prone to the bouts of self-examination that creative people often go through. It was a difficult role to be a revolutionary in 70s against a trend of classic French food and a real belief in the martini and steak lunch. Goat cheese and fresh vegetables were not in fashion. Jeremiah's subtle influence on the evolution of the Chez Panisse menu, from classic French to regional American, was his greatest contribution to the restaurant that acquired iconic status in the 80s and is still respected to this day.

Jeremiah's creative juices went to work on one of the most successful cookbook series the English world has ever seen: the Good Cook Series of Time and Life Books. These turned out to be some of the most influential books I ever had the privilege to absorb, read and use. It is now out of print, but the series had a huge impact on the generation of people that used them. I was so enthusiastic about them that I purchased about 24 sets to give, one at a time, to all my successful apprentices at The Regent. There are over 24 books in the series, so I figured that if I gave one to each apprentice every two months as they changed sections in the kitchen they would receive the entire set by the time they finished their apprenticeship. What better than getting a classic book on soups when you were set to work in that section of the kitchen? The same applied to eggs, meat, fish, bread, sauce, canapés and so on. I would have loved to receive such an educational tool so regularly when I was young and learning my trade. I hope the books inspired my apprentices to achieve and learn about the art of good cooking.

Jeremiah owned and designed many restaurants over the years, but the most well-known was Stars restaurant in San Francisco. Stars was really a American brasserie serving the new American classics that Jeremiah had became famous for. He mixed cooking techniques and ingredients in a manner that helped define California Cuisine. He was strong on big flavours, on roasting, on colourful ingredients and on contrasts of flavour.

The day that we visited him he impressed us with his ability to explain his belief in his food style and his kitchen system, but also with his trust in his chefs, as he never forgot the freedom that he had been given at Chez Panisse. We ate intriguing foods like grilled pork cutlet with braised lentils, pear chutney and curry sauce. At that time it was amazingly revolutionary and a real taste sensation. The contrast of taste and texture was new to us but the whole dish came together superbly. It was full of concentrated flavours, like the spices of the curry sauce, but then with another mouthful the pear chutney. The tenderness of the meat was amazing and when Jeremiah later came to Sydney he showed me how to achieve this by a long slow roasting and then a quick grilling.

Wolfgang Puck was Los Angeles impersonated but Jeremiah was all California: young, brash, daring, opinionated, talented and prone to bouts of 'time out' to reassess his desire and focus. Jeremiah may have received all the culinary acclaim he deserves, but I think that financial success has eluded him which is such a common situation for our profession.

We moved by rental car to the Promised Land, the magically named Napa Valley. It was the epicentre of good food, great wine and stylish living. It was quite a culture shock to me, its sheer beauty and relevance is quite unique in the New World. It is the American equivalent to Burgundy, but without the past history. Here there was not the period of war, starvation and religious intolerance that Burgundy suffered (evidenced today by its very fragmented and traditional society). The Napa, on the other hand, is a kind of island of food elitism in the middle of that sea of mediocre food and alcohol, known as Middle America.

The Napa is one of the most established wine regions of America. The reasons for its success are many, but obviously are based on the right climate (its climate tends to imitate to a certain degree that of Bordeaux), adequate soil and the sloping hills that offer good drainage and exposure to the long sunny days. The Napa Valley is a picturesque tourist destination, offering many attractions other than the wine tasting rooms, including several wine museums. The countryside is so pretty, the houses are so beautiful, and the vineyards are so trimmed and picturesque, that there is a certain artificiality to the countryside. Everything is regulated to ensure prettiness and a sense of uniform style: there are no ugly buildings, no bad roads and no dirty sheds. I guess nothing wrong with this as long as it does not become a Disneyland for the sophisticated grown-up and they do not start spraying the vine leaves green to make them look more vibrant.

I visited Nieubaum-Coppola vineyard, one of the more elegant vineyards in the Napa Valley. Nieubaum-Coppola is an estate that already had a heady reputation as a top producer in the Napa Valley when Francis Ford-Coppola purchased it decades ago. It is the encapsulation of the American dream, the type of house frequently featured in American architectural magazines. The long sweeping drive leads to the majestic established house in the true East Coast rambling wood construction, with the base of the house completely surrounded by an imposing covered veranda and intricate wooden colonnades. The wines produced here have attained cult status, but the beautiful thing is that their wine maker at the time had retained an incredible humility, something not often seen in most of the other wine makers of the region. He originally came from Mexico, had been working for more than 40 years on the land, and the quality of his wines was outstanding.

Our next winery visit was to a vast operation that was established in the Napa Valley many decades ago, totally different to the boutique winery. Whereas Nieubaum-Coppola was owned by a movie maker philanthropist, Robert Mondavi Winery was owned by a wine maker extraordinaire and a wine personality with no equal in North America. Robert Mondavi and his son Michael created Robert Mondovi Winery, quickly establishing themselves as pioneers of the Napa. Over the years, through development and acquisition, Robert's name and winery grew in statue and he is probably one of the best-known wine names in the world.

We drove a short distance up Highway 29 to reach the winery. Across the road an incredibly modern and imposing structure was been constructed; it was to become the famous OPUS One Winery, a partnership between Robert Mondavi and Baron Phillippe de Rothschild of Château Mouton Rothschild. Robert Mondavi developed working partnerships all over the world and is associated with wine production in France, Italy, Chile, and in Australia, with Rosemount Estate.

It is hard to convey the scope, size and influence the Mondavi family possesses in the Napa Valley, or for that matter in the North

American wine market. On visiting the winery in the early 80s it was not quite evident what was to become of this family winery. Robert had organised for us to have us to have him lunch with him with food prepared by the resident chef. Over the years food became an integral part of the promotion of Robert's wine and the winery became known for its food and music festival and strong links with the arts. Its summer music festival has been running now for over three decades and there are also other programs attracting great crowds. There is always pure excitement in the air when the Great Chef's promotion is run at Robert Mondavi Winery, further confirming the prominence of his name and links to food and arts.

Even in this early stage of Monsieur Mondavi's career we could sense a grand vision, a desire to reinvent the soul of a winery and his belief in the potential of the Napa Valley. I did have the chance over the following years to cook for him and his grace and warm always impressed me. I felt privileged to have met him; he was one of those 'larger than life' characters totally dedicated to the improvement in their field of knowledge. Meeting these kind of people, leaders capable of developing great strategies to improve their product or improve their environment, was something that impressed me enormously as the trip went along.

We left the wineries in a slightly euphoric state and we decided to stop at the Oakville Grocery Shop without much thought except that as people interested in food we had been told that we should stop there. Well, that visit transformed my life. I had never before seen produce like the vegetables they sold there. There were tiny carrots, beetroot, squash and parsnip as well as a great collection of local virgin olive oils, fantastic breads and prepared salad. The Coke sign that dominated the outside of the shop was certainly misleading.

Today the store is quite gentrified, but in the early 80s it was a lair of amazing and exciting produce that defined California Cuisine at that time. More than any experience on this trip those tiny vegetables and range of great lettuce leaves made me realise that we had a long way to go in Australia. The potential to develop this produce at home was a challenge I decided to take on then and there. I knew what to do and why in a sense I was sent to California, because we needed to change both the way we cooked and what we cooked.

The store itself dated back to the late 1880s. Its creaky wooden floor and old fashion feel must have impressed millions of customers since its inception as a gourmet paradise. The store has served as an early example for entrepreneurs with a love for food and I imagine it has inspired many of them to open up shops around the world. These days the Oakville Grocery Shop has inevitably expanded, with a thriving internet site offering corporate gifts, a wine store and private labels. The store in the Napa Valley carries one of the most extensive collections of Californian wines.

I will always remember this trip as the foundation stone for my drive to produce, cajole and encourage small growers to develop new produce and make Australian food on par with what was in offer in California. By the end of the trip my head was full of ideas but to have an influence over what was on offer in Australia was going to be quite a challenge. Everyday we had eaten out for breakfast, lunch and dinner at some fantastic restaurant. It was a whirlwind of new tastes, new presentations, new food personalities and new ways of creating a restaurant environment. Jacky and I made a report on all the restaurants we had visited and still to this day it is relevant and inspiring to read.

On the long trip back I started to develop my plan to change the way I cooked food, wrote menus and taught my staff. I could clearly see the need to develop new producers, improve the ones we had and support the small growers who will invariably give you the exotic products that a chef craves. It would not be easy, as my confidence in running the larger kitchen at The Regent was still not quite there, but I could see what was expected of me. The need to innovate was quite clear as well as the need to serve great food. We were given all the resources we could ever wish for, so it was just a matter of creating dishes that would capture the imagination of our guests and restaurant customers. There was a clear belief from Bob Burns and Ted Wright that whatever I served was to be of the highest quality and served in a style that was in tune with the rest of the hotel operation; sophisticated, elegant, refined and unique. This was a big mission but I was so inspired by California that the path ahead was clear and laid out ahead of me.

12

THE MARKETS

I ALWAYS ENJOYED GOING TO THE MARKETS. IT BECAME a point of honour to go every week, both to the Sydney Fish Market and to the newly opened Flemington Market. There is something primal about getting up before dawn and choosing the fish and fruit and vegetables that you will be using that day as a chef. To see the produce in that environment reminds you of your role as a chef: to select the best, freshest food possible and to serve it on your evening menu in a way that differentiates you from other chefs.

My routine normally would see me leave at 5.30am from Newport on the Northern Beaches in Sydney. In those years there weren't as many traffic lights and the focus of the police did not seem to be on stopping speedsters, which I certainly was. In short, for a long trip it took little time to reach the Sydney Fish Market.

The first time I visited the Sydney Fish Market I could not believe the choice of seafood on offer; it was a treasure trove of essential elements for creating good food. A city with such a fish market had to have the potential to be a serious food city. What an asset these markets were. Where else in the world could you have crate upon crate of fresh fish to select from? Maybe Tokyo, maybe the Rungis market in Paris and a few other places around the world, but here it all was right in the middle of my adopted city.

I was stunned by what was on offer but I also wondered where did all the fish end up? I quickly realised that a lot of the fish was wasted or it ended up as cat food because not many of the unknown species were sold. Still, for me there was every kind of fish that I wanted and much more. The famous Saint-Pierre (John Dory), one of the foundation fish of France, was here, as well as eel, rouget (red mullet), whiting, and the best crab selection in the world, including spanner, blue swimmer, mud crab and many others. The seafood was fresh and often sold still alive, like the Balmain bugs, local lobsters and bay scallops.

In these years it was for me imperative to try new species of fish. Most people only ate two types of fish—John Dory and snapper— when they went to restaurants, so to broaden people's palate I started introducing more unusual and unpopular species to the menu. Blue eye cod slowly became a more fashionable fish to the extent that it now costs nearly as much as snapper or John Dory on some days.

The old Sydney Fish Market was full of character, both in its building and its people. The market at that time was a living entity, full of migrant characters strolling through the old building, looking and obviously feeling totally in their element. The men at that time were mostly Greek and Italian, but with a growing Asian element that over the years became quite important to many fishermen as they were buying for an ever growing range of Asian restaurants. I just loved the way things looked and were done. It gave me a sense of belonging to a secret society of men, as not many women were able to work those weird working hours in an environment that assaults most of your senses.

The old auction system was quite mystical compared to today's cold and efficient silent Dutch auction system. There is something rustic and human about an auctioneer reciting, and in some cases nearly singing, the growing price of each crate or lot. It was like a different language that could only be understood by the close-knit family of buyers and fish merchants, as if they did not want the prying fisherman to hear what their crate was going for.

The idea of the auction was that the government was taking 17.5% of the price to pay for the privilege of the auctioning system and the crates they were provided to put the fish for sale in. Obviously there was a great incentive for the merchant to pay the least possible for the fish and it was often rumoured that the old system was subject to unfair practices. Apparently it was common for a buyer to purchase a complete lot of fish at a very low prices because no other bids were made, the merchants having agreed beforehand that only one of them would bid. Afterwards the fish were sold to the other merchants at that same low price.

These were the days of intrigue and uncertainty that made for the power of experience at the market. The auctioning was live, humane, fast, colourful and mostly honest. The overwhelming sense was that the system dictated the pace, not the need to get fish quickly out of the market to the customers. In those days it was not unusual to have the auction still going on in the early afternoon, not having stopped since the early mourning to get rid of stock. The fish suffered, the merchants suffered and the end-user suffered.

Later a new market was built which cut the handling and auctioning time considerably. Nowadays the fish is auctioned by the Dutch auction system, where you start at the highest price and go down, the first to bid at the highest price getting the fish. The Dutch auction system has probably proved to be the fairest system but it has certainly caused the retirement of many experienced auctioneers who gave the fish market its true character.

When I first started visiting the Sydney Fish Market most of the buyers were selecting for fish shops all around Sydney and the state as all fish caught in NSW were supposed to be traded at the Sydney Fish Market. That rigid system was recently relaxed with the privatisation of the new market but at that time that was the law. I found it was better not to say too much at the market; observe and learn and I kept telling myself. The reputation of The Regent was growing in stature every week and as a consequence of having our fish and shellfish order the merchant who was buying for us got much bigger and richer. In those years price was not really the issue; it was trying to get the best and freshest fish from the market. The menus were printed everyday and the fish could be whatever was the best at the market that morning.

I made friends with merchants, fisherman and other chefs. I took advantage of my contacts, visiting most of my suppliers at the source: oyster growers, tuna fisherman and even harbour ones. I would go out early in the morning catching white bait around Rose Bay in Sydney Harbour. I came to know most of the key players over the years but the family who got most of our business was the Manettas. The Manettas were a real clan and their respect at the market was mostly due to their father, Peter. Peter started trading at the market many decades ago and he was revered as a man of integrity, a wise man with knowledge. His company was fast growing once his sons took over the day-to-day running of the business.

Over the years I mostly dealt with George, one of Peter's sons. George was diplomatic, obliging, polite, resourceful and always helpful. I spoke to George two or three times a day, sometimes more. The demand and volume of the hotel for seafood was nearly insatiable. It was not unusual to have an order for 120kg of fresh prawns, 200kg of fish, 120kg oysters and 50kg of smoked fish.

Understandably with orders like this and a finance department that paid food suppliers promptly we were the number one client who was treated with the utmost care. I never exploited that relationship; I was always polite but insisted on the best quality. My fishmonger, José, a dedicated Portuguese who had an incredible understanding of seafood made my job so much easier, ensuring that we received exactly what we had paid for. José would give me his request list for the next day's seafood requirements. I would check it, sometimes but rarely correct it and then pass it on to purchasing to place the order. If I visited the market that morning I could alter the order to choose different fish, but if I did not go to the markets I relied on George to let me know what was there.

Once I arrived at the market my normal routine was to make a quick dash to the auction floor and walk each alley and absorb the unusual fish on offer. The unusual could have been a special crate of extra large live Balmain Bugs, some consistently-sized rouget, some extra large fresh looking tiger prawns, a great slimy hapuku, or crates of live scallops in the shell from Botany Bay. Once I finished doing my rounds I would go and see Michael Sergis, the Manettas buyer, and tell him what I liked. Invariably Michael knew exactly where the product was and exactly what I wanted. If I wanted it badly enough I would get it through Michael or he would contact the successful buyer and make them an offer they never seemed to refuse.

By spending time with the different buyers I dealt with, I learnt how to pick the freshest and best seafood. George taught me that judging the freshness of a fish by just looking at the condition of the eyes can be misleading. You also need to look at the sliminess of a fish, its firmness and other little things, like the amount of black tint in the tail of a snapper, to evaluate how long a fish has been out of the water.

After ruining several pairs of shoes I decided to purchase a pair of black gumboots. It took me a while before I made that decision because to wear gumboots at the market gave you a certain air of permanency that frankly I did not think I possessed. Still, they were the most practical form of footwear to wear to the markets. I think at the same time I got to wear fins on my long swims in the surf at Newport and

Whale Beach: small ironies, but surely the fins were more effective than the gumboots to swim in. I finally felt at home in Australia, wearing fins in the sea and gumboots at the fish market.

—

With our fruit and vegetables I soon became more and more concerned about the quality and freshness of our produce. Delivery was mostly by open bed trucks with the dog walking all over the produce. Pressure was put on them to get them to cover their trucks, but the resistance was surprising, with many reasons given as to why it could not be done. Eventually one company relented and the others followed. These days you rarely see fragile herbs, fruit and veggies being transported in open trucks in 30°C+ temperatures and the traffic fumes of Parramatta Road. I hope I made a small difference.

Over the years I did develop a good relationship with my suppliers. They were very helpful and obliging in most aspects of our needs, but I had a lingering thought that we still were not getting the quality that we needed. When I was second to Jacky we had a terrible time getting baby carrots. We asked all our suppliers if they could grow them for us but it was as if we had asked them to produce square melons. This was a royal battle of will, our purchasing power against the will to change. Why on earth did we want small carrots with the tail still on, they asked? They could not see the reason or the logic and they just could not visualise a baby carrot on a plate.

Luckily for us the purchasing power defeated the will to change and they organised someone to grow the baby carrots. When it came time to harvest the carrots I was told that the wife of a farmer would go behind the tractor to pick the small carrots not collected by the machine. Joe Leblanco, my buyer, was an old fashioned gentleman and a man with a large heart who was willing and committed to get us

FOOD AND FRIENDS IN ROME
SERGE DANSEREAU, ROSEMARY STANTON, SIMON JOHNSON, ELISE PASCOE,
ARMANDO PERCUOCO, STEVE MANFREDI, SUE FAIRLIE-CUNNINGHAM (VOGUE)

YVETTE AND I FIRST VISIT PARIS TOGETHER

YVETTE IN PORTOFINO

FINALLY, CHEESE TO BE PROUD OF,
THIS TIME IN MILAWA, VICTORIA

STEVE MANFREDI, BARRY MCDONALD, NEIL PERRY AND I
IN GIPPSLAND, VICTORIA

THE BIRTH OF REGIONAL CUISINE: WILD MUSHROOMS,
JERVIS BAY OYSTERS AND FARMED SNAILS

JUST THE TWO OF US: BLISS IN VATULELE

MY MOTHER JEANNINE BEFORE I KNEW
I WOULD END UP AT BATHERS'

BATHERS' PAVILION IN THE
CONSTRUCTION PHASE

what we wanted, but the incident proved how hard it was to achieve anything. Before long I realised that I would have to find a new way.

At Flemington Market I developed some friendships with a few of the growers. Most of them were progressive and quite willing to listen to me, even if it was only to get the chance to have a regular order from Joe Leblanco or me. I eventually was able to find growers who were willing to grow specific products on request. I found my very first grower through Jim Morrison, a horticulturalist with the NSW Department of Agriculture. Over the years he was very helpful with finding willing growers who would plant specific crops for me.

I initially approached Jim to see if he could find me someone willing to grow zucchini flowers for me. At that time you never saw zucchini flowers in shops and they were never used at home. It was one of these fringe ingredients used at home by the Italian community and mostly grown by themselves in their backyards. Most people did not know what to do with a zucchini, apart from using them in a ratatouille. I had seen some once at the market and after my Californian trip I wanted to have them.

In my father's garden, zucchini became a big thing and my mother learned to cook with them. It was such an exciting, versatile and prolific product that our whole family learned to eat zucchini in many different ways. My mother even found a book in America which she gave to me recently called *100 Ways to Cook Zucchini*. Our family was fed by the obsession of my mother, and we ate zucchini jam for breakfast, zucchini frittata for lunch, zucchini and carrot cake for tea, and zucchini relish late at night.

Jim recommended Anthony as an able grower; he was Southern Italian and quite possibly someone that could help me. I organised to go and meet him at his farm near Windsor, over an hour's drive from Sydney. For good measure I took some apprentices with me— something that I continue to do to this day to give them the chance to learn and see the link between the farm and the kitchen.

Anthony was a real farmer and quite typical of the time: he was hard working, his skin darkened and weathered by the sun and wind, focused in what he needed to do, and rough in manner to the point of brusqueness. It was sometimes hard to understand his accent, but he was very wiling to listen to my needs and see what he could do to help me. I could see Anthony was a committed and passionate grower, even though he expressed himself with very few words.

Anthony mostly grew artichokes, another very misunderstood and rarely used vegetable at the time. It was not a glamorous farm or a pretty setting; there was no romance to the art of growing these vegetables. I explained to him that I was looking for someone to supply me with good quality zucchini flowers for the hotel and that I was willing to pretty much take what he could grow. I learnt later on to never give such an open-ended commitment!

It only took a couple of months until two large and, to my surprise, new boxes were waiting for me in the loading dock. We normally received recycled boxes: maybe I paid way too much for that crop! Still they were glorious zucchini flowers, big, fresh and very golden, almost to the point of being fluorescent.

I was delighted and they went straight on the menu that day. A few days later I got three boxes and before I finished using that batch I received another five boxes on the following shipment. From using them exclusively in Kable's I had to put them in the café to start making use of them all. Before too long the shipment size kept increasing and I realised I had to do something about it. We were getting into summer and his crop kept yielding more and more of this golden flower. I didn't want to dampen Anthony's enthusiasm and tell him to slow down so I kept accepting them. I eventually had to call other chefs around town to see if they wanted to have a box or two of this exciting product. All of them were thrilled and so was I, because I was confident that I had finally found the way to get the produce I wanted. I took a sizeable portion of Anthony's artichoke crop when in season and I am sure I made him a very happy man despite my temporal panic at seeing my large fridge at The Regent being swallowed up by either a growing stack of artichokes or zucchini boxes.

One of the bigger issues I did have was with salad greens. The existing selection was so poor that it became my mission to have a much better range by the next summer. When I arrived in Sydney, there were really only four types of salad available in the markets: cos, iceberg, curly endive and the 'glamour' one, mignonette. Looking back at that limited range makes me reflect on far we have come in terms of our local produce. It makes me quite content and proud to have played a hand in creating the demand to have more varieties.

Although the mignonette was the star of the early 80s, seen in all the restaurants, it was in actual fact quite an ordinary lettuce. I never really liked it, with its hard broad leaf and unattractive rusty type of colour. These days you never really see it any more. I spoke to Jim about salad greens and he put me in contact with a couple of people, one of whom was working for Yates on their research station at Narromine in Western NSW. Tom worked with me over the next year to find the type of lettuce I was looking for. He said that he had a great range of lettuce seeds that were never grown commercially and if I could select the ones with potential he would pull them out and make them available to me.

At first we selected by name as far as I could identify them, but some of them just had a number so ultimately we decided that they would have to be planted to see what came out. We had green and red oak leaf lettuce for the first time in Australia, as well as Lolo Rosso, butter lettuce, and one with a number we called Regency, based on the hotel's name. We probably had 30 types, but selected about six to trial with a commercial grower based in Narromine, where the hot and dry climate helps reduce the chance of crop failure due to insects attacking the tender leaves of the exotic lettuce we were trying to develop.

The other big problem we encountered was transporting such a delicate crop. My first shipment of these new lettuces arrived completely wilted. It was hard to come to terms with such failure but we realised that we needed to refine our method and try to find a more reliable transport company. Eventually I received a delivery of fresh exotic lettuces, never seen before in Australia. We kept experimenting and I eliminated some of the original ones and trialed new ones over time: before too long we had a good new range of possible commercial lettuces.

Word went around and one day I got the visit from Jean Renée, a seed salesman from Grain de Clause, a French company specialising in seeds and grains for farmers. Jean Renée had heard through the industry that I was a person worth talking to if he wanted to sell his range of seeds. In a sense it did seem strange to be contacted by him. I was not a farmer, did not quite understand how to grow things, and I did not have or own land. However he had been unable to find a farmer who was willing to trial his seeds and he understood the importance and the need to offer a much better range of lettuces and vegetables in Australia. Jean Renée offered me many seeds, explained to me their preferred climate and left me with promises to return to Australia with more samples. I felt I had gold in my hands and was quick to pass them on to the Yates research station to evaluate them. Out of that range many new lettuces came through like Mache, fine curly endive and many other delicate lettuces like butter and young spinach.

A few years later I received a visit by two large men with quite ordinary ties that were worn way too short. Their names seemed quite out of place at The Regent but I was certainly willing to talk to anyone that vaguely looked like they came from the country or could be farmers. To my surprise they were from the Quarantine Department and they wanted to hear where I got the seeds I spoke about to farmers.

I suddenly realised that what Jean Renée gave me could have somehow been smuggled into the country. They were quite persistent, wanting details of my contacts and to be assured that I did not bring these seeds in myself. I have to admit that in difficult situations I am quite calm and can usually make a great case for myself. They eventually left, semi-convinced that I did not act illegally. I think that in the end it was a close call, as I could not provide any written documents of what I had received or supplied. From that day on I realised the importance of protecting our land from potential hazards of the diseases carried by overseas produce. A couple of years later I crossed paths again with the short tied Quarantine men at the airport. They noticed me and I noticed them and we gave each other plenty of space to avoid each other.

One morning in May, it was dark and cold and I was already on my way to Flemington Market. The season change was in full swing, we had received a lot of rain recently, my place was cold and I was starting to use my old metal stove to warm the house. The road from Newport was quiet as it usually was at that time of the morning. I did not stay long that morning at the Sydney Fish Market, as I wanted to be early at Flemington. I was on my own that morning, needing to change my menu to take advantage of the new produce coming to market.

As usual I started my walk in the grower's market; it is here that you find the local growers who bring their own harvest to the market. Over the years I have seen the ethnic balance change quite dramatically. These days you see so many more Asian growers with their produce, whereas when I began visiting the markets most of the blokes were Italian, Greek, and Maltese, with a sprinkling of Australians and Asians. They were always plenty of zucchini, cucumber, cabbage, beans, awful tomatoes, ordinary lettuces, but sometimes there would be some brilliant produce grown either through luck or sheer talent. It was here that sometimes I would find tiny eggplants, broad beans, small tomatoes, the odd bunches of radish or Italian radicchio.

That morning I saw nothing of interest at the market and was about to go to the other sheds where more established distributors were selling their product range. I was taking a short cut to go to B shed when I saw something that looked to me like wild mushrooms. At that time the only wild mushroom I had ever seen was either in a book, in a tin or when I went camping as a Boy Scout, and we certainly never ate them.

An old man was crouching near them and after another good look my instinct told me that I had just put my finger on the find of the morning. I tried to speak to the man but his response was clearly in Greek or Turkish, however I understood that he was telling me to wait for someone, who eventually turned out to be his son. The son explained to me that he worked for a distributor but that his father had come with him to the markets this morning with what turned out to be a mushroom collection from a family picnic in the Blue Mountains. They were a Greek-Cypriot family and it was a family tradition to gather wild dandelion, aniseed, olives and wild mushrooms, mostly in the Blue Mountains.

Apart from field mushrooms, which I previously gathered on my rabbit-hunting trips, I never collected other types of mushroom, as I didn't know whether they were safe for eating or not. I was very excited by my new find and I returned to my kitchen with my precious jewel. My staff were more doubtful, but I was determined they would go on that evening's menu. I paired them with the milk-fed veal and for good measure I sampled the first plate. They had a very orange hue to them, but they tasted very hearty and quite good.

By the early evening I was fairly tired; it had been few days of not much sleep and I was starting to feel all kinds of sleep deprivation symptoms. Ted Wright came to see me at the start of the service and on seeing the boxes of mushrooms he asked what they were. When I replied that they were wild mushrooms his reply was, 'Are you sure they are okay?' The left side of my face was by then very numb, like after a visit to the dentist (no doubt from the effect of lack of sleep). I told him that they tasted good but I could not feel the side of my face anymore. He look at me straight in the eye with a look of 'I do not want to know' and he walked away, probably hoping he would not have to deal with the repercussion of my folly the next morning.

The next day I knew Stephanie Alexander was coming to visit as she was writing an article for The Good Weekend Magazine and I strategically left my boxes of wild mushroom near my office, where I knew she would walk pass. Her surprise and wonder at these mushroom was precious, even if I nonchalantly made it appear like it was just another small addition to my range of produce. To be safe, I did send a sample of these mushrooms to the University of New South Wales to confirm they were nontoxic. They were called lactaire or saffron milk caps and were common in most forests after rain.

Over the next few months I enrolled a few young chefs to go and collect wild mushrooms from the forest and sell them to me. I ended up with many keen sellers with car boots full of wild mushrooms. I felt obliged to purchase all the mushrooms (even if there was more than I could use), however it enabled me to pass on the excess for other chefs to use.

These were the years of pioneering: it was refreshing to find and develop new food products, and find markets for underused ones. Many chefs and merchants have contributed to improve our range of produce, but I was lucky to be there when the need to introduce new produce was at its strongest and when the range was quite restricted. It sounds like a cliché to say that potatoes came in two varieties; washed and un-washed, but it was true; no one at that time would have known what was a Pontiac, desirée or a pink-eye potato. A lot of research, convincing and education was done to provide what we have available to us today. I loved those years and will always remind myself of the partnerships we formed that led to the development of the produce that we enjoy today.

13

COMING OF AGE OF THE CHEF

I N THE 70S THE ONLY CELEBRITY CHEFS WERE FRENCH. YOU did not hear of any Italian, Spanish or English chefs who had made a mark, let alone any American ones. It was the total preserve of the French, with maybe a couple of Swiss such as Girardet and Mosiman. You needed to be French to have any sort of gastronomic credibility and you also needed to have a three-star Michelin restaurant.

During my cookery school days in Canada I spotted in the newsagent a magazine that had an interview with Paul Bocuse. Paul was a chef who was redefining and revolutionizing French food with his Nouvelle Cuisine. I really wanted to read the article, but it was in *Playboy* magazine. After several passes in front of the newsagent over several days I gathered the gumption to buy the magazine, and the interview was a revelation.

Today any chef could be interviewed in a prominent magazine like *Playboy* and it would not even raise an eyebrow, but 35 years ago it was unheard of. Chefs were supposed to cook and confine their opinions to the kitchen, however here was a chef with no fear, no sentimental attachment to old cuisine, or worrying about been seen as a servant to the upper classes. Paul Bocuse was no servant to any one, and his views on food were to change the way chefs bought, prepared, presented and served food. It put them at the forefront of innovation and brought them out of the kitchen to express their opinions on creating great food.

Other chefs followed Paul Bocuse's example; all were French and had their own personal beliefs and style. They all produced cookbooks and a generation of young chefs saw a new future in their profession. Suddenly a chef could be an innovator, a creator and a trendsetter, as opposed to replicating classic dishes. There was something quite liberating and positive in this, but it was also scary to have the responsibility to invent or create new dishes.

In North America the first celebrity chefs made their name by recreating great provinçial French Food, like Wolfgang Puck at Ma Maison and Alice Waters at Chez Panisse. Slowly they moved towards an ingredients-based cuisine, one built more around personal belief. The birth of California Cuisine had these two influences at the core of its style. California had reinvented itself due to the accessibility and quality of its local ingredients so there was no reason why this could not be done in Australia.

To understand the changing role of the chef over the last two decades in Australia we need to examine our society's cultural structure. Our Anglo-Saxon background has a lot to do with the food evolution and the explosion of new food products and the way we eat in this country. It is no secret that food was never a huge cultural asset for the conquering expanding British Empire, however, by contrast, the French have left an incredible food culture in any territory they held onto for any significant period of time. We only have to look at the food of Louisiana, Nouvelle France (Québec), Haiti and New Calédonia, to see that they all have very vibrant cuisines with a strong link to their region. In each instance the recipes and cooking methods that the French brought have been adapted to create their own local style, imbued with the respect of the food products.

In Australia, despite the fertility of the land and the abundance of the seafood, no true local cuisine was ever developed until recently. Instead of using the local abundant ingredients (such as kangaroo and seafood) or adjusting their recipes and diet to the climate, the English continued to cook the food they knew, even though it was highly inappropriate. And 200 years on the Anglo-Saxon style of eating had remained nearly the same as when they left England, having a fondness for roast meats with over-cooked vegetables and potatoes. Where was the light salad using local seafood and fish, especially considering the closeness to the sea of most settlements? Where was the produce that they could have copied from other their other hot climate colonies, such as papaya, citrus fruit, coconuts, Asian vegetables, and the salt fish?

Thirty years ago, with the explosion of the wine industry, restaurants started to thrive and more sophisticated food needed to be served. The advent of French restaurants became all the rage, with places like Claudes, Julliets, Bagatelle, Le Trianon and may others forgotten by history. In Melbourne the trend was the same. It was still difficult to educate people that you could eat such things as garlic snails, rabbit terrine and yabbies in jelly, but at least the food was getting much more diverse. Not surprisingly, Australian chefs took on classical French cooking after being inspired to cook better food.

In Sydney there were no outspoken or daring chefs. Most of us tried to do our duties to a high standard, cooking with knowledge and experience, but in general, social comments on food were left to the supremo of gastronomic press: Leo Schofield. Leo was probably born a gourmand but he was also an intuitive gourmet. He never dreamt of owning a restaurant, let alone cooked in one, but he had a profound influence over the way we cooked, served and ate food in Australia, more so than even the most influential chefs did. He made the chef relevant, but also responsible for what they served. His entertaining reviews redefined what was bad and needed to be discarded—from tacky décor to bad service to ordinary food—but also praised the innovations that some chefs were capable of.

Leo was feared and respected, and his friendship was sought by all in the food game. His small piercing eyes would not reveal much emotion but you could see a great analytical mind at work. He became an eminent guide of the food scene and an enthusiastic innovator and leader of the arts and culture. Leo was able to spot talent and he had the means to make stars out of creative chefs.

Once Leo Schofield introduced us to the chef behind the façade of the restaurant, then the chef's personalities started speak for themselves, either through their food or their opinion. Although the restaurant scene in Sydney was certainly less diverse than it is today there were some quite established leaders who made a real difference to Sydney. The absolute big gun of the city was Berowra Waters Inn, where Gay Bilson ran a restaurant that possessed a strong belief in its sense of place in the culinary world. Tony Bilson was no longer part of the restaurant, but his contribution to date was well-known and he was to become a prominent figure of the Sydney food scene, opening many restaurants; in fact Tony could probably set a record on how many restaurants he opened.

Tony was a food visionary, a thinker who seemed to find the rational running of a restaurant seven days a week a challenging task. It is often hard to combine culinary talent, business acumen and stamina. A restaurant is a very fragile balance between the attraction of a great menu and a reputed chef, and the hard aspect of margins.

Gay was more of a mother and practical survivor than Tony. She was the one at the legendary Tony's Bon Goût who worked in the kitchen doing the critical task of food preparation. She first learned to cook as an obsession, and it then became a passion and a means to having an income. Inexperience was a fresh and precious asset, but she was also capable of balancing the other needs of the business, like managing the books and ensuring continuity of production.

My first visit to Berowra Water's Inn was an eye opener, a delight with its well-known arrival by putty after the interminable drive through the northern suburbs of Sydney. Water views have become an essential ingredient of success of a restaurant and it certainly was the case with Berowra Water's Inn. One of the clearest lessons I retained from the restaurant was the mental and culinary integrity of the dish rather then the produce; ingredients seemed subservient to the recipes. The cleanliness of its presentation and the purity of its cooking were fascinating. It was like there was no fear in what they were serving.

By then Janni Kyritsis was the Chef de Cuisine, a very able tradesman who was capable of working under the rigour of Gay. Janni's technical skills, combined with Gay's culinary discipline, made for a revolutionary pared-down cuisine that was unique in Australia. It was a brave menu that was not designed to appeal to the average customer; if one was not gastronomically inclined it could be a hard restaurant to like. Brioche with bone marrow in red wine sauce was a central dish, but you could also find a simple oyster omelette or a parsley and Parmesan salad. It was not a display of the most famous Australian ingredients on offer but more of a philosophical menu of self belief. I always admired Gay's frankness and the healthy distance she tried to keep from the food press. She was a trendsetter who was happy to slip away for a life of reflection removed from the fickleness of our industry.

When I came in contact with other leaders I try to understand what makes them different, and what sets them apart from others. Invariably it is the ones who are totally focused and have a very defined vision who are successful. Some people have total commitment but they can still falter if they are not prepared to sell their vision. Some achieve success because the sheer quality of their work shines through and it is recognised by the public and press alike.

There will always be giants of the food scene. For each of us in this industry these giants could differ, but the ones we nominate and look up to have achieved beyond the realm of the extraordinary. As the years go by, older leaders fade away, forgotten by the young apprentice chefs and wine makers but their achievements can never be undone and their influence remains.

Peter Doyle would be one of the most unlikely chefs to be a culinary star, but Leo and many other people in Sydney thought his food was all stars. I lived near his restaurant, Reflections, in Palm Beach and had the chance to visit him, some times eating, some times just dropping by in the kitchen. He is a technical person who possesses beautiful presentation skills but also has a talent and knowledge for combining flavours. He had no concern for stardom and I imagine him reeling at the thought of having to perform for a crowd of journalists. There is no denying his influence through his food, even if he is too humble to admit it himself. In my eyes he is the best cook in Sydney, his dishes have a colour, vibrancy and subtle flavours.

In Australia the real catalyst for stardom was Neil Perry. It is interesting to see that at that same time that Peter was at Reflections, Neil was cooking within walking distance at Barrenjoey House. He started to make his mark at Perry's, but reinvented the way we cooked in Australia at Blue Water Grill, due to his belief in fresh ingredients and great seafood.

Neil is so outspoken because of his certainty of conviction but also because he has so much experience from the many different restaurants he has opened over the years. He is without a doubt one of the most creative chefs and people in Australia. Neil and I are both of the same age but we come from very different backgrounds. The fact that we can both achieve success from such disparate roads made for intriguing reviews, but such are the opportunities that one can create in Australia.

Mark Armstrong's Pegrum's was another restaurant that set new trends. Mark's cooking was fresh and innovative, with great classical skills. His restaurant in Paddington was beautiful, small, and intimate. It was a reflection of what was consider a superior restaurant in Sydney, possessing a personal décor, serving dishes not found anywhere else and having a sublime ambience. Mark was creative and full of nervous but focused energy. His desserts were magical and his meat courses were full of robust flavour. He developed into a critical leader in the Sydney food scene by opening the very well patronised Macleay Street Bistro and then the meat-focused Armstrongs in North Sydney. Not happy with this, he eventually opened another Armstrongs at the Manly Wharf, its seafood-based menu reflecting the water location.

Another leader, who I have known since I arrived in Australia, is Anders Ousback. I first saw his accomplishment as a caterer through the pages of *Vogue* magazine. Later I was to experience his food and eventually I was to enjoy his company. He is one of the sharpest operators I ever came in contact with. Anders' catering prowess and the redefinition of the type of food that could and should be served was a wake-up call to our catering industry. He has great intuition to create the next food trend or define and build new restaurant around his style of food. Anders' intellect has ensured he made a success of each place, but his greatest move was always to sell when his places were full and popular. This allowed him to reinvent himself time after time, satisfying his need to create a space built with the right food, décor, environment and the right people to work in it.

One of the absolute giants of the Australian food scene is Len Evans. His career goes back through decades of making people enjoy the good life of drinking great wine and eating superb food. He trampled some people when they stood in his way, but he cared little for people that held him back. He came with a big heart and sharp verbs.

Len knows everything there is to know about running a successful hotel, running a restaurant, making wine and judging wine. He is a great speaker, a confident cook, an accomplished artist and an ordinary golfer. Len is generous, loyal, driven and he is like a father to me. He should be seen as a national icon in Australia. He has given me confidence and talent in writing and delivering speeches, taught me the importance of leading a group to achieve an outcome, as well as the art of food and wine matching. But most of all, I have learned from him to never to stop achieving.

I have also always admired Stephanie Alexander, firstly for her style of cooking, and secondly for her commitment to producing the food herself in the kitchen, working under pressure, night after night, trying to make a living out of a restaurant. She has now found success and recognition through her book writing. Stephanie is one of my heroes and I have enormous respect for her publishing prowess and her dedication to seek the best ingredients. She has been an inspiration and has taught Australia to cook better.

Stephanie has contributed to many magazines and she helped elevate the respect that chefs received from the public. Her writings were intelligent and progressive and they helped all chefs focus on producing better food. Stephanie was one of my early Australian influences, having eaten at her restaurant a few times in the early 80s. I found the food to be well-sourced, cooked with skill and designed with intelligence, reflecting more of her personal style rather then copying dishes that were in vogue either in France or America.

There are many other chefs who have made the Australian food scene so vibrant, that it is impossible to name them all: Tetsuya, Cheong

Lieu, Damien Pignolet, Andrew Blake, Steve and Franca Manfredi, Chris Manfield, Maggie Beer, Gilbert Lau and Jacques Raymond. All of these chefs and many more have had a huge influence in the way we eat today, but they didn't do it on their own. There was another major player that was to have a huge influence over what, how and where we ate in this country: the press.

—

There are not many countries in the world where just one or two publications exert a huge culinary influence over the whole profession. In France there is the *Guide Michelin*, but this is really a rating book, not an influential trendsetter. You could think of some American publications, such as *American Gourmet*, but none had the reach and depth of what we possessed in Australia.

Vogue Entertaining was more than just a trendsetter; it was the food magazine that educated Australia on how to eat, cook, present and serve modern food. It is impossible to diminish its importance and role in making what Australia is today, a vibrant and energetic culinary place. The magazine redefined the way we cook and how we should cook. It pared down food and the style and finesse of the editors and photographers become worldwide assets. *Vogue Entertaining* not only raised the quality level in food publishing in Australia, but it also set new standards for the rest of the world. That world is still trying to catch up to the refined level and quality that *Vogue* produced.

In the early 80s *Vogue* was more influential than any other food publication; it was feared, respected and praised by all working in the restaurant industry. Whenever June McCallum, the editor of *Vogue Australia*, attended a dinner or a function at The Regent Ted Wright was delighted. June never travelled on her own; many other employees of *Vogue* would also attend, such as Carolyn Lockhart (the editor of *Vogue Entertaining*) and Joan Campbell. Joan was the queen of the food page of *Vogue*; the no-nonsense arbiter of what was good or bad and the ultimate panel of one who decided if a dish was worthy of inclusion in the pages of *Vogue*.

Every chef, restaurant owner and hotelier would dissect the pages of *Vogue Entertaining*. They sought coverage of their restaurant in *Vogue's* pages, but to their credit, only the best made it inside. To succeed in having some of your dishes in *Vogue Entertaining* was the ultimate crowning for a chef. Few were selected, but large was the reward in terms of prestige and exposure.

How did a magazine become so influential and creative? How did it attain such an exalted status? How did it attract such a following, with all the top chefs wanting to be featured in its pages? All of this really related to a vision, a style and a determination to be at the cutting edge of publishing. The visionaries of the magazine were June McCallum (who developed the original vision for the magazine) and Carolyn Lockhart (and subsequently Sharyn Storrier Lyneham) as editor. They all drove the concept of the pages to the pinnacle of style by hiring the best photographers and stylists. They carefully selected the stories, events and food that would be featured and they developed the *Vogue* style of shooting the food.

On the coal face of many food pages was Joan Campbell, one of the absolute giants of the food scene in Australia. I shot many features with Joan and her abrupt style matched with her no-nonsense manner. She certainly did not suffer fools easily. My first feature (organised by Ted Wright) was quite daunting. I was told how important she was and how anything we presented needed to be perfect; it was enough warning to scare anyone. The trick was to remain calm and composed, and to show off your best skills.

I made it to the dining room where no less than three assistants were there ready to help the photography. The amount of lights, tripods, boxes, cameras, transformers, screens and trolleys was staggering; it was as if we were in a fully outfitted studio. There were little mirrors on pivoted bases to shine light in hard-to-get-at corners of the food, white boards taped on flexible microphone stands and tables loaded with Polaroid packets.

Then we were made to show every plate we possessed and every piece of cutlery on display to Joan so that she could select what we should serve the food on. Joan herself was sitting in the tallest chair they could find for her in the dining room, and this gave her an even more regal air. Years later, when we swapped comments about Joan between chefs, we would call this 'Joan sitting on her throne' (she did have a bad back). I was lucky that she did not pronounce her customary 'What slop is this?' on the presentation of my first dish. I survived the first shoot and eventually grew to love, respect and admire Joan. She mellowed with each feature we did together, but she also got even crankier with her bad back.

Shooting the food was almost a full-day event. I quickly learnt that every small imperfection would show and that all the meat, vegetables and fish needed to be as perfect as possible. Many dishes needed to be redone, time and time again, either through the sudden lack of natural light or because they just didn't look quite right. All of the photographers that I worked with were extreme perfectionists: people like George Seper, Michael Cook, Rodney Weidland and Geoff Lung. They were inspiring to work with and I guess it was their personal style that helped build the reputation of *Vogue* to a great extent. The images of food displayed a new level of style, a new way of assembling ingredients, or they showed the food from a special function that *Vogue* had agreed to cover.

In short, the pages of *Vogue Entertaining* were an evocative mix of food, leisure and travel, with an insight in the homes of the social set of Sydney. Joan and many of the editors, food directors, stylists, assistants and creative directors (with the photographer in tow) would travel the country to cover the new, the exciting and the unheard of. New resorts, superb locations, just opened restaurants and fabulous sites would be visited and featured. The people at *Vogue* became the best-connected networkers around, knowing about every new product, restaurant, hotel and resort before anyone else. It was fascinating to see the influence of a magazine at work.

It is not surprising to now see so many new food magazines around, as *Vogue* was the benchmark and probably a gold mine for its publisher Condé Nast. Everyone eventually wanted to imitate *Vogue* and this caused the birth and premature death of many short-lived magazines that could not dent *Vogue's* circulation.

Carolyn Lockhart eventually moved to *Australian Gourmet Traveller* and slowly built a following for her fresh new style and more relaxed approach. *Australian Gourmet Traveller* was published more frequently and consequently it was seeking more stories on food, wine and travel. It was less eclectic and more accessible for the general public. It featured food you could cook and produce at home as opposed to the absolute cutting-edge food of *Vogue*. Both magazines vied for exclusivity and it became a minefield deciding which magazine to offer a story to. In general only one magazine would cover each story and if you happened to offer it to both magazines thinking that they would both cover it you were playing with fire.

To this day it is still surprising to have overseas people tell you how incredible our magazines are and have much they are read in New York, Montréal, Paris and London. They have achieved the near cult status that so many overseas magazines would love to possess.

—

The other publication that was growing in stature and relevance was the Good Living section of *The Sydney Morning Herald*. Leo Schofield always had enormous relevance with his restaurant reviews but the rest of the section was really coming of age by producing more focused features on food products, restaurants, service stories and people.

Short Black came into existence and became the ears and voice of the restaurant industry. It revealed the moves of the chefs to new ventures or restaurants; it exposed feuds and informed the public about great events.

Good Living made itself relevant through the sheer reach of *The Sydney Morning Herald*. They could publicise an event and ensure a good patronage or they could lay bare the fall out of restaurant partners. Pretty much every thing was fair game as long as it was new, fresh and relevant. Often stories were inaccurate and embarrassing, but no matter, they filled the page with informed gossip. Every chef and many of the general public followed their pages to keep abreast with what was happening in the industry.

I would say that *Vogue* was by far the most influential publication in the early 80s, *Australian Gourmet Traveller* in the late 80s and early 90s, with Good Living in the late 90s and early 2000. These days the quality of the colour print of *The Sydney Morning Herald* makes it a real alternative to magazines (even if the quality of the broadsheet will never reach the glossiness of magazines) and their stories are immediate, varied and punchy. In a magazine the sense of decorum is much higher, emphasising the beautiful and successful, whereas the broadsheet is more interested in the unpolished edge of the real story. Where the broadsheet could be nasty and self-righteous the magazines needed to be pious and supporting. You never would see a bad review feature in their glossy pages.

The influence of the leading chefs and the press has developed Australian food to a world-class level. As a food culture we have developed enormously over the last two decades, largely because of these chefs and these publications. With a food public who were interested in and well informed about food, and chefs who had a public profile and opportunity to express their opinions, the Australian chefs had finally come of age.

14

THE FOOD CRITIC

W ITH THE ADULATION THAT CHEFS RECEIVED IF THEY WERE elevated to food stardom came an increased scrutiny of their food and restaurants. The more people became interested in chefs and their food, the more their trend-setting ways changed the way we ate. All chefs go through long periods of struggle to educate themselves. They gain experience in various restaurants, learning different cooking styles, techniques and recipes, until they eventually lead their own kitchen, if they have the ambition and talent to do so. It takes them time to develop a following and without press coverage or reviews they will have a hard time letting the public know they are open. Quick death could soon follow if they do not reach the radar of the press.

A profile can still take years to develop even if you have great food. I never sought publicity or coverage in my first decade in Australia. My focus was always on creating great food, searching for new producers, or helping producers in developing new ingredients. Working in a large hotel I got to brush shoulders with a department that I never heard of before: the PR department. I originally thought that they were the spokespeople for the hotel in situations such as a fire or a calamity. After becoming the Executive Chef I realised that one of their prime roles was to handle the local and overseas journalists, ensuring they received the best impression of the hotel. After gushing over the view from their room, the amenities, the level of services and the art and finishes of the hotel, the story they could write was in effect quite lean. They either needed to write about the city, its geography and history, but not so much about the hotel, even if it was to feature in their article.

Sonia Smirnow was our PR lady. She was a real 'mother earth', a clever publicist who had a gentle and honest manner. Everyone loved Sonia; in a line of work where people often were nasty, offended and resentful, and where fragile egos dictated people's behaviour, she was universally respected and liked. Sonia was a powerful influence behind The Regent becoming 'the hotel' of Sydney where all the artists, stars, and big wigs would stay. She was constantly asked to provide accommodation, press conferences, dinners or cocktail parties by the publicists for the movers and shakers, and she often became the de facto publicist for the personalities who did not travel with one.

Over the years Sonia handled so many world leaders, Hollywood stars, and people of the moment that it is hard to see who made more of a splash. Michael Jackson came with his bodyguards and personal macrobiotic chef flown from LA. There were also many others who can't be revealed as their privacy was so well preserved. But over the years there was a constant roll of celebrities and great achievers, including: Pavarotti, Tom Cruise, Nicole Kidman, Harrison Ford, Mel Gibson, Quincy Jones, Sir Andre Previn, Lady Margaret Thatcher, HRH Prince Philip, Julia Roberts, Meryl Streep, Sir Kenneth Branagh, Prime Minister Bob Hawke, Prime Minister Malcolm Fraser, Sir Don Bradman, and Dame Joan Sutherland, just to name a few!

We had a constant stream of dinners, cocktail parties, charity functions and little private gatherings for these visiting celebrities.

Often the food would seek to represent what they liked, where they came from or where they worked. It was fun and challenging to tailor the menu and food for these events and it needed a good depth of research and knowledge to achieve this.

One of the more unusual celebrities that I developed a menu for was the raw food guru Leslie Kenton, who came from England to promote her book. I spent a great deal of time reading her book to get instilled with her philosophy before I felt prepared to write a menu using only raw ingredients. It was something I certainly would not have done on my own and I felt I had learned a new approach that could possibly be useful for the future.

On her second visit (after the birth of her second child) she totally amazed the audience by revealing that she had eaten some of the discarded placenta of her newborn child. If this was not enough of a shock, she added that if people were skirmish about raw foods they could cook the placenta with onions and garlic to make it more palatable! Her reasoning was that most wild animals ate the placenta on the birth of their babies and it had to be beneficial. I do not think she convinced many people to take up her belief.

—

The more I come in contact with celebrities the more I understood the dynamics of the press: their need for stories and the process of an interview. Sonia could see me gaining confidence in my food and she could see what I was trying to achieve with my search for new producers and the link I had with our growers. She probably saw the potential for promoting our food and restaurant by getting them photographed. In those days most commentaries were done by the journalist and the chef spoke only through their recipes, dishes and the published photos of their food.

I started to do more and more dishes that were photographed by not only local magazines, but also by overseas publications such as *Italian Vogue, American Gourmet* and *French Elle.* In fact there were so many photographers and journalists that I truly lost count of how many features we did. Our food reputation was growing and Sonia made sure that if journalists were staying in-house free of charge then she would get excellent coverage for her favours. One of the roles of the PR lady was to give free nights in a room to journalists and organise what they should cover in exchange for the hospitality. She ensured that they met the right people in the city, had access to radio or television programs, and managers who they could meet from the local press to give them a run down on Sydney's best spots.

My relationship with Sonia grew and grew and I was saddened when she eventually moved on. All of the publicists who followed her were dynamic women, each with a different style, but all with the same commitment. To succeed in being in charge of the PR of such a prestigious brand as The Regent was one of the best assignments in the city.

One section of the press that you could not control was the food reviewer. They were supposed to come incognito but they were often recognised by the staff. Once they were in your restaurant there was little that you could do to lift your game, as it was too late to change your menu or to scrounge for better ingredients.

Reviewing a restaurant is very much like reviewing a ballet, operatic performance or a new CD. Your personal likes and dislikes as a reviewer affect your judging criteria as much as your experience and your personal approach. Reviewing can not be formulised by breaking every segment of judging down into a ratings chart. At the end of the day it is really on gut feeling that you base your review. There is also the perception that reviewers are influenced by the perceived trendiness of a restaurant, with a new restaurant having a dynamism that a four-year-old restaurant does not have. These perceptions will affect their review as it would affect the perception of a first-time customer.

When your restaurant has no rating you are always hoping to be reviewed. This is more likely to happen to a restaurant if it is a new, if a well-known chef has moved or if the restaurant is in the news for some reason. There are many food guides in Australia and all have their place. Many are short lived or they only make an impact on the restaurant industry, not really reaching the public. The only guide that seems to count is the one published by *The Age* in Melbourne or *The Sydney Morning Herald* in Sydney as *The Good Food Guide*. They are (like it or not) for the chef the guides that mean everything, the ones that have a huge following.

By the very nature of what food guides do they are controversial. Their rating at the end of the day is very subjective, but there is also no question that they try to have a fair rating as their credibility depends on it. Most potential restaurants worthy of inclusion in *The Good Food Guide* are visited at least once, and sometimes more. The reviewers are old industry hands who know their food and contribute their comments and reviews to a small panel. This panel consists of the editors of each guide who then rate and edit all of the reviews. On them fall all the responsibilities of producing a serious but credible, entertaining but also factual guide. The guide is not only used by people to assess the worth of a place and decide where to go, but also to locate the restaurants.

Most chefs have serious misgivings at some point or another about the fairness, validity, accuracy and worth of these guides. Many have suffered at the hand of the reviewers and most leading chefs have lost their three-hat rating at some point in the past. Neil Perry, Tim Pak Poy, Liam Tomlin, Dietmar Sawyere, Peter Doyle, and I have all been there, waking up with the unexpected shock of losing our top rating. Even if we could not comprehend the reasons behind the loss of that hat, that is the way it will be for the next year. These days I think it is better to try to stay on one or two hats then have three and lose one. The damage your restaurant suffers in these situations is heart wrenching and can be sometimes be fatal to a restaurant.

It was to my great surprise that in *The Good Food Guide* of 1990 I received the top rating of three hats for Kable's Restaurant. I never thought that a hotel restaurant could ever achieve that acclaimed rating. Ted Wright's attitude that we should act like we were a restaurant in a hotel (rather then a hotel restaurant) had been validated. Kable's had become too important to dismiss in a city with a growing sense of knowledge in food and a populace demanding better service. It was with a subdued mind that I received our new rating because like every chef I knew that it really was a team effort and that I was only one part of a team that had made this success possible. Never had a hotel received this rating previously and it certainly justified all the effort we had put into Kable's. The previous year I was named chef of the year, an accolade that filled me with pride.

Leo Schofield was in my opinion probably the greatest restaurant reviewer we have ever had. Over the years he built a formidable knowledge of cooking and with his dissecting comments, social barb and witty turn of phrase he succeeded in elevating *The Good Food Guide* to an uncontested position. His weekly reviews were eagerly read by a receptive public, but were also followed by all the chefs. Chefs often tailored their dishes to what they perceived he liked. However this could be a fatal mistake as Leo could instinctively see the worth of a kitchen; and I knew it was better to cook accordingly to the strength of your belief, not to the perceived trend of the day.

I always felt that Leo Schofield was a person who rated restaurants with more balance than other reviewers had done, either past or present. He paid attention to things such as the level of service, the knowledge of service, the hesitation or familiarity of the waiters, but he could also assess the depth of the wine list, and the quality of the glassware or cutlery. He noticed little intangibles like if we had silver instead of stainless steel, the quality of the plate and the balance of the menu. Did the menu contain spelling mistakes, have repeated ingredients, and was there a lack of vegetable dishes? He also noticed welcomes or good byes at the beginning and the end of the meals. None of this distracted him from his assessment of the food, but he noted these points and made sure that they formed part of his assessments. He was ruthless, entertaining, supportive and informed at the same time.

Leo eventually acquired such a powerful voice in the Sydney food scene that only he could give up his job as the restaurant reviewer for Good Living and *The Good Food Guide*. The fact that he gave it up had more to do with a new direction he wished to take in his life, eventually becoming Festival Director of the Melbourne Arts Festival. It was quite a shock for the chefs and restaurateurs of Sydney to see him move to Melbourne, which in the eyes of Sydney people was quite a conservative food city. As soon as the shock of his departure was over everyone was gossiping about who he would be replaced by.

Terry Durack was a bit of an unknown to Sydney, but he was soon to establish himself and his personal brand of reviewing. And now that Terry has gone to work in London, Matthew Evans is in the hot seat. I always believe in accepting the bad as well as the good when it came down to reviewing, but there are still some times when you wonder how much objectivity goes into each review. Preconceived ideas will effect a rating and the whole reviewing process is often more of a perceived view rather than a true reflection of what we are.

Sydney is one of the rare cities in the world where the opinion of one guide is so strong. Its permanent reviewer has an all-powerful position and the ability to make and break restaurants. In most other world food cities you have several reviewers for different publications, each with their own opinion. Hopefully Sydney will one day be in the position where our food culture is vibrant and strong enough to allow several reviewers and guides, making for a far more balanced view of our local food scene.

15

THE BIRTH OF AUSTRALIAN CUISINE

T HE NEED FOR BETTER, FRESHER, MORE DIVERSE AND NEW ingredients became a constant of my daily routine. Little by little I was achieving the goal I had set years ago on my visit to California. My range of options to base my menu on was ever expanding and my reputation as someone looking for quality was spreading at the markets and in food circles.

Growers, merchants, researchers and distributors were contacting me to see what I was looking for or to establish if a certain produce had potential. I tried and tested and evaluated many varieties of new or forgotten apples that you may now see grown commercially again. I convinced growers that there was a market for corella pear, witloof, sorrel, milk-fed veal, vine-ripened tomatoes, and different varieties of potatoes. It was time to broaden not only the range of vegetables but also their varieties.

My search for new produce took me out of my kitchen and in touch with the producers. These were people trying to make a living out of growing or selling what they believed was great produce, but they often did not know how to find a market or convince chefs that their products were superior.

One of the producers who contacted me was an oyster farmer called Eric. After a conversation where both of us struggled though our respective accents (Eric with his thick Australian one, and me with my strong French Canadian tone) he told me that he had a lease in Jervis Bay allowing him to collect wild oysters. Eric explained the oysters were flat mud oysters, not seen anywhere in Sydney to date, and that no one had shown any interest in purchasing them. I made an appointment to visit him down in Jervis Bay (a few hours south of Sydney) and decided to take some of my apprentices with me to see the potential of these wild oysters.

There is something so rewarding to be at the source of a product, to see the real heroes of good food and to see its harvesting. Eric was waiting at the Jervis Bay pier with his partner, their boat having just returned from their lease in the bay. Attached to the side of the boat were heavily loaded sacks of oysters. One was pulled on the pier, opened, and to my delight big muddy oysters with a green tinge spilt onto the pier. Using a bucket of seawater we cleaned a few oysters with a brush.

While we were cleaning the oysters Eric explained the speculation that was going on in the small fishing community. Some people, he said, believed that these oysters come from France, and were probably dropped in the bay by La Pérouse. Indeed there was a real similarity to the Belon oysters from Arcachon in France, where many of the French explorers' boats departed. In any case, I started to use the oysters, never being too sure just what to call them. I eventually settled on plain Jervis Bay Oysters. Sometimes they were enormous in size and needed to be made into soup but their flavour was always impressive. We now know that they are a native Australian oyster called Angasi Oysters, as opposed to the more common native Sydney Rock Oyster. The folklore of the French story was great, but in this case inaccurate.

We were now ready to open a couple of the oysters and since my first taste at school I think there is no other food more exotic than an oyster. The fat oysters were pried open and I gulped the full body with plenty of sea salt. It was just fabulous, if a tad large. I was so pleased to be at the source and have the chance to be one of the first ones in the restaurant market to use them. Quick negotiations settled a price and a transport arrangement. The oysters were going to be a perfect addition to my menu, either served freshly shucked or crumbed and fried and served with a salsa or roast capsicum dressing.

I took the opportunity of being in the Nowra district to also visit one of my earliest local cheese makers, Gilbert Pesenti. Gilbert was making camembert and in those days he was one of the first to produce a local fresh camembert. At that time most camembert came in a tin from Denmark and it was unusual to have such a beautiful fresh product.

Gilbert was one person who was using his French skills in cheese making to establish a factory in a region with a great reputation for the quality of its milk. Gilbert needed help in promoting his cheese and that fitted so well with my need and commitment. His cheese was a vast improvement on the Danish variety, but maybe not quite up to the French standard that one could sometimes find in the delicatessen. Nevertheless, it was a locally-made, fresh product that one could exalt over. Gilbert sold his camembert at a point of perfect maturity so he was serving as the producer and as affineur. On cutting his camembert the insides would gently run on the cheese board, which was a great deal better than having a French cheese with a chalky core.

My love for cheese was rewarded, but I knew his was only a small start and until we could have a good range of Australian boutique cheeses we could not consider ourself an innovative and complete food culture. Having a good range of cheese would show the deep skills and produce our country could have and so working with cheese makers became a passion for me and I made it my mission to help their development and the promotion of local variety. I financially supported these producers by eventually moving to exclusively using Australian cheese at The Regent. This was eventually achieved when I felt we covered most styles and had enough quality and range to overtake the imported choices. It was considered by the public and the food press to be a great accomplishment, one of which I am very proud. These days it does not mean so much, but in those pioneering days it was a bit of a revolution to claim that our range of boutique cheese could rival their European counterpart.

A few months after my trip to Nowra I decided to visit another of the upcoming cheese factories, but this time in Tasmania. I made plans to go with a few of the other chefs from Sydney and Barry McDonald (one of my suppliers of special products who was trying to develop a large range of products to distribute to the restaurants in Sydney). I had planned as usual visits to several of my producers: Aldo, my meat supplier, based in North Carlton in Melbourne; the King Island cheese factory in Tasmania; and Jeff, my lobster supplier, who collected lobsters on Bernie and King Island.

With Neil Perry, Steve Manfredi and Barry we decided to go to Melbourne first to visit some of the good restaurants and then go on to Tasmania. Neil was at Blue Water Grill at that time, redefining the way to serve fish in Australia. Steve was well ensconced with his mother Franca, wife Julie, and brother Franco, in the kitchen of which was considered the most innovative Italian restaurant of Sydney.

We all decided that a visit to Stephanie Alexander's restaurant was the place to start. Duré Dara, now a long-term friend, greeted us with her familiar hospitality and we sat to a succession of dishes that left us amazed at the skill of the kitchen. Stephanie's presentation style and menu was a welcome departure of what we were used to. She served oysters with a superb jelly and a steamed chicken with seasoned salt that I well remember to this day. The flesh was white in the extreme and of a silkiness that could not be achieved by western cooking methods. Stephanie was in her Chinese period and her love for new cooking methods and foreign ingredients made for a welcome change to the predictable fare. The boys drank too much and I ate too much, but I at least had the sense to avoid the hotel bar in view of our 5am wake-up call to catch the small plane to King Island.

I never have a problem waking up early, but looking at the faces of my colleagues it could have been harder if I had accepted their invitation to stay at the bar until the wee hours. The trip was rough and, for the most part, conducted in the dark. As usual Melbourne was gloomy and cold—I seemed to be unlucky with the weather every time I visited our southern cousin—but at least we landed safely at King Island airport in the light of the day.

The now famous King Island dairy industry originally began by default. A large mainland purchaser stopped buying the basic cheese they had contracted this dairy-producing island to make. So the local dairy farmers decided to reinvent themselves to prevent their livelihood and economy from collapsing. The entire milk production of the island needed to be redirected into producing a boutique product to attract better margins. Through sheer vision, their production moved from basic commercial and unbranded cheddar to a unique high-quality product. They did this so successfully that they created what is now one of the most recognisable food brands in Australia.

Back then, the cheese and dairy producers of King Island were starting to make a great impression on the public. The chefs were already convinced of the value of their double brie, because it had a kind of inconsistency and rusticity that was typical of the great French unpasteurised double brie. The King Island double cream was a unique product, unseen previously in Australia.

We met at the airport and were driven to Loorana, where King Island Dairy is situated. Over the next few hours we were shown all the facilities and the production methods for the different cheeses. We got the chance to sample and venture our opinion on new products, and let them know the kinds of cheeses that we would like them to make. We were listened to with intent and we could see our opinion was very much valued. It was interesting to see the huge facilities and the impact an economic decision could make on a community like this one. The first milk cooperative was formed in 1902, which meant that the island had been involved in dairy production for over 100 years.

The island industry was always struggling to remain viable and relevant, looking to diversify into new areas and produce value-added foods. Fortunately, the range of food products is quite extensive for such a small island. King Island produced beef, cheese, pork, honey, pepper, rock lobster, abalone and scale fish. They also harvest Bull kelp, which after drying is trimmed into granules and shipped to Scotland to be turned a gelling agent to be used in ice-cream or toothpaste.

Neil, Steve and Barry were starting to show signs of weakness due to their overindulgence and were quite keen on taking the next flight to Melbourne. I wanted to remain and visit the West Coast, where the Bull kelp was harvested. We said goodbye and I went to investigate the harvesting process of the kelp. Apparently it was ripped from the seabed by the waves and then washed onto the shore of the island. It is huge, growing up to eight metres in length. Special tow trucks pull the long brown leather-like strips and take them back to the factory where they are air-dried and eventually processed.

I decided to have lunch on the beach, having gathered a live lobster at the local seafood shop. I was going to cook this on a beach fire and eat it with my supply of local cheese. The news travelled fast on a small island and it was not long after I had found a great spot and was starting my fire that the local press show up. They could not quite believe that a chef of my stature was firstly on the island, and secondly prepared to cook his own lunch. To me it was certainly not abnormal, but for them it was a perfect marketing opportunity. They took pictures of me wrapping my local lobster in kelp to protect it from the fire and after a good roasting it was ready for lunch. With a few cold beers, the cheese from the factory and the bread from the local bakery it could not make for a more perfect lunch or for the journalists, a more perfect story.

I made my way back to the airport after a great day on the island. Seeing that I was the only passenger I was given the prized co-pilot seat. The pilot did all his customary checks and we finally lined up to take off, engine blaring, when a truck came in to view and a message came over from the tower control room. A fisherman had just arrived and he was hoping to get his fish aboard. I got out of the plane and was stunned by the intended cargo: it was three huge crates of lobster. The crates were each the size of at least two big coffins and all of three of them were full to the brim with freshly cooked lobsters. There was no way in my eyes that this load would fit in the plane. The pilot and the airport attendant removed the other four seats of our tiny plane and used a forklift to load the crate aboard. They just fitted in, with no more than one inch on each side of the plane spared. With each crate loaded I could see the plane getting lower to the ground. When the last crate was loaded I sensed that we were in for a difficult and nervous take off.

We got back into our seats and after revving the engine we made our way to the grassy strip that served as a runway. The engine was gunned to the max, the breaks were released, and slowly the plane made its way down towards what to me seemed to be a small hill. It certainly did not feel like we were aiming at the sky. After a long time, when we were nearly at the hill, it finally started to feel like the plane was trying to take to the air. That we eventually did take off must have more to do with a sudden gust of uplifting wind then the laws of physics, because I did not see anyone weigh the contents of the crate to ensure that the weight was within the capability of the aircraft. I began to think that Neil, Steve and Barry had made the right decision by leaving earlier.

The next day we reassembled in Victoria and made our way to two more cheese factories, this time in Gippsland, where one of the best blues in Australia was produced. At South Nerrin at the Tarrago River Cheese Company we come in contact with a great family-run operation, where all your senses were assaulted on entering the maturing room for their great blue cheese. We entered into plenty of discussion about the ideal cheese, debating whether the cheese should be dry on the outside or wet like a Bleu D'Auvergne. We then made our way to Jindivick, where the great triple cream cheese made by Laurie Jensen was made. Again we sampled, evaluated and commented on the worth for other type. The Regent was a great consumer of cheese and my opinion was sought and welcomed.

Our trip to Victoria and Tasmania reinforced my belief that we could develop regional produce that was high in quality and quite specialised. Producers were seeing that there was a demand and the quality of their produce was allowing us as chefs to develop a local cuisine based on seasonal ingredients. I was excited and proud to be involved in the birth of a truly authentic Australian cuisine or at least the birth of a superb base of Australian products.

—

My range of produce was getting better all the time. Not long after my trip down south I was contacted and asked if I was interested in purchasing fresh snails? Well this was a turn for the books, something unseen in Sydney and a bit challenging. I organised for a sample, having a choice of either live snails or ones that had been precooked on the farm.

I chose live and the next week I received a Styrofoam box with holes drilled in the top and a large sticker saying 'Fragile-Live Snails'. I can only imagine the comments that the different handlers from Walcha (near Armidale) to Sydney made. Still, the snails were in perfect condition, purged and ready for the evening menu. They were a good curiosity for some and a gastronomic delight for others. I eventually visited the farm, which did not really have any meaning for regionalism as they could have been grown in my backyard in Sydney, but at least it provided a good income for someone living in the country.

One of my most exciting finds were products from Western Australia. Someone contacted me from the Fisheries Research Department and wanted to ascertain the commercial viability of a new species they just found in the deep water off the Western Australian coast. I obviously was quite prepared to look at it and to my surprise and joy it was beautiful scampi. It did not take me long to pick up the phone and confirm that this was like striking oil in the high sea. It was another missing link that was slowly completing my big picture. The delicate shellfish had previously only been found in the chilled water of the North Sea and to have them here, even if they needed to be chilled to preserve their freshness, was way better than using an imported product that was foreign to our shores.

My second find was the great marron from the same state. Marron are indigenous to Australia and originally they were known as a pest of the Western Australian waterways. Someone decided to farm them and eventually went commercial. Warren Moore offered me some samples, probably knowing that I would literally jump at them. What he sent me were monster beasts, nearly a kilo each.

Marron are funny beasts: aggressive, territorial and mean spirited, as well as being carnivores, happy to eat other marron. Warren explained that if you put one thousand yabbies in a pond and come back one year later you will still have one thousand yabbies. If you put one thousand marron in the same pond you would end up with just one huge one, as their natural tendency was to fight all their neighbours to the death. That process would go on till the ultimate warrior was left standing or actually crawling in the muddy pit still looking for an adversary. Still, as a culinary delight there is not much better, especially when you consider the marron cannot be found anywhere else in the world. France, Canada and the US might have the sweet northern Lobster, but we are the only ones with marrons.

—

Australia is blessed in many ways, especially when it comes to food, and we have certain advantages that most countries do not have. Because of our size and our position across several climatic zones we are able to grow practically everything. We have a very small population that is easy to feed and despite our small continental shelf we have a huge continuous shoreline. We have pasture in abundance and we have fertile land close to our big cities. We can claim to be a green exporter but also have a boutique industry that produces cheese, game and specialised vegetables. We have integrated markets that provide very fresh products and we have young chefs that are creative and unburdened by specific traditions or culture. Like every great food country we have a wine culture with specific regions and innovative wine makers who seek to produce outstanding wine to compliment our food.

It was not always like this. Many pioneers have worked tirelessly to create a wine industry. Murray Tyrell, Max Schubert, Len Evans, and so many others built this industry for our great benefit. More than anything, the quality of our food was inspired by the impressive improvement we made in producing quality wine. The natural association between these two elements of food and wine elevated our quality of life and made Australia a better country.

Foie gras is one of the few food items that we still do not produce here in Australia. It is produced in France, the Czech Republic, Israel, and many other countries, but not in Australia. A few years ago it started to be produced in America, and despite my reservations about certain ethical objections I decided to explore the possibilities of producing it here in Australia.

John Meredith had become a friend years ago. His duck farm and processing plant had supplied me with tens of thousands of ducks, geese, guinea foul, pheasants and quail over the years. I used Poussin from his farm as well as free-range chickens. He sourced me one of my absolute favourites—the hare—and could supply me with fresh turkey or farmed rabbit if I needed those items. I could get chicken liver, duck liver, and great goose liver from him but why not foie gras?

John, like many country people, is a conservative at heart and he struggles to make a living. The fluctuations in the market, the need to extend credit, the cost of raids by foxes and the closing of some of the restaurants he supplied (leaving him with unpaid bills) made him even more conservative. I tried to get him to expand, market himself better, renew his processing plant and put more trucks and staff on the road. John understood my reasoning but was always reluctant to implement my suggestions. Today I perfectly understand his reluctance; now that I am running my own business I have a much deeper appreciation of the pitfalls of increasing your costs, managing your cash flow and producing profit to make ends meet. My enthusiastic recommendations were, in a sense, naïve and idealistic.

John asked me to become a partner in the business and we set up all the paper work, signed all the documents and developed goals, but in the end we never went ahead with it. I could have easily seen myself working on the farm, caring for the flocks and enticing the chefs of Sydney with great produce. The dream of producing foie gras was at the time at the top of my agenda. I slowly realised and I am sure John did also, without a major injection of capital it would have been hard to achieve all the objectives I set out to achieve. My position at The Regent was always going to be difficult if I remained as chef and then also became a supplier of the hotel. Ted Wright was a very supportive person who totally understood my quest for better produce, but would someone else be as understanding? Once I really thought the idea through I realised that it was just not going to work at that time.

John and I still at times talk about the potential of producing foie gras. We went as far as visiting France and their foie gras producing region; we got all the literature on its production, but we always stopped short of starting some form of production. In France force-feeding is taken to the extreme. It is a tradition of the countryside, used by their duck farmers to produce a very large liver in the duck. This can only be achieved by force-feeding, which could certainly be controversial in Australia. In America there are plenty of rules and community groups ready to pounce on anything slightly controversial or unethical and yet there seems to be no issue with the production of foie gras. At the end it has to do with getting the animal to ingest more then he is willing to eat. I always believe that one day my project will somehow be achieved.

John's ducks, in the meantime, were just amazing. His breed was unique to Australia and needed to be produced by artificial insemination. He got the ducklings from a crossbreed of French Rouen, American Mallard and English Kaki Campbell, with maybe some Native Black Duck. This duck we brought in massive quantities for Kable's. The public appetite for this duck was insatiable but John's supplies were limited: eagles and foxes took their toll, as well as diseases and the heat and cold.

I became known for my duck dishes and passion for that game meat. This duck produced a lean meat, as opposed to their fatty cousins found mostly in Chinese restaurants. The meat of these ducks was tender and fresh and best served medium rare. That method of cooking was suited to the more sophisticated clientele of Kable's, where people could choose to eat bloody duck breast (like a French Magret) or instead fall back on white veal or pheasant. It was not suited to banquet style meals where people didn't have a choice, as I was to find out in our first year of operation.

When Jacky was still the Executive Chef he wrote a menu for a society function. Many of the social set of Sydney came to The Regent and because it was a lunch, it was mostly attended by women. This luncheon turned out to be one of the most disastrous functions we had ever held. I had just came back from a day off and in making my way to the function I could see the bloody duck breast being served as a main course. To me the duck seemed particularly rare that day, but it was too late to do anything as they were already being served as I arrived in the banquet kitchen.

Well it did not take long for the thirty waiters to come back with a growing pile of uneaten duck from the customers. What began as an embarrassing rejection by few of this main course turned into a flood of returned meals, with nearly everyone returning their plates. I had never seen anything like this and there was nothing we could do. The banqueting manager was stunned, speechless and turning paler as more and more plates were returned to the kitchen. Jacky took a very Gaelic approach, thinking there was nothing wrong with the cooking of the duck, blaming people's ignorance and generally settling into a state of denial. I wisely disappeared out of the banquet kitchen, which was probably quite unsupportive, but I could not bear it any more. I learned a valuable lesson that day: never serve to a large group anything that the majority of people would not like. It is far better to be on the side of caution than to have this type of rejection from your guests.

It was always extremely difficult to serve fish at lunch for our large functions, especially when you were feeding anywhere between 300 to 500 people. Fish was the logical dish to serve but relying on fresh fish made it quite difficult to write a menu with certainty. There was usually no way I could find three hundred portions by lunchtime. Fortunately a great change was about to happen in Tasmania. In the sixties the fishery department imported from Canada some live trout and salmon with the intention of analysing the potential to set up commercial production in the Snowy Mountains. The trout were farmed in Canada with great success and they had a great potential here. The fact that it took nearly forty years to achieve that goal says a lot about our eating habits of that time: meat was king and fish was for the few.

I keep hearing that freshwater trout were being raised in Tasmania with great success. They were being acclimatised gradually to salt water and at a certain stage were transferred into sea pens to raise them to an extraordinary size for a freshwater trout. Being such a large consumer of fish and one of the largest seafood purchasers, I was targeted as a potential market right from onset. The first time I saw ocean trout it was another turning point for Australian food and indeed for Australian cuisine.

The ocean trout was a wonderful fish to use. It was our first pink-fleshed fish that promised to be in easy supply and with a long season. I was delighted to have something new that could be supplied to me in a quantity that I required, making it possible for me to finally be able offer fish to large functions. The sweetness of the flesh, its deep red colour, the beautiful grain, perfect saltiness, perfect portioning size and the thickness of its fillet made it the perfect fish for my purposes. Even more interesting, Atlantic salmon was soon to follow, and suddenly we were rich in choice, with a whole industry developing around these fish.

It was in these golden years of discovery, innovation and creative thinking that I became known for my support of small producers, my drive to develop new produce, increase the range of our food and serve it with respect for its true flavour. I was having fun and the public really responded to our offerings, with probably a fair amount of national pride guiding their choice.

In all the years that I searched for, developed and commissioned special crops I always tried to share my bounty with other chefs. I did this to sometimes help develop a larger market for my small producers or to share my joy of new finds like wild mushrooms, zucchini flowers, new lettuces, baby vegetables or anything unusual. I remember visiting Peter Doyle with white asparagus, a vegetable that most Australian chefs had never seen in its fresh form. His reaction was so precious and typical of a person recognising another key element for better food. I made friendships through sharing my food finds and earned some respect for that commitment.

One day Stephanie Alexander visited me at The Regent, while on a quest to find stories for her page in the weekend insert for *The Sydney Morning Herald*. Stephanie came on that fateful day that I had purchased the first wild mushrooms I had ever seen in Australia. It was also the time that the ocean trout were arriving, and the season for fresh white asparagus (which I was the only one using). The range of produce I could gather amazed Stephanie. It was much easier for me, with such a large volume and an imposing purchasing power, to offer the best and newest. Restaurants did not have the time to invest in developing new produce nor did they have the necessary volume of sales to be able to influence the growing pattern of farmers, so it was only natural for me to have made a difference in improving our lot.

Stephanie wrote a beautiful article that started with a photo of me in front of all my precious new produce, titled 'The Birth of Australian Cuisine'. This was the confirmation of our arrival, not only as a nation of food lovers, but also as a nation of superb food producers.

16

KABLE'S AND THE CHEF'S TABLE

KABLE'S RESTAURANT WAS ON A PATH TO GREATNESS EVEN before the first customer was served. There is probably no other restaurant in Australia that had the same level of planning, review and assessment for every single component of the place that Kable's had. If a customer asked for a tea with lemon, how should he squeeze the lemon? At Kable's it was decided that the lemon wedge should be served wrapped in muslin ready to be squeezed with a beautiful little silver tool made in Switzerland.

The best plates, glasses, silverware, tablecloths and serviettes were ordered. The chairs were analysed for comfort, style and colour, with more than one hundred tested. The service procedures were entrusted into the capable hands of the company service expert and a team was recruited from hundreds of candidates. Each and every single service step was rehearsed and trialed. The restaurant was eventually opened, but not for the public: it was open for days on end to the staff to give both the kitchen and the floor staff a chance to build confidence and test their skills.

The style of food was very French at first, but modern French as opposed to the classic dishes seen around town in the more traditional French restaurants. The produce was superb and of amazing quality, as anything less was rejected. There were the best bartenders to prepare the cocktails, experienced bakers to make the fresh bread and skilful chefs making beautiful consommé, sauces and desserts. It was like living in the era of Escofier, where there was a total rebirth of the commitment to do things like they should have been done, regardless of cost. The only thing that was asked of everyone was to serve the best.

One of the little advantages The Regent had over other restaurants or at least other hotel restaurants was the access we had to a print shop. The print shop employed three people and produced every single piece of printed material that the hotel needed: parking tickets, welcome cards from the general manager, triplicate purchase orders, the valet list, sales brochures and, of course, menus. All of this and many more printed items were produced in-house. To have the ability to reprint our menu twice a day (sometimes even three times a day for breakfast, lunch and dinner) was such a bonus for us. It gave me the chance to purchase anything that I felt was the freshest in the morning from the market, instruct my chef of this impending arrival and have a menu description ready to be printed by 10am.

It became a real ritual for me to rush twice daily to the print shop before service and make the necessary changes to the menu for that day. Not all the dishes would change daily but over two weeks the menu would probably have made a complete turn around. There is nothing more special in my eyes than to go to a restaurant and see the menu either handwritten or printed with the date on it. It normally indicates that the chef has gone to the trouble of sourcing the ingredients daily and making full use of the seasonal produce. That tool was one of the most important aspects of Kable's success and it gave me the chance to showcase the full scope of the produce I could purchase.

The Kable's wine list was fast becoming one of the best in the city. As well as a commitment to gather the best wines in the marketplace, we also had unlimited funds to purchase rare bottles of expensive vintage wines and classic French Grand Cru. Ted Wright attended wine auction after wine auction, outbidding other buyers to get the best. It was often like at Flemington Market, when the first case of mangoes or cherries was auctioned. Ted loved buying 16th century Armagnac or a case of one of the better years of Chateau d' Yquem, which was the best desert wine in the world, produced in Burgundy. Today the list would make most sommeliers cry with jealousy seeing the wine selection and the prices on offer at that time. You could find a 1926 Château Margaux for $680, a 1959 Château Palmer for $280, a 1980 Clos Vougeot from Bouchard Père et Fils for $125 or a 1975 Grange Hermitage for $75. Or if you wanted to make a splash because these prices were too low you could select a double magnum of Château Lafite Rothschild '59 for at the time a staggering $2,400. Today these wines would be priceless.

The service team was lead by Willy Haska, the sombre and precise restaurant manager. Willy got his training from Jean-Pierre Dosse, who was the specialist who set up the standard of service for any new restaurants that were opened in The Regent group of hotels. Jean-Pierre was a tyrant at work, expecting all the staff to work seven days a week, morning to night, until in his mind the restaurant reached a perfect score. He was a sticker for written standards, something that I aspire to achieve but never quite got there. He drilled the front of the house team, made up mostly of east Europeans, into a cohesive and polished team. The team that Jean-Pierre formed was as professional, informed and capable as one could wish to have. They were supported by a large number of waiters, plus a bevvy of hostesses, florists, cleaners, polishers, valets and many other trades needed to keep the restaurant in perfect shape.

The first Kable's menu was written by Claude Boudoux. He gave a direction to the food and Jacky and Cheong were to follow the path that he laid. Claude had selected Cheong to be the Sous Chef for Kable's by asking all of The Regent's Sous Chefs when the hotel was about to open to cook a dish that they felt should be served in the restaurant. Cheong won that contest hands down because of his talent and experience.

Claude was a fabulous chef. He possessed an amount of experience that was unequalled by anyone in The Regent hotel company. He worked as Chef Saucier on 'Le France', the ship that was considered to have the absolute best food in the world. He worked for the Hilton in Québec City as Executive Chef, followed by the leading role in the kitchen at the Four Seasons Montréal, where the hotel acquired a formidable reputation for his innovative food. He was at The Regent Montréal when he was eventually tapped on the shoulder to become Corporate Director of Food and Beverage.

When Kable's eventually opened the chefs were surprised by the diners' response to the food, which was not as enthusiastic and appreciative as they had hoped. They soon discovered that the food portions were way too small and that the diners demanded larger servings. If this was not enough, the amount of complaints Ted Wright received about the absence of a steak dish on the menu was enough to make Ted a very nervous GM. It did not take very long for this to change and they soon added a steak dish to the choice. It was getting very hard to explain to the Australian people that the menu was not an appropriate place to have steak, especially when rabbit or venison was on the menu (which in the eye of the typical Australian was such an inferior meat to a well-cooked beef tenderloin).

The reputation of Kable's food quickly spread around Sydney. The general population of Sydney saw The Regent as a new attraction, a new place to visit, even if only to admire the foyer of the hotel. The architectural style was clean, fresh and different to expectations. Bellboys opened the doors of the foyer, the live classical music was a great change from the muzak of most other hotels and the fresh flowers were at that time a novelty that made every guest feel special.

The simple lines of the furniture and desks were a kind of cross between Scandinavian and Asian styles. It was pleasing to the eye and a big departure from what could be found in other public buildings.

There was a real sense of theatre when you arrived for dinner at Kable's; it was quite a special event. If you drove up to the hotel, the commissionaire would open your door and handle the parking of your car. The walk through the foyer up the majestic marble staircase further reinforced the sense of occasion. There was a place where you could dress up and make an entrance. Everyone felt special. You could easily picture Fred Astaire walking down the stairs or Cary Grant, cigarette in hand, deep in a discussion with other well-dressed men. There were beautiful women having a cocktail in the Club Bar, with cigar smoking businessmen concluding deals. You would often arrive at the same time as a Gala Dinner, with the procession of the beautiful people of Sydney streaming into the Ballroom. The sense of arrival was unequalled in Sydney.

Once you arrived at Kable's a beautiful hostess would be waiting at the entrance of the restaurant, clad in a long black silk skirt with a height defying split. The restaurant manager, Willie Haska, would be expecting you, having memorised the names of all the guests expected within each half-hour slot. Regular guests would be welcomed by name, once their custom became frequent. The hostess would then either offer you a drink in the foyer of Kable's while you waited for your guests, or they would take you directly to your table if you were having a 'dinner a deux'. The sheer plushness of the place would then just envelop you. Just making it to the table would have impressed any guest and first-time patron to a level that could never be forgotten.

The hostess would introduce the captain that would be serving them for the night. A drink of Kir Royale would be offered on a complimentary basis and served in an elegant champagne glass. The serviette would then be unrolled and put across the lap of the diner, and after they received their drink, the menus would be presented.

The first impression of the menu was the quality of the paper: it was thick and textured, a beautiful off-white, with the date standing proudly at the top. It was for Sydney and for most restaurants round the world a novel approach. None of those standard menus printed in Singapore every six months allowed you to use the freshest ingredients that you could find at the market that day. Kable's had a short menu that showcased our philosophy of sourcing the best food produce. There were two items that were always on offer in Kable's: the best Iranian sevruga caviar with blinis, and fresh grilled lobsters. The rest of the menu would change more or less according to the available produce and the season.

Dishes typical of the Kable's menu included medallions of lobster with pawpaw seed dressing and fresh melon, or an appetiser of roast duck saddle with mango and a ginger, orange and passionfruit dressing. The mains were simple and ever changing: you could see John Dory with tiny vegetables and a noilly prat sauce or a roast breast of chicken filled with a prawn mousse. In those days many dishes were stuffed, filled or coated with a variety of mousses. Fish was paired with meat and meat was paired with seafood. It was an odd combination but it was all the rage of that era.

John Purbrick, the sommelier, was a man with maturity, wisdom and knowledge on his side. He was the son of Eric, the very famous Victorian winemaker who owns Château Tahbilk, north of Melbourne. The winery was one of the oldest in Australia and Eric was a giant of the wine industry. Being larger than life and with no chance to outshine his father, John became one of the better known sommeliers of the era. His grey hair, mouthful of silver capped teeth and impeccable tuxedo made any recommendation hard to resist. He set a standard for wine service that is probably to this day unequalled in Australia. He was beautiful to look at and his attentive diners passionately consumed every sip of his advice. John's cellar and his access to great wines kept us amazed and intrigued.

Once the food order was taken and delivered to the kitchen an amuse bouche would be served. Every night this would change, but it included dishes such as tiny morsels of tartlette, crisp fried prawns or goats cheese salad. The bread would then arrive in a stunning silver metal weaved basket. The bread was another first for Sydney: it was the crispy lavosh bread, an unleavened thin, stretched bread dough sprinkled with poppy and sesame seeds. It eventually appeared in other restaurants and was also produced in a commercial form, however when it first appeared at Kable's it was considered daring, elegant, different and scrumptious. Its crispness and addictive quality became legendary, with people calling the kitchen to order some for dinner parties at home. For years no-one had our secret recipe and the only place you could find the bread was at The Regent.

In the kitchen Cheong would receive the order from the waiter who was working under the captain, being overlooked by the assistant manager, who was watched by Willie. It was all very hierarchical in the dining room, but even more so in the kitchen. The order would be called in a loud voice to all chefs, from the far away cold section to the busy entrée section and up to the noisy saucier section where the meat was cooked and the sauces were made. In between were the entremetier section, heating the soup, consommé and preparing and serving all the needed vegetables. There was a small army of chefs all very busy keeping up with the two lead chefs plating the food.

The dining room got busier and busier as the service went along, reaching a total crescendo around 8.30pm. By then most of the orders would be in the kitchen and not only did Cheong have to call the meal order, but he also had to call the pick-up. Within a couple of months Cheong's voice was incapable of sustaining the full service, causing all sorts of trouble. The chefs had no access to the written docket and had to rely on their memories. If one dish for one table was wrong it could ruin the next few tables and in some instance the whole night. So it was not surprising that one morning a microphone was installed with strategically placed speakers to help keep the chefs in line and inform them of their order. If Cheong was off I would take charge of the kitchen.

There was a valid point that the kitchen was too small. The main kitchen not only catered for Kable's, but it also catered for the room service and for the mezzanine level, where I soon introduced a new menu. This was three restaurants out of one kitchen. The pressure on the chefs was enormous, especially because Australians did not eat early like the Americans and they all wanted to come at 7.30pm. Even if they were told that no 7pm, 7.30 or 8pm bookings were available, and that they could only book for 9pm, they would say yes and show up at 7.30pm regardless. There was a constant battle between the kitchen and Willie on how badly spread his bookings were, but nothing ever changed, in fact I still have the same problem these days. Even though the people taking the reservations were not responsible they still got the flak over this.

The skill levels of the chefs and waiters kept improving, the popularity of Kable's kept growing and life was probably very good for the accountant of the hotel. One of the biggest problems Ted faced every Saturday was the irate phone calls from so-called mates, friends, businessmen, stars, agents, secretaries and house guests requesting or actually demanding access to a table for the evening. Ted bunkered down in his office and handled each call with grace and patience, explaining the situation faced by the limited number of tables, chairs and space. It was a good problem to have, but Ted hated to displease anyone and this made the start of his Saturday quite challenging. The chefs kept pleading for years to limit the number of bookings, as we did not feel capable of handling more than 100 guests a night. Often on these demanding Saturday nights we served 120 or even 130 guests: that is an enormous number of people to serve as only one person could cook the fish or the meat due to the limited stove space.

Kable's had reached the peak of its performance and once I eventually became responsible for the entire kitchen I decided to instill my own style of cooking with always an able Sous Chef at my side to run the Kable's kitchen. My big chance had come and it was time to install my philosophy about better produce and the development of a cuisine based more on regional food and with a sense of place and time in the Australian society.

One Friday we once again had a fully-booked restaurant and pressure from all sides to take more bookings. Sometimes a booking would grow from four to six then eight, causing all sorts of problems. From day one the rule at Kable's was that we did not take any large bookings. The single biggest table was 12 people and only one of this size was available. Trying to cook for anything more than 10 wrecked havoc with the food service; food could be overcooked or could not come on the plate at the same time from the various sections of the kitchen. Large tables slowed down the whole night and for this reason they were avoided in our booking plan as much as possible.

On that particular weekend the restaurant manager for the evening was Branko, our very composed and experienced restaurant manager, following the departure of Willie. He was struggling to fit in all the bookings, when he received a phone call from a regular guest who wanted to increase his booking at 8pm from 12 to 14 people. Branko could not find his booking on the list and despite looking at the phone log and other possible dates that particular booking was just not anywhere to be seen. The customer apparently got quite aggressive and despite Branko telling him that no place could be found for him he just said 'Thank you, I'll see you at 8pm' and hung up the phone.

Branko's exasperated air and the difficult predicament that he found himself was more than I could bear. We tried to juggle the floor plan to see if somehow it was possible to fit more people in. My plan was to sit six people at a table that normally would fit only four, a table of three could sit at table for two (instead of using the larger table of four), but in the end it was to no avail; there were just not enough chairs.

It was getting late in the day and we realised that we had a serious problem on our hands if we could not find a solution. I checked the small function rooms; they were all full. I checked the Presidential Suite that possessed its own dining room and discovered that was to be occupied. Solutions were being eliminated faster than we could come up with more options. I then said 'Why don't we use the Garde Manger table as a place to seat them'. The Garde Manger section was near Kable's kitchen and was unused in the evening. I knew that I could get enough barstools to sit the 14 guests and if Branko gave me some waiters I could handle the guests. Seeing that our options had run out, we decided to face the music with the guests, falling back on the table in the kitchen if we were desperate. The hope was that either he would not show up or some of the other guests would not come. Maybe he had made a booking somewhere else after hearing Branko's serious predicament.

It was with nervousness that the service started. It was a weekend, the hotel was full, the ballroom had 500 people in for a Gala dinner, the coffee shop was booming and the room service was already getting a steady stream of orders. No matter what, it was going to be an ugly night.

Eight o'clock came and Branko called me from the front and said, 'He's here.' With apprehension, I replied, 'Bring them to me.' The host was a very well-known businessman (who will remain unnamed) and on walking through the dining room he was recognised by a couple of tables and drawn into conversation with these other diners. Meanwhile his guests were lead into the kitchen. They were surprised and stunned at the same time by the size, cleanliness and set-up of a professional kitchen. This was probably the first time that most of these people had ever seen a commercial kitchen of that size and they just loved it. Branko lead them to the Garde Manger and the beautifully set stainless steel table with the silverware and sparkling wine glasses all around this central workplace. They knew this was going to be a special evening.

The host was eventually led into the kitchen. I was watching from the depths of the kitchen for his reaction and I could see his face and demeanor change when he realized where he was seated. Before he could explode he reached his guests and they all applauded him spontaneously, thinking that he had organized this especially for them. He decided to just go with it, although I could see it was reluctantly. I told the kitchen staff to serve them quickly, as I knew we would be hit hard by the full service to come and it was better to get them fed and out of the way.

The appetisers came out of the kitchen fairly quickly. I had decided not to give menus to the guests as I knew if they ordered a la carte it would take too long for them to order and then to serve them. Instead I decided to cook all the appetisers minus the caviar, giving me 18 entrées. I instructed the waiter to place the entrées randomly in front of all the guests and then to put the balance in the centre of the table, as I had made a few extra entrées. To ease this new approach I went personally to the table, explaining all the dishes and what I intended to do. I told them that tonight they would be sampling different dishes in a different environment and if they did not like what they had in front of them then they had to try to exchange it with other guests, to plead, beg or borrow. Somehow it worked and the people decided to go with it: they shared, sampled from every plate and generally had fun eating the entrées.

The kitchen was by now at the busiest part of the evening and I realised that I wasn't going to be able to serve their main course before the big rush. The kitchen was already well and truly bogged down and there was no way I could serve their main courses any time soon. I pushed the kitchen guys to work faster, I helped plate up, but the wait for their mains was getting embarrassingly long, with no sign of being able to start cooking for them anytime soon. I resolved to go and apologise, wondering why I had attempted to fit this table in.

On reaching the table I suddenly thought about offering them the option to get up and see the service in the kitchen. They all enthusiastically agreed, even though the host was still looking unimpressed. The service had reached a peak when there were main courses going out but also a great deal of appetisers. It was the most difficult time of the evening and the guests could see the panic on each chef's face, the sweat soaking their uniforms and the flames rushing toward the exhaust in an impressive and frightening size. Because the waiters were carrying so much food I decided to move the guests to the back of the kitchen as it offered me more chance to kill time as well as getting them out of the way. Now the guests were even closer to the cooking of the food; their fascination was growing and they were eagerly asking questions about the way things were being done.

Eventually the time came to return them to their table and serve their main course. I checked with my chef as I went past but he told me that it would be impossible to feed them for at least another hour. Things were getting worse and I needed to kill more time. I gathered the whole group and moved them away from the Kable's kitchen. I passed in front of the washing-up section, with a huge board that displayed broken crockery with the price on it: $37 per main course plates, $32 per tea cup, $30 per wine glasses, $12 per high ball and so on. I explained that we broke on average about $700 daily in crockery and glasses, and that this amounted to a staggering $225,500 a year. People were stunned that it could cost that much, they were starting to realise just how much it costs to operate a hotel of this calibre.

We then moved to the room service area, where dozens and dozens of trolleys were set with salt, pepper, cutlery, napkins, basic plates, jam and honey jars, ready to be used for the next morning's breakfast. I explained that most guests ate between 7.30 and 8.30, with a few romantic stragglers eating later. This put an enormous amount of pressure on the room service and the kitchen, as it was a very inefficient way of serving guests. It took one waiter per room order to deliver the food. It took a long time to wait for the ever-busy service lift to go up and probably the same amount of time to wait for it to go down. A waiter could spend 30 minutes just serving one continental breakfast. Room service was considered a lost leader—meaning that it was an area of the hotel that constantly lost money—but we had no choice but to offer that service. It is one of those little indulgences that people expect of a five-star hotel. Having dinner for two with the view of the harbour, a bottle of wine, and the lights dimmed down was just so romantic. Most weekday guests were businessmen who preferred a hamburger in front of the TV late at night, rather than eating alone in the restaurant.

That night I had noticed that one of the guests from that table was staying in-house. The man was fun but demanding and he was a perfect target for my sense of humour. As a trick I wrote his name on the room service board where all guests' requests were listed. They read like this: 'Mr John Smith: return guest, tea with lemon only, likes steam veg with main meal' If they were a special person (such as Robert Holmes a Court) they were listed as SP.

I wrote beside his name: 'Mr Ian Smith: R1917, be careful, extremely demanding and a difficult person who likes to be called Sir'. As his fellow guests were scanning the board they eventually saw his name and one person screamed 'Ian, look you are on the board as a special person'. Everyone was laughing and Ian just blushed with embarrassment, even though he knew that was not quite true. Then they read the comments about him being difficult and not only did they laugh but they gave him such a hard time until I eventually told everyone I was actually playing a joke on him, and that created even more laughter. This was a practical joke that I eventually played many times when I perceived there were difficult guests attending the Chef's Table.

My next stop on the tour was the pastry shop and the ice-cream room. Some of the Pastry Chefs were there, working to finish the desserts for Kable's and the room service. Soufflés were coming out of the oven for a large table and it was an impressive sight for my guests. When you make soufflé you normally prepare a batch and produce extra soufflé, as there are always a couple that do not rise perfectly. That night there were about half-a-dozen spare soufflés, so I quickly gathered some spoons and all the guests plunged into the leftover ones. One of my Pastry Chefs was churning mango ice-cream and it was just another little bonus that they could try this ice-cream, even though they did not have main courses yet.

I decided to call the Kable's kitchen to see if I could bring my guests back. The answer was still no; things were at their worst down there. I needed to prolong the tour, so I took them next to the silver polishing room, where two of the kitchen stewards were dipping and polishing beautiful pieces of silver: all the tea pots and strainers, cutlery, function platters, flower vases, butter dishes and all the other silver pieces that needed to be polished twice a week. There were tens of thousands of silver pieces in the hotel, and it was a mammoth job to ensure a beautiful finish on all the silver. Everyone made jokes about bringing their silver in to be polished, which I welcomed them to do.

We stopped next at the chocolate room, where I got my Pastry Chef to show them all how we produced all our in-house chocolates. Vats of tempered chocolate were glistening and boxes and boxes of finished chocolates were lining the shelves. A couple of the women could not resist sampling items.

I decided to take them down one more level to our banquet kitchen. Ron, my Executive Sous Chef, was serving a huge function which was quite a sight. There were at least 50 waiters, plus a dozen chefs in the kitchen. Main course was about to be served and Ron was controlling the process with total focus. The chef and helpers were lined up in two long lines, with food ready to be plated between them set on the huge stainless steel table. Ron suddenly yelled 'go' and a procession of hot plates made their way down the line, with each person responsible to put an item in a precise point on that scorching plate. At the end of the table Ron and my other Sous Chef sauced the finished dish and it was scooped up by the waiter to be delivered warm and perfectly presented at the table.

Another phone call to the kitchen told me that it was at least 15 minutes before they could start cooking my guest's meal. I decided to make my way at the end of the corridor where our George St Bar was. As I opened the door I could feel the enormous vibrancy of the place: loud pumping music was blaring, hundreds of young people were packed like sardines in the bar, all standing and drinking. There were seven bartenders behind the bar, trying to cope with the sheer volume. It was such a contrast to the rest of the hotel, even to me it was amazing to see so much business being done in the hotel.

We next moved to the lobby kitchen where the service was full on. Plates of club sandwiches, chicken and mango salad, and desserts were being prepared and delivered to the tables. Anne, my second female Sous Chef, was busy checking all the food and ensuring the good standards were maintained.

I then moved through the back of the hotel and through a huge glass wall we could see a big darker room with half-a-dozen telephonists answering and directing calls, fetching faxes and posting messages. Email did not exist in those days and dissemination of faxes in a hotel was an extremely labour-intensive burden, as all guests would constantly phone the telephonists to see if a fax had arrived or if they could send one. A bell captain was then sent to their room to fetch a fax to be sent away. Thank goodness for email!

We finally returned through the emergency stairwell and re-emerged at the back of the main kitchen. I reached the Garde Manger, sat the guests and miraculously the main courses started arriving. People burst into automatic applause. I could see the host was starting to relax and a little wink to me give me the indication that we were back on track.

That evening could have been a total disaster. We chose to try to accommodate our guests, although we were pretty much forced into it. Still, the spirit instilled into us all, by Bob Burns and Ted Wright was that service was the be all and end all. That night out of adversity we created a bit of magic.

A week later I was checking my upcoming menu for a function when Beverly, my PA, told me there was a lady waiting to speak with me. The lady quickly told me that she had special guests coming to Sydney and that she wanted to come to the Chef's Table! I said, 'What Chef's Table?' She said, 'I know you have a Chef's Table in the kitchen because one of my friends attended it last week.' So out of the blue we had a booking for something that did not exist. She was so persuasive that I had to take it.

In the early 1900s in old Europe, in the time of the glitzy hotel, the Executive Chefs were treated as kings and their offices were always located next to an eating room, with full view of the kitchen. That room was used for meetings and the meal that the team would have together. Sometimes the chef would invite journalists, other chefs or food personalities to show off his food and this became known as the 'Chef's Table'.

Over the next few months, leading up to Christmas, Branko booked more and more Chef's Tables. In late November the Chef's Tables were becoming more frequent and they were starting to ruin my routine. I could not get up at 5.30 in the morning, start work at 7am and do the Chef's Table two or three nights a week. I resolve to talk to Branko about cutting back on them and to my total dismay he told me that from the second week of December we had about four to five Chef's Tables a week. I was stunned; how could I do these plus my normal work? I put in place rules to restrict them to three nights a week, and even that was a big ask of me. The consequence of this was the waiting list grew longer and longer, eventually reaching six months for a booking. A nightmare had just started and I was at the centre of it.

To say that the Chef's Table was a phenomenon was an understatement; it seems that the whole of Sydney attended that table at some point in time. A few years in I resolved to stop it because I was totally exhausted, not just physically with the constant late nights, but also from the mental pressure of somehow repeating the same story every time for the benefit of the guest. Each night I tried to change what I said to remain fresh, but there is a limit of how many ways you can say the same thing.

I told Ted Wright that I thought that maybe it was a great time to stop it. His response was, 'Do you know how much revenue it takes a year?' I said that I thought that it was around a quarter of a million dollars. He replied, 'Serge, do you realize that that amount is very close to your present salary?' His message was obviously that if the Chef's Table was to disappear, my job could be in jeopardy. Well, maybe that is not what he meant to say but my reply was, 'Okay, what about another year!' I had a very good sense of self-preservation!

17

YVETTE AND VATULELE

Y VETTE CAME INTO MY LIFE AS A FRESH BURST OF LOVE. I AM
certainly not an impulsive person, but I knew when my heart was
pulling me in a certain direction.

I first met Yvette in Sydney through a mutual friend. Yvette was
running several very successful Melbourne pubs, having previously
worked for Peter Rowland (the King of Melbourne catering), working
at the famous Jean Jacques Restaurant on St Kilda beach and as
Executive Assistant Bar Manager at the newly opened Grand Hyatt in
Melbourne. But I was not aware of any of this when I first met her.

I had decided to take my staff for dinner at the new Bilsons
Restaurant in Circular Quay. To my surprise Aldo (one of my suppliers
from Melbourne) was also there, having dinner with a beautiful
woman called Yvette, who was also from Melbourne. One of Yvette's
pubs was across the road from Aldo's factory, and when they realised
they were both visiting Sydney at the same time Aldo invited her to
join him for dinner. As they were both in town the next day I invited
them to have lunch at Jonahs at Whale Beach, near where I was living

on the peninsula. I found Yvette to be beautiful and full of joy, but she already had a boyfriend, who was a triathlete. So that was that.

One year later I visited Melbourne and Aldo invited me to lunch the next day. I wanted to go to Stephanie's and I made a reservation for three: Aldo, his wife Stacey and myself. Unbeknown to me, Aldo had changed the booking to four so that I could enjoy Yvette's company again. We had a very pleasant lunch and on my return to my hotel I organised to send her a bunch of flowers to thank her for her company and to wish her a happy birthday, as she had said it was her birthday the following day.

It was another year before I saw her again. Just for a change, it was Aldo who was the instigator of our next encounter; I think he was trying to send me a message. I was with my parents (who were visiting from Canada) and my friends John Meredith (the duck grower) and Roger, staying on a farm in Wee Jasper, near Yass. My mother loved the idea of staying on a property in Australia and I had arranged to take three weeks off work: two to spend with my parents and one to do a consultancy at Vatulele Island in Fiji. I had a speaking engagement for the Meat Board in Melbourne one of the nights we were staying on the farm. The previous night we all went rabbit shooting until three in the morning and after a few hours sleep I drove to Canberra to catch a flight to Melbourne and speak at the dinner, which was held at The Regent.

Aldo picked me up from the airport and told me that because he was coming with Stacey, his wife, he thought it was a good idea to invite Yvette as well. Here we go again, I thought, the message was getting very clear. Because his work was across the road from Yvette's, we stopped by to confirm what time she would like to be picked up, and while we were there one of Yvette's employees wished her a happy birthday. It was one year to the day since I last saw her.

I returned to the hotel to prepare for my speech and have a shower. Before I went up to my room I decided to send her some more flowers to wish her a happy birthday. Not knowing how much to spend I asked the concierge to send $100 of cut loose flowers; I wanted her to be able to use them around the pub. Well $100 worth of flowers was not seen as excessive in my book, but I didn't realise that in Melbourne in summertime, $100 of loose flowers was apparently a gigantic bouquet. I only learned about this months later. Anyway, it made an impression.

The dinner came, the speech was done (not one of my best) and finally Yvette and I could have a one-to-one chat after dinner. But before this could happen, I had already promised to visit Marchetti's Latin, as all my Sydney friends were going there for dinner because they had come down to Melbourne for the harvest picnic the next day. They had a private room upstairs and as we walked up I could hear a sudden great burst of laughing. Someone had just made a joke about it being late in the night and was referring to what I might be doing on my own. At that precise moment I arrived with Yvette; it was an inopportune moment to walk in. We did not stay long as it was late and Yvette was not very comfortable with so many people she did not know. Questions from friends, like 'So, who is this blonde?' also made me uncomfortable.

We decided to go to the downstairs bar at nearby Mietta's, but Mietta was at the door and recognised me, so for the next hour she proceeded to show us around the whole building with a precise description of the whole operation! I did not think this visit would ever end, but we finally left without even a drink, but being extremely thankful for her generous tour. Once we were in the street Yvette said that she would like to take me somewhere were nobody would recognise me. We ended up at a groovy little bar (the type that you only find in Melbourne) and finally we were alone together at two in the morning, the first chance we had had to talk privately so far. After some light conversation I asked her directly why her boyfriend wasn't with her on her birthday night. She told me that he had a race the next morning and so he needed to go to bed early. I thought to myself 'silly man'.

I was booked on a 7am plane but realised that I was never going to make it, so I changed the time to 11am and I caught up with Yvette in the morning for a great walk in one of Melbourne's magnificent parks. I could feel that rush of attraction coming over me in seeing Yvette again. I promised to call her as soon as I got to Sydney but first I had to get back to Wee Jasper.

I arrived that afternoon and cooked dinner for everyone. After dinner we were supposed to go shooting, but I decided that I had had enough and excused myself and went to my room. There was no phone at the property as the house we were staying in was an unused worker's house. My mobile did not have any coverage and despite the fact that I was dying to speak to Yvette I could not do so. I fell into a heap and that was the end of me for that eventful weekend.

When I returned to Sydney I phoned Yvette and discovered that after our evening together she had gone home and ended her relationship with her boyfriend. By that time Linda and I had already taken different paths and I felt ready to start a new relationship. I was due to go to Fiji in two days, but I realised that I just could not face one week in Vatulele without Yvette, so I decided to ask her to come with me. I knew it was too soon and really rushed, but here was a chance to go away together to an incredibly romantic island. I gently insisted that she consider it, despite her protests that she was too busy at work. I did not know that Yvette was long overdue for a vacation and she had promised herself to take one for months. She phoned me back the next day and we were on. She threw caution into the wind, a bikini into a bag and we were off to Vatulele.

There is no more romantic destination than Vatulele. It is the only resort on that tiny island to the south of Fiji's main island. It has only twelve romantic bures on the beach, the sand is pure white, the water warm and impossibly turquoise. We landed by seaplane in front of the resort, on the perfect white sand. I was not working in the kitchen for a couple of days and the tradition was for the new arrivals to eat at the side of the general manager, Martin, on the communal table that sat all the guests. We covered numerous topics that night and Yvette and I were discovering so many things that were right about each other to the consternation of Martin, who jokingly asked us had we just met on the plane: it was near enough to the truth.

We had the most blissful time on the island. My intention of spending a lot of time in the kitchen went out the window, especially since Martin kept insisting that I relax and not worry about the kitchen. Still, my professionalism was pulling me one way and my heart the other way. I am normally never late for anything, but for the entire week we arrived late for every single meal. It was embarrassing, but I was on another planet for that week.

The resort was partly owned by Henry Crawford, who was a successful film producer. Henry's dream was Vatulele, which he took years to build and it was voted one of the best resorts in the world. It was at his invitation that I ended up with my bare feet on the beach, living a dream that will never cease to amaze me.

———

One year later we decided to return to Vatulele to get married and on that occasion we were to be even more amazed. The year had flown, with both of us working very hard. Yvette had taken over another pub and was in the process of transforming it, like she had done with her other successful one. She flew into Sydney every Saturday evening and returned on Monday morning. I would occasionally go to Melbourne as a surprise on a Wednesday night, taking the last flight out of Sydney and returning on the 7am flight the next morning. We did this for four years, even after we got married!

I asked Henry if he would mind us getting married at Vatulele. He was delighted and very generous in his offer, the only small concession he asked was if we would not mind having *Vogue* cover the wedding, because Henry wished to publicise the resort but did not have the necessary budget. I could hardly say no, despite the fact that we had not told any of our friends, parents or family of our intentions. There was no way I could have any of my family at the wedding living so far away in Canada and Yvette also wanted to have this for just the two of us. That suited me, despite my burning desire to tell the world I was marrying Yvette.

For five months the secret was kept, but just two weeks prior to going to Fiji Simon Johnson called me and said, 'Serge, there is a rumour that you are getting married'. I replied, 'Simon, look it means nothing. Maybe next year, but not now.' He tried again and again, but I was not going to give anything away. He finally said in exasperation, 'Look Serge, I know you are getting married, because there is a wedding cake ordered for you for Fiji.' I was totally surprised by this, how could this happen? Henry knew it was totally private and that we did not want a wedding cake! We wanted bare feet on the beach, no friends, no family, and above all, no fuss.

I needed to find out where this rumour had come from so Simon finally told me that Henry had asked Joan Campbell to recommend the best wedding cake maker in Australia to make a cake. She had refused to advise him unless he agreed to say whom it was for, then she immediately phoned Simon once she was off the phone from Henry. Not only was Joan a good friend, but I lived a few steps away from her house in Darling Point. I had kept the secret for five months, seeing Joan and Simon weekly, if not more. It was typical Joan to find out just two weeks before our wedding. I had to discourage Simon from coming with all my friends.

We finally arrived at Vatulele and the whole affair was incredible. It rained for four days solid, but the day before our wedding the sky turned blue, the sea flattened and the magic returned. Over the next two days the stage managing of Henry was incredible. After the kava offering (with a full tribe of oiled Fijians in grass skirts) we had the wedding day itself, with a stunning Catholic missionary presiding over the ceremony, his black skin littered with tattoos, contrasting with his white collar. Then the full village choir sang at the great love feast that was held after.

The most stunning moment of it all was when I was told by Henry to wait on the beach at the water's edge. I could hear the regular beat of the tam tam drum coming from the hill above the resort and suddenly I saw a beautiful blue wooden boat with four Fijian warriors dressed in grass skirts, rowing it to shore. Yvette was in her pretty gold corset and tulle skirt, sitting serenely with two gorgeous village children; it was the perfection of a romantic ideal.

At the end of the day, when the photographer was taking his final picture, a sun flash appeared on the horizon when the sun was setting on the water. All the Fijians acknowledged this sign and told us there could be no better luck. I could only agree with them, having the chance to marry such a stunning woman.

18

THE VISITING CHEFS

ONE OF THE EVENTS THAT MARKED THE ARRIVAL OF SYDNEY as a world food city was the start of the visits by guest chefs from France and America. Up to that point, the only chance to eat the food of these three-star Michelin chefs or the leading American chefs was to visit their restaurants overseas. The big trend in Asia was to invite prestigious chefs, preferably from the elite of French restaurants, obviously at great cost for special promotions.

One of the leading chefs of America at that time was Jeremiah Tower, now at his famous American brasserie 'Stars'. Ted had secured Jeremiah to come and hold a weeklong promotion at The Regent. This event created a real stir in the food press, in other hotels, in other restaurants and with most chefs in Sydney. It was not often that we had a living legend visit our shores, as the long distance and the misguided belief of the backwardness of Australians in food matters just did not make us an attractive destination for these chefs. To have Jeremiah Tower agree to hold a promotion was at that time a real gastronomic coup.

To think that Jeremiah was at the inception of Chez Panisse as fifty per cent owner seems strange. Most people would think of Stars as his signature restaurant. In these early years Jeremiah was like many creative Californians, a dreamer with not much practical experience. The fact that he got a job at the newly opened Chez Panisse—a very bohemian restaurant with friends of Alice Waters taking turns to cook—was more fluke than good sense. With very little professional training he still appeared to be more experienced than the other dreamers in the kitchen were. It did not take long for these people to depart, probably glad someone could actually turn the gas on and somehow cook something. The restaurant was always struggling and in lieu of pay he instead got his half partnership. Over the next five years he went from strictly Elizabeth David recipes to more personal interpretations of other European dishes, finally evolving a style of cooking that was based on the local ingredients and created the birth of California Cuisine.

Everyone was wondering why such a chef would agree to come to Sydney. Jeremiah had actually spent his teenage years in Sydney. He was raised for many years in Vaucluse from American parents, and remembered going to Pruniers in Woollahra in the forties and fifties and developing a love for food and restaurants.

Jeremiah's dishes were simple but unusually striking. He balanced fresh ingredients and vibrant colours and was the first American chef to introduce us to chilli, as chilli was all the rage in California at that time. His food was a continuing evolution of American classics mixed with spices and Asian flavours.

He prepared a ceviche of snapper with a coriander purée and a Chinese black bean sauce that was puréed with fish stock and smothered with butter. It was my first contact anywhere with fermented black bean, apart from their use in Chinese restaurants. He showed the daring of someone who was prepared to use any food to create great flavours.

His menu contained grilled scampi drizzled with a 'herb goddess sauce' (a silky smooth mayonnaise, thinned down with a vinaigrette and coloured with a parsley purée). He made great use of grilled capsicum purées to enhance sauces and meats, as well as other flavours like garlic purée, basil, tomato, anchovies, chilli and black bean. He made steak tartare with beef sirloin and drizzled them with a spicy Cajun remoulade. He used my wild Blue Mountain mushrooms in a warm spinach and bacon salad and he made soup with duck, pistachio and grilled lemon. It was all very avant garde at the time, with new presentations and flavours at its central core. His desserts were scrumptious and typically American, such as Stars Fantasy Cream (berry and marscapone cream), warm tropical fruit compote with ice-cream, pear with sabayon and raspberry sauce and shortbread with apple. The people loved it, they loved him and he ended up loving Sydney again.

Jeremiah was due to visit me with his team a couple of days prior to the start of his promotion in Kable's, and he arrived in my kitchen, lead by Ted. He had an easy manner and a very good sense of how the kitchen worked. He had bought three chefs with him: his Chef de Cuisine, a kitchen chef and his Pastry Chefs.

Jeremiah accepted my suggestion to visit the fish markets to confirm the menu and to ensure he knew what he would be working with. Our visit the next morning was a revelation for him as there was nowhere near the range of fresh fish back in San Francisco. He marvelled about the choice of fish, the set-up and proximity of the market to the city. It was certainly going to make his life much easier in refining his menu.

Together we planned our joint lunch menu for the food press one day prior to the start of our promotion. Our idea would be that we would each do a dish, not so much to compete but to show an equal partnership and our love of cooking. Jeremiah had his team brief my chefs on the menu and the recipes to be prepared and all of this went without an incident. My team was strong and fully prepared for the task at hand and the produce we ordered was the freshest and best quality you could find at the market.

On looking at the bookings I realised that this would be a great event for Kable's and for Sydney. We were fully booked for a week ahead, with many big-name chefs coming to dine over the week. Jeremiah and I struck a friendship that remains true to this day. His first duty was to prepare the food for the journalist's lunch, but once he realised that all the dishes were under control he concentrated on spreading his charm and knowledge to the many people who wished to talk to him.

During the week, as soon as the service was over, we would wander into the restaurant and speak to the people who had asked to speak to him and then to the chefs and restaurateurs I could see in the room. Jeremiah had immense ease with people, being able to speak on practically any subject and always sounding happy and informed. I certainly learned from him the need to approach people and remain accessible. People can sense your genuine willingness to speak to them and they respond to that.

I have never been a believer in the huge consumption of alcohol, although I do have the occasional beer after a hard day at work. However I usually don't drink at work, especially because in this industry drinking can often get out of control. Well, my position on drinking at work was certainly challenged when Jacky bought a chilled bottle of Pommery champagne to Jeremiah just before lunch started on the first day. I do not know if Jacky was forewarned that Jeremiah liked a glass of chilled bubbly, because he certainly enjoyed that drink. For the rest of the week we received a new bottle every day and I got used to Jeremiah's savouring (I would not dare say drinking) of the champagne. Jeremiah's mood improved as he consumed the bottle: he was more animated with the customers and his talk was more interesting, deeper in meaning and more fluid.

The days went fast and the services blended into each other. We reached the end of the week without major problem or gaffes. The food was innovative, modern and from a different mould we were used to. The success of one of the first visits from a celebrity chef was complete. The local press featured him extensively and his quotes were to the point and challenging. Above all, he charmed Sydney with his tales of his teenage years spent around Sydney Harbour and the difficulty in living with a semi-aristocrat family who kept uprooting themselves.

To me and to my chefs it was a rewarding period, especially because their chefs got along so well with mine, visiting Sydney and its night-time watering holes, as all young chefs like to do. For Ted and the management of the hotel it was a very successful event in terms of revenue and public relations; the idea of bringing an American star to Sydney was seen as a very innovative coup.

—

It became a must for Ted to have an annual visit from a prestigious chef who did not fit the conventional mould. Our next chef was Ken Hom, the telegenic Chinese American Chef who was hugely popular in England. More than any of the other visiting chefs, Ken became a close friend to me. He was a true inspiration and guide, as well as a great source of advice on writing books, agreeing to do promotions and structuring recipes. Ken was born in Chicago, but lived in Berkeley, California, where I often stayed at his home on my visits to San Francisco. Ken was part of the 'brat pack' who worked at Chez Panisse in its gipsy years. He lived with his long-term French boyfriend, Daniel, and their famous dog Titoune, the Alaskan husky with the beautiful blue eyes.

Ken was actually born in Tucson, Arizona, after his family migrated from difficult circumstances out of Guangzhou Canton in mainland China. His father soon passed away, leaving one-year-old Ken (now an

American citizen) fatherless. Ken's mother struggled to earn an income from low-paying jobs due to her lack of English and her limited work skills. She eventually made her way to live with her extended family in Chicago, where Ken was surrounded by cousins and nephews. He grew up eating traditional Chinese food and could observe the preparation in the commercial kitchen of his uncle's restaurant. His knowledge was acquired working in these kitchens, although that type of work certainly did not appeal to him. But flavours and traditions remained ingrained in him and they were to become useful after he finished his university years in California.

Ken quickly realised that he aspired to a more fulfilling life than slaving in a Chinese restaurant. Catering for friends and friends of friends was a vocation and eventually this turned into teaching cooking in his incredibly well-stocked kitchen and then to book publishing. Ken published many dozens of cookbooks and he was one of the first famous chefs to have a cooking series on the ABC. His series was a huge success, as were his associated books. He was the model for many of our contemporary television chefs. Ken's stature grew and by the time we agreed to have him at The Regent he was a food consultant for Hong Kong's Cathay Pacific Airlines and he held promotions all over the world.

Ken was always an extremely stylish dresser and a man who thrived on connections and contacts.. Having stayed at his different homes spread across the US and France I realised he was a real clotheshorse. I have never seen so many clothes, and while he was not quite an Imelda Marcos, his shoe collection would serve me many times over. I understood that in his line of work it was imperative for him to look good, but this was obviously a pleasure and thrill and quite possibly an addiction to seek the best. Ken loved labels and the quality that went with them. He was always encouraging me to borrow some of his clothes and he would advise me on the subtle differences between a shirt from Comme des Garcons, Montana, Versace, Armani or Tom Ford: all things I could not afford.

This is not to say Ken did not focus on his food; he was an excellent cook with a very intuitive palate. His strength lay in his food style, being one of the first to blend the cooking produce and techniques of the East with the West. His 'East meets West' cookbooks were true best sellers, a wake-up call to the gastronomic world of the potential for this esoteric and magical blend of techniques. What made Ken a great proponent of his East meets West style of food was his love of French food and the admiration he had for the disciplined and stylish French approach to food. Ken became a Francophile early in life after his first visit to France, when he was photographing medieval monuments throughout Europe on behalf of The University of California. Ken became fluent in French and today mostly lives in France, as he feels more comfortable with that culture than any other.

Ken literally opened up the Chinese kitchen to Westerners and educated many of us in the cooking techniques and methods of this great cuisine. Up to that point the world of the Chinese kitchens was fairly closed, having a totally abstract kitchen hierarchy, vastly different kitchen equipment and kitchen set-up. Their ingredients were only vaguely familiar in name and appearance, and few people knew how to use Chinese ingredients such as bitter melon, raw duck, pork belly and garlic chives. Thai ingredients were somewhat more understood than Chinese ones. His many books described ingredients that were to this point unknown to the Western eyes and his recipes were a modern version of Chinese techniques blended with familiar Western cooking methods. The fact that he taught Charlie Trotter in the use of Chinese ingredients shows the respect he has from his peers.

Ken was the public precursor to a form of cuisine that was to take California, Australia, Asia and most of the Western world by storm. Suddenly there were Asian ingredients and techniques introduced into chef's repertoires everywhere, but it was not all good news. Like nouvelle cuisine, with its eventual excess, East meets West was to stumble eventually with an overzealousness of many inexperienced chefs.

I never believed a cuisine could be universal unless it is based on an established cuisine such as French, Chinese, Thai or Italian. Made-up cuisines lacking roots and mixing different cooking techniques are more like marketing exercises for chefs or establishments that are searching for an identity. Examples of these include Australian cuisine and my all-time pet hate, Pacific Rim cuisine. Authentic new styles of cooking come from the chef's personal belief and experience, building on tested cooking methods combined with local produce to create recipes that have a meaning, a sense of belonging and a balance between technique and composition.

Like Paul Bocuse, Ken Hom eventually returned to creating more traditional dishes, discarding the shock value of clashing cultures to produce what I consider a great style that complimented his skills and certainly the produce available to him.

Ken and I worked together on many occasions to create menus that would pair together our great produce with his skills and recipes to create menus that people really enjoyed. They was always a sense of trust between the two of us, him relying on me to suggest a menu from his book and me relying on him to teach my staff how to cook the food with his skilful oriental cooking techniques.

I have never served so many ducks in my life as when Ken Hom did his first promotion at The Regent. To achieve the perfect crisp skin necessary for Peking Duck we needed to blow the ducks to separate the skin from the flesh. If you possessed extremely strong lungs and lips and were not afraid to get in contact with the more intimate parts of the ducks anatomy, you could become a specialised Chinese duck blower, but needless to say I preferred to try another technique. Looking at the bookings for the week ahead I realised that we would be busy with Ken's visit to Kable's so I quickly doubled my order of ducks from John Meredith.

I then proceeded to phone the engineering department to see if we could borrow a compressor, which I knew they had. The weird wheeled contraption arrived in the kitchen within an hour and Udo, my German dynamo of a Sous Chef, proceeded to stuff the duck with chopped ginger, orange peel, salt and spices, then skewering the open cavity of the chest. After the customary dip in the boiling soya bath and high heat roasting he put my device to good use, inflating the superbly trussed duck to separate the skin and achieve that perfect result.

One of Ken's strongest attributes is his capacity to network and build relationships on every continent. Not having the desire to have a restaurant of his own, he chose to consult and hold promotions within airlines, hotels and restaurants around the world. He is so successful at this that most of his living is now derived from these activities. He is able to design a chain of simple restaurants (like he did in London, based on Chinese favourites), write cookbooks, hold promotions in hotels and consult to organisations. He never seems to stop, constantly amazing me with his new contacts. He is on friendly terms with Alain Ducasse, having regular meals in his kitchen in Paris, and has free access to accommodation at The Dorchester in London, where he is considered a friend of the hotel.

A few years ago I was in Singapore for a promotion and I was watching television in my hotel. The meeting of the European leaders held in London was being broadcast with the Chinese supreme leader Jiang Zemin in attendance, which was a very big deal in Europe and London, where Tony Blair was holding the summit. All the leaders were lining up as Tony Blair welcomed them to a Chinese banquet and standing beside Tony Blair, shaking hands with all the heads of state, was no less than Ken Hom! This image was broadcast worldwide on CNN and other news channels over the next 12 hours. I was just stunned and totally amazed.

I asked Ken about this a few weeks later. He replied that he had made friends with the Blairs and they had asked him to prepare the food for the banquet in honour of the Chinese leader. Ken said he could tell that when the Chinese leader looked in his eyes he was wondering why he was shaking hands with the cook! Ken was dressed in a beautifully stylish green Chinese suit and I just can imagine all the ambassadors scratching their heads and thinking 'who the hell is this guy?' It was a great moment and it was pure Ken.

We continued to hold promotions, always trying to go against the grain or trend. My next promotion was with Annie Féolde from Enoteca Pinchiorri in Florence, a three-star Michelin chef, one of the rare ones in Italy. I developed a great friendship with Annie that will last forever. Her food was a breath of fresh air and a good chance to renew our preconception of Italian flood. Her menu and food was complex and vibrant and certainly veered away from the expected.

Ted Wright had an innate sense to pick chefs that did not fit the mould of the predictable. Yes we could have had Paul Bocuse, but for him a female French chef running a three-star Michelin restaurant in Florence was much more daring and would probably excite the public more then an established star. Annie proved to be everything and more that I could wish for. She was beautiful looking, in a near-regal way, she was approachable, talented and obviously very passionate. Her stylish disposition and precise knowledge of Italian cooking and produce was a refreshing approach to all of us who experienced her food.

In later years I had the chance to visit her restaurant several times and spend time with her around Tuscany. I remember the first time she received me on Via Ghibellina in the 17th century Palazzo which is now a restaurant owned by Annie and her partner, Giorgio. She showed a genuine happiness to see me and made me experience her restaurant in a very generous manner. In the mould of all three-star Michelin restaurants, the setting is without parallel, but with an Italian twist. The linen is from Frette, the cutlery from Broggi, the porcelain from Richard Ginori and the silver from the famous silversmiths Cassetti and Braganti. The restaurant is small but the capacity increases in summer with the use of the great courtyard of the Palazzo.

Annie's food is refined but very much Italian. The rusticity is gone, but the flavours are pure Tuscany. I saw amazing pasta being made in the kitchen, smelt superb white truffles from Alba and could only admire her dexterity using fresh wild mushrooms. The food I ate made such a refreshing change from French food, dishes like 'chicken giblets with egg and lemon' or 'cannelloni of Gorgonzola on red mullet with clams and red wine sauce'. Her desserts included 'chestnut roulade stuffed with cream and pistachio sauce' and her famous finishing touch of 'a tiny cone of gelato', which was served in an amazing silversmith rack that looked like more like a miniature candelabra. The food would leave anyone enthralled as long as you were capable of accepting that calibre of service and sophistication from an Italian restaurant with prices more reminiscent of her French counterpart.

Giorgio's cellar is something else to see. Very few are privileged to walk down the stairs to the basement of the palazzo to see this amazing and unique cellar. Giorgio's collection and wine list has won him most of the wine awards of the world, including the Grand Award from the *Wine Spectator Magazine* and the accolade of so many wine writers, with most of them considering his collection probably one of the best in the world. What left me stunned was not only that the cellar was stocked with amazing vintages of Krug, Latour, collections of Domaine de la Romanée-Conti, Tignanello, Barbaresco from A. Gaja, with incredible vintages of Château Pétrus and Château d'Yquem, but the opportunity to select a series of wine from his incredibly clever set-price wine menu. There were more then twelve wine menus that offered a variety of prices and different amazing selections from

Giorgio's cellar. One could select the 'special degustazione di quattro vini', starting with your choice of white such as a Montrachet 1986, then Domaine de la Romanée-Conti, followed by a Brunello di Montalcino 1990, then an Echezeaux 1986. To finish you could choose a Château Palmer 53 or different vintage of Château Ausone, Latour, Petrus or Lafite Rothschild. The selection on offer on each menu is so incredible that it would leave any guest, wine lover and wine writer totally stunned by the selection. It provided the opportunity to sample amazing wines, matched to a stunning menu from Annie. It was a place that I will never forget.

—

One of the most formidable chefs of that era was based in France and he was to be our next visitor. In the end it proved to be one of the most challenging and rewarding promotions but it was also a lesson on the true meaning of ego and greed. Alain Senderens was the uncontested leader of French chefs. His pronouncements on any topic—the state of French cuisine, its historical strength, the creative evolution of food, and the understanding of pairing of flavours with food or wine—was lapped up by both the French and the international press.

He was a very quotable person who stirred debate and tried to intellectualise his cooking and the reasons for blending produce. His historical research on recipes, going back to the Roman occupation of France, and his dissertation on ways of eating over various eras fascinated the French. Here was a man who analysed, dissected, reconstructed and reinvented dishes with an historical or analytical view. He was seen as a genius, a savant, who ended up in a kitchen instead of a laboratory. He was a speaker with the view of an ecologist and the manner of an aristocrat.

In situations such as this upcoming promotion, most of the preparation was done prior to his and his team's arrival. He dictated the number of team members that he brought with him and the recipes were established after a long consultation process, based on the produce I could supply. A suite was reserved for him, a Rolls Royce was despatched to the airport to fetch him, and the red carpet was actually rolled out for his landing at the hotel. This was a serious event for the hotel and for Sydney. Monsieur Senderens came to visit me in the kitchen immediately after arriving and I was struck by his small height. I had always assumed he was taller from the pictures I had seen, but what he lacked in physical stature he certainly made up with mental rigour.

We went over all of my produce and its link with his recipes. I was only one of two French-speaking people in the kitchen, the other one being Nichan, my Pastry Chef. The burden of setting up a menu and instructing the chefs, the printer, the public relations department, the waiters and the press fell on me. I was not only the Executive Chef of the hotel, with an operation to continue running (including large banquets and other restaurant productions) but I also became Alain's offsider, personal assistant, translator, muse, guide to Sydney and recipient of his anxiety.

The press were falling over each other to interview him and appointment after appointment was set up over the next few days to meet them. I organised my customary visit with him and his staff to the Sydney Fish Market before firming the menu. His amazement was contagious, new dishes came to the fore after gushing over the rouget, scampi, jewfish and other seafood on display. He was like a child in a toyshop, which was great to see. Markets often have that effect on chefs. The final dishes were prepared, the menus were printed and the service staff were briefed. Alain's staff positioned themselves strategically in the kitchen in their area of expertise and I then spent my next ten days with him, at first from 7am till midnight, and then once the menu was firmly established from lunchtime to midnight. I continued to come at

7am to make sure my normal work was proceeding and that I could get my hand on all the seafood I needed for the menus.

Alain brought with him a strong personality and a determination to do things his way. He was an eccentric at heart, everyday wearing a different coloured pair of glasses: bright blue, yellow, green or red. All these glasses had a matching watch of the same colour and I hate to think of the cost of his ensembles. Alain also constantly smoked the fattest cigar one could ever smoke, even in the kitchen. If his ponytail was at the time daring and controversial, his smoking was certainly much more questionable. All my staff were probably wondering what I would do about it but I realised that I would just have to accept it. In the end I decided to do nothing, and he smoked constantly, apart from when we went and visited nearly every table in the room at the end of each service.

The food he produced was eclectic and extremely clean on the plate, probably losing a bit of its impact without the backdrop of his restaurant, the famous Lucas Carton in Paris. I had visited his restaurant a couple of years earlier on my first ever trip to France. It was the first three-star Michelin restaurant I had been to and by then it was the most famous of the French restaurants in Paris.

I have never seen a sense of arrival like the one that I received at Lucas Carton. It was probably overdone but it certainly left guests with a lasting impression. The restaurant had a small door that led you into a cubicle, before you reached the main entrance. The front door had to close behind you (like in a secure jewellery store) before the main door could open. For what seemed like interminable seconds, maybe minutes, the door in front of you remained closed, then suddenly the door would slide sideways to reveal an amazing sight of over 30 waiters, Chef de Rangs, the sommeliers and the Maître d'Hôtel. It was a grandly-designed entrance, one that was offered to every guest and conducted with military precision to make an impact on your arrival. The room was stunning, the food was stunning and the service was obviously unequalled by anything I had ever experienced before. If this was what a three-star Michelin restaurant was offering then I was in for a treat for the rest of my trip.

At the end of the evening I requested the bill in French and on its receipt I deposited my new American Express card. I never believed in credit cards and as this was my first credit card I was quite proud to deposit it in the beautiful little silver tray in front of me. The Chef de Rang came over and he froze on seeing my card. He then composed himself and gently asked me if I had anything other than American Express. I was surprised by his request but on telling him that was the only card I had he told me that he would see what he could do. It was all a bit mysterious for me.

I was wondering what could be the problem when he finally came back to our table. Before he deposited the slip for me to sign he said, 'I am terribly, terribly sorry, but we seem to have damaged your card!' And then he quickly added, 'But not to worry, we succeeded in getting an imprint so all is fine!' He then put my card in front of me and I could barely recognise it; it was as if a train had run over it. My card was scratched, bent, squashed and unusable. I was just stunned and left alone to comprehend the implication of this totally unfortunate, but predicated incident; they were quite clearly indicating their disapproval of my American Express card. It certainly made an impact on me as I realised the implications of using this card in France. My next two days of my trip were ruined trying to source another card in a countryside obviously at war with an American institution.

—

My work with Monsieur Senderens continued and by the end of the week I was spending more time on my translating duties. The first interview was for *Australian Gourmet Traveller* magazine, where the journalist had been warned of Monsieur Senderens' formidable intellect and came prepared with intelligent questions. I knew that Alain spoke passable English, as he sometimes would correct me when I passed information about his restaurant to my chefs, but in interviews he would never venture a word of English.

The first question was always a chance for the parties to test each other. It was relatively easy for me to translate, but then the questions would become more insightful and the complexity of his answers would became more challenging. His French was impeccable and his verse was deep and complex. I struggled to find similar English words and turn of phrase and to retain the essence of his reply. The more complex the questions were the more esoteric and profound his answers became, sometimes stretching into many minutes. This was becoming a game that I could not win. He would often answer with diatribe longer than five minutes, based on the reading of historical books mixed with passionate belief and an educated French turn of phrase. The journalist knew, I knew and Alain knew that there was no way I could translate, let alone summarise, his deep thoughts of the last ten minutes. I did what I could do to translate his last points along with a few of the others that had stuck in my mind. It was beautiful French but it would have needed an international translator of complex diplomatic language to achieve anything close to his words. All the journalists were left in no doubt that they should learn French if they were to get more of his intellectual prose.

He had a beautiful turn of phrase, coming out with expressions such as: 'In food, like in music or art, you have two disciplines at play: technique and creativity. Technique is easy to learn—you just copy the recipes—but it is creativity that makes great chefs.' 'A good chef, like a good lover, must know when the timing is right; if he is too early or too late it is no good.' 'Food is like a painting, it must have harmony in everything as it is the only art that stimulates all five of your senses.'

Alain's egotistical and self-absorbed personality developed over the week, with many demands made, often without my knowledge.

Whatever Alain wanted the hotel was quite happy to supply to him with: free champagne, gifts to tables, accepting his guests in the restaurant at the hotel's cost and restocking his cigar collection. But there was even more happening that I was not aware of.

After service, when I'd left the kitchen for the night, Alain and his team (with a few of my chefs) would gather in the restaurant to taste wine. Alain would direct the Maître d'Hôtel to fetch him some of the best vintages, including Grange, Henschke, old vintages of Leeuwin Estate and a few old Bordeaux. Not knowing what to do with the embarrassing bills, the Maître d'Hôtel charged it to Alain's room, as he was the one ordering it.

The day before he was due to leave, Alain asked me to ensure that his payment for the promotion had been finalised, so in the afternoon I went to see Max Dickens, our Financial Controller, to go over his invoice. We were stunned by his request for US$42,000 (in cash) as a fee for his services; not bad for just one week of promotions! This fee was in addition to our provision of free accommodation, laundry, meals, telephone calls, first class flights and transportation and similar accommodation for his four staff. Max was stunned, but that was the agreed amount so it was to be. There was a question of tax and after getting advice from a big accounting firm it was resolved that it was Alain's responsibility to declare that amount. There was also a lot of concern about the safety of that amount in cash being carried by him through customs, but again it was resolved that it was his problem. Max had to visit several banks to gather that amount of cash in US currency and it was with anxiety that Alain visited Max's office, where the cash was quickly exchanged. Alain, with not so much as a thank you, disappeared out the door.

The last day of the promotion was on a Saturday, and after two weeks of working from 7am till midnight I resolved not to come into work until midday. Maybe sensing that his stay was at an end, greed for some reason had overtaken common sense. When I arrived at the hotel around lunchtime Ton, the resident manager at the hotel, (Ted was overseas) had left a message for me to call him. I went to see him in the office and what I heard just made my stomach churn.

Alain had gone to the front desk in the morning and asked for his bill with the current charges. It was customary that before a guest chef departs we scan their bill and remove any charges that we had agreed could be covered by the hotel. On seeing his bill Alain apparently threw an enormous fit, right in the foyer of the hotel. He was incensed that he had been charged for wine, mineral water and phone calls. Ton resolved to rebate all the charges to avoid a further scene but I was just left speechless when Ton showed me the thousands of dollars of wine that was charged to his room.

I could not comprehend why Alain did not wait for my arrival to sort this out, instead of causing such a scene with his host, especially after receiving his cash payment the previous day. It was as if now that he had his money he was not going to part with any of it, including the legitimate cost of his phones calls. It was a very disappointing display, especially since the hotel did everything to make his stay as fulfilling as possible and that I personally looked after him so well with no regard to cost or my personal time.

I confronted Alain when he came down for the last evening's service. I told him that doing what he did was in my eyes way beyond the bounds of behaviour expected of a man like him, especially after all the work my staff, myself and the management of the hotel had done for him. His reply was that never in his whole life had he ever paid for wine! I told him that his greedy attitude went against the spirit of friendship and accommodation and that the wine would have been rebated anyway if he would have paid me the courtesy of letting me know that he had consumed it. For me it was not about the cost but it was about his lack of respect for a host who at every step had done the right thing by him.

It was a shame that this promotion finished with such an unfortunate incident, but in all other cases the visiting chefs became close friends and to this day we remain in touch. The value of these visits proved to be a great bonus to everyone involved, including the public. It is impossible to totally reproduce the feel and atmosphere of another restaurant, as in most cases the service and décor are part of the package of why a restaurant is successful. The food on its own, out of context of the restaurant is not a truthful reflection of the experience of visiting a celebrated restaurant, but the food should be the major factor that attracts diners to a restaurant, and in most instances the dishes of the visiting chefs were wonderful. The sense of anticipation from my staff and my suppliers and the opportunity to work with different cooking methods and techniques made each occasion a time to remember.

19

THE BENEFIT OF LOYALTY

I HAD PASSED MY TEN YEARS AT THE REGENT A WHILE AGO and I was getting anxious to remain sharp and relevant. I had heard that a new hotel of exclusive standards was being built uptown and I was wondering what the future held for me. Should I stay a chef, become a grower, move to the Hunter Valley and open a restaurant, or become an executive and run food operations like Claude Boudoux did for The Regent? I just did not know what was right for me to remain relevant, sharp and focused. I felt that I shouldn't be afraid of change and I was ready to explore other possibilities.

I had met Michael Whiteman a couple of years ago when for some reason he was sent by Bob Burns to evaluate our food program at The Regent. Michael is from Queens in New York and he possesses an analytical mind that could frighten the best prosecutor in America. He is a man of a few words who reserves his intellectual musings for his report. His words were as sharp as an icepick, as deadly as a poisonous mushroom and as entertaining as Bill Bryson. The fact that my food and kitchen was the target of his verve only tempered my amazement at his insight. Michael used a few well-chosen sharp sentences to convey his reproach. 'You make your own ice-cream but it's got water crystals in it. Why? It is better to buy your ice-cream if that's your result.' 'We ordered two green salads: one was loaded with vinegar, the other with oil. Why not pair these two siblings? Unless the chefs like dysfunctional families.'

He firstly went incognito, ordering food from room service. 'You offer little boxes with 15 minutes increment for service time at breakfast, so why does it come 12 minutes late?' He then visited our café. 'You date the menu but there were only two changes over three days, so what is the point?' Even Kable's was cause for comment. 'Is this Australia or America? "Good evening, my name is Myro, and I will be your waiter tonight."'

We were all offended but at the end of the day the exercise was really about making you think. You could not argue with Michael's points. After my initial shock I worked with him on how we could do things better and be more truthful to our aims of quality and consistency. Michael was actually one of the partners in the most successful firm of restaurant designers in America. Not only had they designed some of the best restaurants in New York and America but they also designed, owned and ran Window of the World in the fateful Twin Tower building in New York.

Michael was associated with Joseph Baum, the famous restaurant designer from New York, who gave so much credibility to their firm. Their portfolio of work and constant demand from developers, architects, hotel owners and restaurateurs to review, re-design, construct and develop concepts for new and old space made then travel the world. One week Michael was in Singapore, designing the food court of new venture, the next he was in Los Angeles, putting the finishing touch to the whole food program and restaurant they designed for Guggenheim Museum. It was heady stuff that could not fail to impress me.

Years later, after developing a great friendship with Michael, he let it slip that whenever I was ready for a move they would be happy to have me for one of their projects. I was visiting New York when they were about to re-open one of the most famous New York restaurants, The Rainbow Room, in the newly renovated Rockefeller Center. They took me to visit the place and I was just amazed at the sheer size and scope of it. The central element of the Rainbow Room was a huge dining room with a revolving dance floor, where they intended to renew America's love for big bands and formal dances with great food, but there was also a multiplicity of private dining rooms and function rooms. The access to the kitchen for the waiters was through two long escalators traveling between floors to provide a more efficient delivery system then a dumb waiter lift. This was a big chance to make a new move in my career, to run a very prestigious operation. Did I have the ability? It was all very tempting and over the next few days I debated the benefits of moving from Sydney to New York.

In the end it was the quality of my life in Australia, my love for the water and the beaches, and my ability to make a difference to our food culture that made me stay put, as well as the fast pace and huge cost of life in New York. It would have been fun, challenging and would have satisfied my need to take on a new project but it was not to be and I am sure that I made the right decision.

The Park Lane Hotel, that new mega hotel that was to rival The Regent in size, quality and innovation, was opening soon and it started sending feelers into the market to see who would be interested and capable of running this huge operation. If I wanted to stay in a hotel this was going to be a good option and a natural progression. I was obviously torn by the possibility of leaving The Regent, but the pull to have the chance to renew myself and take on a new challenge was stronger.

I met with Michael Carr, the super confident hip executive of the hotel, who was an integral part of the design and opening team. Michael had a contagious enthusiasm for this new hotel and we struck a good rapport after a few meetings. I was starting to understand the proposed facilities and they wanted me to assemble the team to run the whole of the food operation. It was very tempting, especially considering the attractive package they were prepared to offer for me to jump ship. I obviously could see that it was going to be a coup for them to snatch me from The Regent and Ted's clutch.

What happened next was a turn of events that would culminate in one of my most difficult days of my life. The Park Lane Hotel were to appoint a General Manager any day and I decided to wait to meet him before we concluded our deal. In the meantime, Ted Wright approached me in my office and said, 'Serge, I know the Park Lane will approach you. Make sure you speak to me before you make a decision.' I could only agree to this.

I received a phone call from Michael, asking me to visit the new General Manager. When I walked into his office I was stunned to come face to face with Ton, the old resident manager of The Regent Sydney, who was also my squash partner of many years. He had left The Regent some years ago to work for another company. In all honesty I did not know if I was going to be comfortable working with Ton, as I did not feel that he shared the same kind of vision that Ted did. He effusively told me how great it would be to work together and how fantastic this new hotel would be. He put the contract in front of me for me to sign and right away I felt trapped. I had insisted with Michael that I could never make a final decision before I discussed this with Ted Wright; this was a courtesy that I owed him. Ton would not have a bar of this; he announced that he would keep the secretary as long and as late as necessary for us two to revise the contract, but the contract needed to be signed that night. I told him many times over the next few hours that was not the agreement, but Ton being extremely stubborn and a hard hitter was not going to let me go.

Through sheer exhaustion, wishful thinking and a need to finish the meeting I ended signing the contract, but as soon as I did this I regretted it. My regrets only grew when I left Ton's office, late in the night, to meet with Michael, and he told me that I could not have the extra equipment that I had requested. I had reviewed the kitchen plans and the list of equipment and could see there was a great need to refine and change some of this. I eliminated what I thought was superfluous (there was a lot of that) and I added some that I thought was absolutely essential. Well in the end they had accepted all my cuts but they would not provide me with any of my essential list. That, in my eyes, was a deal breaker. I left confused and still had to face Ted Wright the next day. My nightmare was getting worse.

The next morning I gathered the courage to face Ted and resign. It was not the way I envisioned things, but that's what I was facing. As I entered his office he said, 'Tell me one thing. Can we talk?' I said yes. He said, 'Serge, I have been loyal to you for ten years; will you be loyal to me?' What could I say? He matched the salary I was offered, essentially doubling my package to remove any doubt over my resignation, and it was left to me to undo my words of the previous evening. My day got worse, having to now face Ton, but that was the cost of my error.

I stayed with Ted for another five years until he left to open his own hotel chain. His departure was a great loss to the hotel and in a sense the end of an era, as the Four Seasons Hotel had purchased Regent International Hotels. To all of us it was like a hostile takeover, despite the assurance of the executives from Four Seasons Hotel.

Just before Four Seasons purchased The Regent, I was asked by the general manager of The Regent Singapore if I could do a promotion with my team at their signature restaurant 'Maxims'. Maxims was from the same stable of restaurants as the famous Maxims of Paris. The décor was a carbon copy of the Paris site, but strangely it was in Singapore. Singaporeans love brands and labels, and the name 'Maxims' was the ultimate food name. The agreement was that I was to fly in with three of my chefs and all of my Australian produce to do a one-week food promotion. The logistics of doing this was quite daunting, having to not only export all of my fresh produce (including meat, seafood, dairy and fruit and vegetables) but I also had to ensure it would be allowed to be imported into Singapore.

It took me weeks of negotiations to get marron, yabbies, lobster, jewfish, blue eye cod, snapper, lamb, mushrooms, double cream and so many other food products out of Australia and into Singapore, but in the end it was all ready, along with the recipes, costings and service procedures.

Three weeks before I was to depart for Singapore, Stephen Lewis (our new GM who had replaced Ted Wright) sent me a note from Four Seasons head office requesting my participation in a promotion to open the new Bloomingdales store in California. Stephen's note said, 'Serge, I guess you are going.' I sent back the note saying, 'Stephen, sorry, I'm doing a promo in Singapore, but maybe next time.'

Stephen was actually the first employee of The Regent of Sydney. He had worked, like most of us, for years under Ted Wright, leaving to head our new hotel in Okinawa and then to open the new Regent Auckland. It was the realisation of his dream to be appointed General Manager by the executives of Four Seasons and so I imagine Stephen did not want to displease our new owner at head office. He sent me back a note saying, 'Sorry, Serge, this must happen!'

Well, what a predicament I was in. The timing was atrocious and I could not cancel Singapore as the publicity was already underway. I was to be in LA on the Monday and my Singapore promotion was starting that Thursday. The fact that it took nearly one day of travel and you lose one day across the dateline meant that I would arrive in Singapore just a few hours before the start of the promotion. I guess there was no choice.

Bloomingdales were taking over three JC Penny stores: one in Palo Alto, near San Francisco, and two other ones in Los Angeles. They wanted to have a few international chefs doing cooking demonstrations to celebrate the opening of their new stores. I sent my recipes and product list to the person in charge in San Francisco and I expected no problems.

Air New Zealand was the sponsoring airline and when I received my tickets I realised the extent of my misfortune. Despite the fact that there were plenty of direct flights out of Sydney, I was to fly first to Auckland, then to Nadi (in Fiji), then Rarotonga and finally to Hawaii and LA. It was the longest Pacific crossing by air I could imagine and it took forever. I arrived in LA exhausted, but despite the fact that my accommodation was not available in San Francisco I decided to make my way there in advance to check that everything was okay. I flew to San Francisco airport, rented a car and drove to the super picturesque and very gentrified Palo Alto, home of the University of Stanford.

I drove the pretty streets looking for the new Bloomingdales where I was to do the promotion. I eventually found it on the periphery of town, walked in to the food department and asked for my contact. I was told that she just left for a vacation. I blurted out, 'But you only just opened the store this week?' 'Yes,' she replied, 'but she worked really hard to set this up so she took some time off.' I tried to compose myself and asked, 'Where is the kitchen?' It turned out that they no longer had a kitchen, they now leased it out. When I asked about my food produce, I was told that the chef normally brings it! I explained that I had come from Australia, but she replied, 'Sorry, I do not know what I can do for you!'

Two options were running through my mind: too get back on the plane or to put my head down and get this promotion done. Well I was not good at being a prima donna so I chose the later option. I then found out that because I was going to demonstrate my dishes on a Saturday, I was to prepare 400 tiny portions, not the 80 that I was originally told. Here I was with no kitchen, no help, and no produce, in a strange city with an impossible goal. The next few days were going to test me, but first things first; I needed to find a kitchen.

I drove in search of an idea, when across a huge parking lot I saw a motel. I parked the car, walked to reception and asked for the chef. I introduced myself, told him of my predicament, and pleaded for him to let me use his kitchen overnight. He agreed and I told him that I would be no bother. My only big request was that he help me source some seafood. We sat down in his office and after making many phone calls we could only find fresh scallops and yellow fin tuna in San Jose, over an hour's drive away.

I jumped in the car and I made it just on closing time. They weighted up the produce for me and said 'cash or cheque'. I did not have US$536 on me; neither did I have a chequebook that I could use in America. They refused to give me the seafood until they got their payment. Here I was, roaming the street again in my rental car, this time trying to find a bank but they were all closed. I made my way to a motel, asked for the general manager and after explaining my sad story he gave me the cash on my credit card. I finally picked up my seafood, stopped at what seemed like a groovy fruit and veg store in Palo Alto and then made my way back to my motel and my borrowed kitchen.

American kitchens are quite different to Australian ones. For a start, the cultural mix in the kitchen is a surprise. Many of the chefs did not speak English, being Mexican and from South America. The ones that did speak English I had a hard time understanding and the sheer size of most of the kitchen staff was quite unnerving and a departure from what I was used to in Sydney. They did not seem to have a kitchen hierarchy; it was more like a bunch of friends with their extended family working together. There were a lot of open boxes of pre-

prepared food: portioned steak, crumbed turkey cutlets, pre-roasted beef, ready to fry potatoes, powdered soup and sauce poured from wine-like casks. Still, everyone seemed very happy working together and evidently the customers were happy with the food on offer.

I was probably seen as an oddity, making scallop ravioli (using Chinese gow gee dough that they probably had never seem before), sashimi of tuna, and passionfruit timbale (using fresh pulp from a fruit they did not use much). I worked through the night, preparing my demonstration dishes and the 400 little portions needed to provide a tasting morsel. My work was finally ready and packed in empty boxes that I gathered from around the kitchen. I slept for a couple of hours, and then had a quick shower after the front desk manager (who worked the night shift and acted as receptionist, security guard, fire safety warden, auditor and porter) decided to take pity on me and offer me a room.

I made it across the street by 10am for my scheduled 11am show. Bloomingdales was a big arrival out West and they expected thousands of people to view their offering of this East Coast name. The food department was quite typical of any large retailer and the idea was that I was to do my class at 11am, watched by a couple of hundred people roving around the store. The public announcement over the intercom further increased the size of the crowd over the next hour and after completing my demonstration I tasked myself to feed the crowd.

The whole idea of doing this promotion was to lift the profile of all the participants. There was no question that Bloomingdales was profiting from this, but I am not too sure what we got out of this one. When people asked me from what restaurant I came from and I replied that I was from The Regent in Sydney, Australia, a puzzled look remained on their faces. Australia, pre-Olympics, was mostly a big blur for Americans. There was always that confusion between Australia and Austria and generally not much incentive for the public at large to know about a country so far away. Still, I guess they enjoyed the food and a quick chat. Free food samples seemed to be a bigger thing than picking up printed recipes or seeing the demonstration. I finished serving all my portions and then needed to make a place for the next chef a couple of hours later, which was none other than Jeremiah Tower. I left a message for him, having to go back to my motel and re-do all of my food preparations for the next day's class. I was exhausted.

I had organised to stay at Ken Hom's place in Berkeley that night and he had planned for us to to have a dinner with a few friends. I finished my work around 6pm and made my way to San Francisco to go to Berkeley, across the Bay. Well rain started to pour in a torrential way, slowing the traffic to a crawl. For four hours I inched my way along the highway and what seemed to be the longest bridge in the world. I could not believe that a modern metropolis in America could suffer such poor road planning. I arrived at Ken's at 10pm with dinner in full swing, but at least he comforted me with one of the best bottles of Pomerol from his cellar, which I slowly sipped, thinking of anything but the days ahead.

I did my repeat performance the next day and then flew into LA and the welcoming arms of The Regent Beverley Wilshire, our great LA hotel which served as a famous backdrop for the Pretty Woman movie. At least here I had better backup for my two gigs at the Bloomingdales stores in the city of the stars.

On my last night in LA I went for dinner with a former Sous Chef of mine, Jean Marc Pollet. He was now working for the Peppers Group in Port Macquarie. It was great to have him around and we decided to dine at L'Orangerie, a famous restaurant in the French mould. The place was very glitzy with a bevy of waiters and a menu that was conservative in the Modern French way, but also carrying stratospheric prices.

At the next table there were six people; the men were sporting ponytails and the women were incredibly beautiful. I recognised one of them as being a model who had caught my eye a long time ago. I

A HEAVILY PREGNANT YVETTE AND HER
FRIEND RACHEL INSPECTING THE WORKS

A SIGN FROM THE ORIGINAL BATHERS'

MY NEW PASTRY KITCHEN

THE LOVELY NEW KITCHEN UTENSILS, A CHEF'S DREAM

NEARLY THERE: THE REALISATION OF A DREAM

YVETTE, CÉLESTE AND MYSELF ON THE OPENING DAY OF THE NEW BATHERS'

SIGNING THE CONTRACT WITH VICTORIA

RON AND XAVIER: MY TWO CHEF DE CUISINE

SALLY HARPER, MY SOMMELIER

ANDREAS, MY GREAT RESTAURANT MANAGER AND RIGHT-HAND MAN

RELAXING AT HOME

BALANCING WORK AND FAMILY LIFE

YVETTE, SASHA AND CÉLESTE

THREE GENERATIONS OF FOOD LOVERS

MY FAMILY IN THE POOL

love shopping when I am travelling in Europe with Yvette, especially buying Italian shoes and I am always the first one in a shoe shop to encourage Yvette to purchase. I am also a great lingerie buyer for Christmas and birthdays. Because I am such a regular buyer of lingerie from a certain store in Sydney they send me catalogues every year. One of the voluptuous women modelling an Italian brand was the one I recognised at the next table.

But what really stood out to me was my initial underestimation of them, because by the end of our meal we had heard them converse fluently in at least five different languages. Their original conversation had started in German and all of them participated in it. At some point of time we noticed that their conversation changed to French then to Spanish and eventually to Italian, and they spoke to the waiters in English. We were amazed that the whole table could speak so many languages. It was a good example of how rewarding a European education combined with a will to travel and learn different languages at a young age can be.

—

The next day I was to fly to Singapore to start my promotion at The Regent Singapore. That plane trip was the first chance I had to take a break and try to catch up on a couple of hour's sleep. I have never been able to sleep on planes but through sheer exhaustion I did on that flight.

When I arrived in Singapore my team was already in the kitchen, having arrived a couple of days ago. Terence, my great Kable's Sous Chef, was there, instructing the restaurant chef on the recipes, and the fresh food was starting to arrive. At least everything here was in perfect condition: barramundi from the Northern Territory, Wallis Lake oysters, venison, duck, asparagus and mangos. It was very different to my experience in California and my trial by neglect.

The next day I briefed the very professional service staff and with Anders Josepson, the famous wine merchant from Australia, we prepared the wine and food, matching menus to the various bookings already planned. I was able to match my Balmain bugs with great Leeuwin Estate Chardonnay, hare with superb Mosswood Cabernet and beef with intense Henschke Shiraz. Everything was running smoothly until the Maître d'Hôtel came into the kitchen on our second day of service to tell me that two gentlemen were at the bar asking to speak to me.

I meet them, not sure at first of what they were trying to ask me. They explained that they were with the entourage of the Mexican President (who was on his way to an APEC meeting of the heads of state of the Pacific Region) and that they needed food. They explained that the former Executive Chef of the Raffles Hotel had recommended me to them. They had two planes, one for the Mexican President and his ministers and one for the accompanying journalists (in total nearly 200 people). Apparently they never ate airport prepared food and they wanted to order food from my menu, and for us to pack it for the aircraft stewards to be reheated on the aircraft.

They told me they wanted 50 servings of all the dishes on my menu. I was quite uncertain about the whole affair, so as a way of getting out of it I asked how they were going to pay for it. They said they would pay in cash in US dollars, full price off the menu and that they would give me half in advance and the other half on delivery. The deal was not very good for me as I would need to work all through the night again with no sleep to prepare their requests, but the revenue for the hotel was unbelievable. This was US$24,000 in cash and it produced the biggest food and beverage revenue in a day that the hotel had ever had. We worked all night to ready the little aluminium containers they brought with them and the next morning they came with a van to pick up their food, paid the balance and disappeared. The down side of the deal was that I was left with hardly any food for the rest of the week and

I spent the next day trying to source replacement products to carry on my promotion.

It always seems exciting to do a bit of work outside your normal work environment but it is never easy to work with a different kitchen crew, different equipment and with products that are often not the same as or of the same standard as those found in Australia. Still it is great to be a culinary ambassador for Australia and our restaurant and it does give me the chance to take a breather from the routine.

I came back to Sydney totally exhausted from the promotions. There was my kitchen brigade, waiting for me to inspire them, and thinking that I had a good rest overseas! Such is life.

20

END OF AN ERA

I WAS BACK IN SYDNEY FROM MY OVERSEAS PROMOTIONS AND after a couple of days of rest I got back to work. It was now one year since Ted had left and the long-term management staff, the true Regent people, could see the changes ahead. At that point no-one knew whether the changes were to be positive or negative.

Bob Burns' dream to build and operate 25 of the best hotels in the world had come so close to realisation. He built more than two dozen hotels, but in an industry where your competition was always trying to steal your management contracts it was hard to expand while maintaining some of the best standards in the world. Bob was about to open three significant hotels, having spent years developing these key sites. The Regent Milan, situated in a centuries old convent in the heart of the fashion district, was unique. The Regent Bali was a classic Bob Burns project, with each of its rooms possessing a superb plunge pool, a bathing pavilion, a day pavilion and another pavilion for each bedroom. It was built like a Balinese village, and eventually it received a hotel rating that toppled most of the other resorts in the world.

The newly planned and designed Regent New York was, in retrospect, a financial folly. It was supposed to put The Regent hotel group on a serious footing in the North American market. The price tag of one billion US dollars made it both a hotel to be noticed, but also a burden for the future owners. The money was not spent on glitz, but on a great architect who produced classical lines, elegance and an imposing foyer with a clean design. This was the most significant of The Regent hotels, and the one that made The Regent company very attractive for a takeover.

Before The Regent New York could open, the biggest investor in the company suffered from the burst real estate bubble in Japan; The Regent Hotel group was now on the market. Many investors vied for the company, but in the end an extremely experienced hotel company purchased it. It was sad in a sense not to see the grand vision of Bob Burns fully realised, but he had still achieved a lot. From nothing he created one of the greatest hotel companies in the world, one that set new standards of hotel luxury and one that will be remembered for a long time.

Those of us who were privileged to work for the company, especially during its Golden Years of the 80s, will know they have experienced something unique that probably will never be repeated. The sheer idealism and commitment to great hotel service and offering our guests the best we could produce was unwavering and stimulating in the extreme. We were all blessed as employees and I am sure most of The Regent guests also felt they were blessed.

The Four Seasons hotels were making a great mark in America. They were in a race with Ritz Carlton hotels to be seen as the prominent quality hotel chain in America, and eventually also in Asia. When The Regent International came on the market, the people at Four Seasons realised that by buying this mostly Asian-based company they could expand very quickly in Asia without starting from a zero base. There was also the bonus of acquiring the management and naming rights of some key hotels, especially the New York property that was nearing completion.

Four Seasons did not possess a Four Seasons named property in New York and the thought of acquiring the billion dollar designed hotel with some of the largest rooms in that city made purchasing The Regent incredibly attractive. The fact that they now controlled more than a dozen new properties in key markets around the Pacific and Asia made Four Seasons a major force around the world.

The inevitable problem of a competitor purchasing an independent brand is that it unsettles the whole management structure of the company that is being taken over. It took a huge amount of reassurance from Four Seasons to settle everyone's nerves at The Regent. The two companies would be operated independently, with The Regent retaining a President based in Hong Kong, one who would be appointed by Four Seasons. Wolf Hengst was the ideal person to be appointed as the first President: he was intelligent, worldly, calm and a perfect gentleman. The fact that they would only draw resources out of Four Seasons as they needed them made for what seemed encouraging words.

The main problem over the next few years was the incredible culture shock Four Seasons had in seeing how The Regent operated. The Four Seasons Group operated in a mostly unified market in North America, possessing similar accounting systems, labour laws and clientele in each hotel. At The Regent each hotel was operating in different countries, with different cultures, customs and needs, different taxation regimes, labour markets and very different clientele. Australians could be so different to the Chinese of Singapore, Malaysians of Kuala Lumpur, Fijians of Nadi and Thais of Bangkok.

The need to create new rules for each hotel made each Regent hotel operate very independently to each other, with little supervision from Head Office. That freedom obviously had worked very well because most of the General Managers stayed a long time in each property.

Four Seasons, on the other hand, were not keen for their General Managers to stay for a long time in their individual hotels. The fact that Ted Wright had been General Manager for nearly 15 years and I was still the Executive Chef was a telling statistic of the staff satisfaction and loyalty within The Regent group.

I think Four Seasons were also amazed by the number of employees working for each property and in each individual department of each hotel: The Regent Hong Kong had over 160 kitchen employees. Doormen who constantly opened doors by hand for every guest who walked through the front door was seen as excessive by some, but at The Regent it was just a part of the company standards.

Over the next few years everyone tried to compromise and make the relationship work, but it was always going to be a difficult. Four Seasons brought many benefits to the group; their financial expertise and stability, continuous management and standard systems were certainly more developed than what was found in The Regent. The discipline of their General Managers to conform to the company line made for a much more predictable company that was easier to invest in than The Regent. If it was more predictable it was also less fun, but times were changing and the days of free spending and a constant search to do better were over.

I got along with the management staff of Four Seasons because my food operations were running very successfully, even though I pretty much ran them my own way. But because we made good money and our restaurants were doing well Wolf Hengst told all the other Vice Presidents to let me be and let me continue to operate as I had in the past. I was certainly grateful for his support.

Despite this, we all had to justify to a certain extent the way that we did things and why we needed to continue to operate that way. We all made great efforts to accommodate the financial demands of our new bosses but I always drew the line when I knew that a decision could diminish the quality of my work. I always refused to cut my kitchen staff and it was a source of total frustration that I would not do it. The same applied to the style of food we were supposed to serve. To be told that on every menu I was to offer dishes that did not contain salt, butter, oil, sugar and cream was to me just a quick fix for the occasional customer. People are intelligent enough to ask for what they wished to have; I did not need a corporate stance on every menu. I was threatened and told in no uncertain terms to provide this on all my menus but I never complied.

I knew that they would eventually catch up to me, despite my friendships with the new President of The Regent. It was time for me to gracefully exit the scene. It was not that the Four Seasons was wrong in its approach, quite the opposite. They knew better than me what the future held and a much tighter operation was definitely what was needed to make the hotel a viable operation. It was just that I had always run a restaurant within a hotel and I was not prepared to run a hotel restaurant.

I was being pestered by the Human Resources Department to take my long service leave. I had been working in the hotel for over 15 years and it was customary to use your extra two months holiday after reaching your 10 years of service. I decided to take this leave and use the time away from work to assess what the future held for me. It was time for me to make a change.

21

FOOD & FRIENDS

I T WAS A GREAT TIME FOR ME TO TAKE MY LONG SERVICE leave and Yvette asked me what did I want to do with it? My first instinct was to have a rest, but three months off work was a long time. After I gave it some thought I decided that it would be good to refresh myself by visiting all the friends, chefs, wine makers and other contacts I had in France and Italy.

While I was starting to plan this luxury trip I was approached again to do a cookbook. I had refused a couple of times previously because I really wanted to produce a book that was more than a few trendy pictures and some quick recipes, which was the trend of that time. The publishers had heard that I was going to travel in Europe and they asked me if I would write a book on my travels. That idea sounded better to me and suddenly my travels took on a new dimension; now my trip needed to be planned and appointments were made, as they liked that formality in Europe. Over the next few months my schedule became fuller, with day after day of meetings, lunches, dinner tastings, and visiting farms, markets and other small producers.

I was getting excited by the prospect of my trip, and while I made sure I was able to see many of the people I knew, I also planned to visit regions that I had never previously been to and factories and producers that I had an interest in. It was developing into an amazing journey and because friends in Europe had also organised for me to meet other wine makers and food personalities, my schedule was getting too full for any relaxing time. Apart from Paris, at the start of our trip, we were to be on the move every day or second day for two months, packing and unpacking our way through these two beautiful countries.

I was asked to take some snapshots during our travels, but to me snapshots sounded very unprofessional. There was no possibility of taking a photographer with us, and the idea of purchasing photos from a library did not fit in with my vision of the book or do justice to our travels. In the end I resolved to take the pictures myself. I purchased a decent camera and because I had absolutely no idea how to use it I decided to enrol myself into a basic camera craft course.

I had worked with many photographers over my years, but apart from maybe seeing an appropriate angle for a picture I had no idea on what to capture or what depth of field meant and what to do about light, choice of film or any of the technical aspects of taking photos. A four-evening course in basic camera craft will not make you a star photographer, but it was enough for me to learn what I needed to know. I was also advised by one of Sydney's leading photographers, George Seper (who I had regularly worked with on many features) on the type of film to use. He said to use 100 Fuji for colour and Kodak 400T MAX for black-and-white. He advised me to keep things simple, not to use the flash, and to veer towards black-and-white when in doubt. His advice was to pay off.

When I came back from the trip I gave the developer 200 rolls of film, which were delivered to George to review. I had no idea if any of them would turn out. When I went to see George he just said, 'Serge, you got some great stuff in there'. I said, 'Sure', thinking he was trying to make me feel better, but he repeated, 'Seriously, you got some great stuff'. At least I could pass them on to my book designer without feeling too ashamed. In the end the designer decided to only use my photos for the entire book, expect for a couple of dozen from Geoff Lung, which were mostly the food shots we did in his studio.

—

The travel arrangements were organised, hotel rooms and accommodation were booked, reservations for lunch and dinner were done and most importantly appointments with the people in France and Italy were scheduled. We were finally ready to commence our travels through these two magnificent food and wine countries.

In France Ken Hom had lent me his apartment at the foot of Montmarte in a quite cul-de-sac near one of the best street markets of Paris. For a few days we cooked for ourselves, shopping daily in the boulangerie, poissonnerie, boucherie and traiteur of this great street full of diverse food shops. We visited friends, chefs and people like Jacques Vernier (a great cheese affineur) and the late Lionel Poilâne, to me one of the most remarkable food friends of France. His bread and bakery are unique and an inspiration to any food lover. I met Monsieur Ducasse and spend time with him in his Parisian restaurant and visited the incredible central Rungis market that can not fail to impress.

We scoured the vineyards of Champagne, stayed with the owner of Louis Roederer, Monsieur Rouzaud, at his private house and tasted several vintages of Krug with Rémi Krug. I spent time in Alsace learning how to make fois gras and I toured the vineyards of Chablis and Burgundy. I stayed and ate at the great Michelin-rated restaurant of Jacques Lameloise and Georges Blanc and collapsed in the bed of the superb small hotel. I had barrel tasting at Pétrus, hunted truffle with the Pébeyre family in Périgord and was honored by being hosted at a Chef's Table in Monsieur Ducasse kitchen at the Louis XV in the Hotel De Paris in Monaco.

In Italy I was amazed by the view from my room at the Splendido in Portofino, the Villa D'este in Lake Como and the Cipriani in Venice. I learned how parmagiano reggiano is made in Emilia-Romagna, how risotto is harvested in Verona and how traditional balsamic vinegar is aged in Modena. I spent time touring Tuscany with Annie Féolde, I stayed in one of the Antinori's 14th century castles in Umbria, and I learned the intricacies of olive oil pressing in Terni. I saw the field of durum wheat in Le Marche, their harvest and the milling of the wheat into fine pasta flour, and I observed the making of artisan pasta.

I finished the trip in Rome, worn out and full of knowledge. It was an exhausting trip that turned out to be more work than pleasure, but it made for a fulfilling and inspiring experience. I was ready to come home and compile the stories of our trip and turn it into a book.

—

When we were in Cognac, there was a message in my room from Victoria Alexander, the owner of The Bathers' Pavilion in Sydney's Balmoral Beach. I knew Victoria professionally, but not on a personal level. I happened to live in Balmoral Beach with Yvette when we first moved in together. I remember the long, ten-year saga of the renovations of The Bathers' Pavilion, which was just a short stroll from our new apartment, and the constant public debate and opposition to the renovations.

I had even sent a letter to Mosman Municipal Council in support of the renovations and of Victoria's plan to operate as a restaurant. Because the opposition were making quite outlandish claims about the dangers of operating a restaurant I felt I had to step in and voice my opinion in support. In any case, according to Victoria, the letter came at a crucial time for her when she was quite discouraged with the council, and my letter gave her new impetus to carry on.

Victoria had apparently thought of approaching me as a partner in her new business, knowing my reputation. She chose to call one of our mutual friends, Maggie Beer, to see what it could be like to work with me. I think Maggie's opinion made a difference to Victoria, so she took the step of calling me in France to offer me the partnership. There was a strong possibility, I told her, but it would be better to wait until I finished my travels to talk about it. I did not realise that this would cause her to agonise over what to do next. In any case, she waited for my return (nearly a-month-and-a-half later) to continue our conversation. I felt that if I was the right person for Victoria then she could wait for a more thought-out discussion face-to-face.

On my return, we met at my apartment at Balmoral and she explained the situation with the council and the details of the final decision to allow the development. She felt everything was reaching a conclusion, but having been thrown so many times previously she was clearly wary of the future. She proposed a partnership and I said the only partnership I would be interested in would be an equal one of 50/50, with me running the operation. She said it was exactly what she had in mind. Well that pretty much summed up our agreement; now the waiting game was on to see the result of the last appeal.

In the meantime, I was quite happy to focus on writing my upcoming book, get my kitchen back on a new footing with the inspiration I had gathered from Europe, and make a life with Yvette in Balmoral. The book proved to be an exhausting process. Firstly, I had never used a computer up to that point. At The Regent I had an assistant in my office who helped me do all the administrative work. Because I did not wish to mix my work on the book with my work at Four Seasons, I had to rely on Yvette to edit, correct and polish my English. My rambling quasi English often left her perplexed, but over eight months we worked through it.

The final manuscript was 120,000 words of material that was edited and debated to the last single word by Yvette and me. It left very little work for the editor, apart from cutting all my historical chapters on the specific regions of France and Italy that I had visited. They were judged superfluous to the book (I was not supposed to be an historian, even though that part appealed enormously to me) as it was supposed to focus on the food story.

Food & Friends was a striking departure of what was available in Australia. It won the Julia Child Best Cookbook design in America against over 450 other submitted books from around the world.

Things were getting difficult at work. I was losing my patience with the constant search to cut costs to our operation and I refused to conform to the directives from departments like human resources and finance. I was going to do things the way I was taught and the way I felt the food program should go. I was not going to cut back my kitchen staff or introduce meatloaf to satisfy the perceived needs of the American clientele for homely food.

Pride, along with the need to protect my team, their expertise and the quality we extended to our customers, was more important to me than risking my job. My long-term staff, many of who had worked together for nearly two decades, was my principal preoccupation. They all looked up to me, and even though in today's corporate world resistance is futile, for me it was worth fighting as they all had been loyal to me for so long.

Unfortunately the hotel was aging and the process of renovation that had started nearly ten years before, with an $80 million renovation, never succeeded in completing all the hotel floors. Since Four Seasons had taken over and found a new American investor for the property plans had been in place to finally restart and complete the much-needed renovation. This time they planned to close the entire hotel to effect this because the last time the renovation had stretched for over six years and affected many of the guests. The plan was to close the hotel for six months, renovate and reopen. A certain bonus for all the staff was that they were to remain on full pay, but that is the pitfall of owning a hotel.

My timing was either perfect or very bad (depending on how you want to view it) but Victoria called me announcing that the court case was over, she had won the last appeal and that Bathers' as a restaurant was to go ahead. There were a few months planning before The Regent was to close and Bathers' was to open. I knew that I was going to leave the hotel, but I needed to remain there a little bit longer. My plan was to finish in February and after 18 years at The Regent I felt I needed to give three months notice to ensure my succession was handled properly. In hindsight four weeks would have sufficed and it would have been better for the new Bathers' project.

—

Over the next six months I worked as hard as I could for The Regent and despite the inevitable rumours and the newspaper reports that I was contemplating leaving Stephen never asked me directly. Like me, he was playing a game of cat and mouse; presumably it was better that I left on good terms before The Regent closed its doors for renovation than getting into a legal skirmish about dismissing me for contemplating leaving. We both played the game perfectly to preserve our dignity and positions and a few months before closure I announced my resignation from The Regent. It made big news but everyone at the hotel, from the president to Stephen, made all the right noises and my departure was a dignified affair.

Ron, my Executive Sous Chef, José, my fish monger, Ray, my butcher, Nichan, my Pastry Chef, Yep, in the cold kitchen, Udo, my uncompromising Sous Chef, and so many other long-term employees were to be left behind. For them the attraction of having six months off during the renovation on full pay was quite attractive, and in any case they did not wish to risk their long service leave.

I always felt that Ron, my assistant for the last ten years, would have been a terrific replacement for my position. Not only was he one of the first kitchen employees of The Regent, but he was also one of the best chefs I had ever worked with. His cooking skills were extraordinary, as was his experience and knowledge, however he had a limited knowledge of the administrative side of running a large kitchen and certain lack of confidence at times. These were two weaknesses I possessed when I was first put in a position to run the kitchen and I believe Ron could have overcome them as well.

Whatever the reason, the Four Seasons did not wish to appoint an Executive Chef on my departure. In view of the impending closure of the hotel for renovations it was somehow understandable. From Ron's point of view, however, it was a very frustrating experience. I guess they had a plan and it was not going to be revealed at the time of my departure.

The day I left The Regent I felt liberated. The politics of the hotel were getting oppressive and I had lost my enthusiasm to fight futile battles. I was tired of constantly having to justify the need to preserve my standards with the bean counters or other people in the company with their own agendas. It was the end of an era and of one of the most professionally rewarding experiences of my life. As I said before, I had the Golden Years of The Regent.

22

THE BATHERS' PAVILION

Y OU SOMETIMES ONLY HAVE ONE CHANCE IN YOUR LIFE TO
design something on your own and I was not going to miss my
chance. Yvette and I finally moved in together into one of the most
picturesque settings in Sydney. Our apartment in Balmoral Beach
was tiny, but I had the chance to design everything on my own, from
the kitchen to the bathroom, from my beautiful home office to the
full veneer built-in wardrobe. I spent a lot of time thinking about
each little detail, from having lights in the wardrobe that started
automatically when the door opened, to the light switches and
patterns in the parquetry floor. We put in an integrated sound system
and an extremely functional kitchen, with recycled timber benchtops,
superb stainless steel walls and benches and a large kitchen mirror that
brought the great view of the beach into the kitchen. That is the type
of indulgence you can have when you have no children!

I have always felt attracted to design, architecture and the process
of building, so I put all of my free time into focusing on my small
apartment. I was extremely lucky because I had a very compliant

developer who loved food and was quite happy for me to build my own kitchen. That I was involved in designing the floor finish, the colour scheme, the tiles on the terrace, the internal doors, and light fittings never seemed to concern him. To the contrary, as he saw my apartment being built he adapted some of my ideas along the way. I was so involved that eventually the site foreman gave me the key to the building. In normal circumstances a buyer would never be allowed to roam the site at will.

On some of the nights, when I was inspecting the sub-contractor's work at the end of the day, I would hear my name being called from outside the building. It was the developer, John, imploring me to unlock the door for him. He would say, 'Serge, even I don't have a key to my building, you amaze me.' Still, I think he liked the way I operated and the shape and quality of what I was producing. All of this designing and working with builders was going to come in handy when I went to build the new Bathers' Pavilion.

One of the most pleasant aspects of living at Balmoral Beach was the chance I got to take nightly walks with Yvette. The promenade is such an easy and absorbing walk to hundreds of people who have a regular walking pattern. The same applies to swimming at the beach; you have the 6.30am crowd, the 7am ones and the ones who swim at 7.30am. They swim before work or when the sun rises, they swim together or on their own, but they are like clockwork. When walking you always cross the same people or the same dogs with their walking partners, as dog walking is an integral part of Balmoral Beach.

The Esplanade was completed with great controversy in 1930, at about the same time the pavilion opened. It is said that the Esplanade was built to provide employment in the lean years between the two great wars. Once the pavilion opened, literally thousands of people would flock to the beach, coming by tram from the city. The pavilion was essential in providing shelter and changing rooms, with rental lockers for the swimmers of the day. In those days swimming would have been a much more complicated affair, with sizeable bathing costumes required for the women; it was the hey day of the pavilion. However, it did not take many decades for the change rooms to fall into a state of disrepair and soon they became obsolete due to the changing customs.

From the first time I saw the pavilion I fell in love with it. Here was this majestic, complex, imposing structure with an architecture that was obviously of a different era. It possessed a strange mystique; the building was only partially occupied because parts of it were either condemned or in such a state of disrepair that they could not be used. Its windows revealed an eclectic restaurant with a blend of rustic pieces, great paintings, rugs, aged wood and fireplaces. Bathers' instantly appealed to romantics and the people in search of a unique experience: it had character, appeal, history and a view to die for. It was a beautiful restaurant with more personality than most other Sydney restaurants put together. Every night when Yvette and I did our walk we sensed the warmth of the place and I have to admit the thought of running that restaurant crossed our minds a few times, such was its incredible appeal.

So it was with a sense of irony that I got Victoria's phone call years later asking me to join her in designing and reopening the new Bathers'. Victoria's dream was to create a small exclusive hotel, with maybe a dozen rooms and a small restaurant, in the mould of La Colombe D'Or in St Paul de Vence on the Côte d'Azure. Alas, that dream was fraught by many legal challenges and an inability by so many people to accept or understand her vision, so after ten years of legal process she had to alter her grand plan. Now the entire building was to be used as a restaurant or in fact many restaurants, something that was beyond Victoria's capacity to operate on her own.

We had reached a mutual agreement by July 1998 but the accountants struggled to make sense of our vision. As the holder of the new lease why would Victoria part with half of the business? Well, there are serious consequences and money risks of owing a restaurant and not being the chef. For a chef to do proper justice to a restaurant he needs to commit himself to a point where he needs to feel a sense of ownership with his kitchen. To achieve this he needs to be constantly there to handle the produce, his chefs and the menu. The hours he needs to keep to make a difference are unsociable, brutal and in a sense illogical. You have two options; either pay your chef a huge amount of money to be the best chef you are able to find or you make him a partner.

If you keep your chef as an employee and the chef becomes very successful then you as an owner are at the mercy of his reputation. If he decides to ask for more money what do you do and if he decided to leave what effect would this have on your business? These are very difficult issues to handle, especially if you are going to invest millions of dollars in setting up a new restaurant.

If the chef is an owner it gives the restaurant a soul and defined style, as well as a sense of security for the other owner and the employees. That was the path Victoria had chosen and I was grateful to have that chance, but at the same time I was careful to set my role clearly. I was to be responsible for the running of the whole operation, as that is the only way I can operate successfully and with integrity.

—

Yvette had become pregnant during my last months at The Regent. I had never really thought about having children. I always presumed that if it happened it was meant to happen, but I was delighted when we found that we were expecting a child.

Yvette's labour started in front of Bathers' at 2am, while walking with me on a hot restless January night. Bathers' at that point was all boarded up and in full demolition mode, the work having finally started. I had been involved now for several months in the planning, design, and budgeting of the new Bathers' and I was now also involved in the preservation of the building and the renovation of the interior.

My little girl Celeste was born on Australia Day and we now always joke that she will never have to work on her birthday and that she will always have special fireworks! I was thrilled to have a girl because I did not want a son to put me through what I put my parents through when I was young and restless. I had a few months before the opening of Bathers' to enjoy this little bundle of life and to get used to the sleepless nights. Still, it was great to start our family, with challenging times ahead.

I had worked for months since my resignation on the plan for the new Bathers'. Victoria was to work out the feel, look, colour and fabric of the building, while I was to work on the flow, kitchens, bars and back of house. My other main role was to manage the construction process and ensure we came within budget and on time. I worked very closely to help produce the budget with Victoria and her accountant, as this was no small project, with a combined total construction and fit out bill for over four million dollars. In short, Victoria was going to give it a spirit and style, and I was to create great food and make the whole business work efficiently.

Victoria had worked for years on the flow of the building, the partition of the spaces and the definition of what could be done with the building. The council had definite parameters for the business with a 'plan of management' and she needed to fulfil this with her design. One of her great achievements was to get the council to hire Alex Popov as the building's architect. Alex's buildings are well-known in Sydney, producing strikingly simple forms that have free flowing spaces. Alex produced for the council the plan for the presentation and renovations of the Pavilion.

237

I worked with Alex to produce a design that made sense as a restaurant. He is a man of total integrity and honesty, and when it came to the difficult process of taking the concept from the conceptual to the fine design Alex was reluctant to engage in it. A restaurant needs amenities that inevitably spoil your clean lines: practical serveries for the waiters (hidden from the view of the customers), cashing up and ordering sections, linen stores and dirty linen drop offs, wine and coolroom storage for the bar, waiter's stations, shelving for glasses and wash-up areas.

My impression was that it was all too messy for Alex to contemplate and he let me know in his own way that he had accomplished his role by providing a great shell and it was now up to us to fill it. I'm not too sure that Alex was prepared to be pulled in different directions by me, Victoria, the builder and the council. He is certainly more comfortable in building houses for a single client instead of having a multiplicity of opinions to deal with. Despite Victoria's sadness with Alex not completing her restaurant she understood the necessity of his decision. I still worked with Alex during the construction process and his insight and good humour were always a pleasant escape from the hard drive of getting the work done by the builder.

In the end we hired a restaurant designer who understood the demands for form as well as practicality in design. McConnell Rayner are experienced architects in this sort of project. They had built Banc restaurant, which was a very sensitive restoration of a former bank in a grand space in Martin Place, as well as many other projects that gave them depth of knowledge.

The council had settled on a builder who specialised in public buildings, most notably schools and jails, and a project manager who was precise in his paperwork but preferred to avoid confrontation. It was going to make for an interesting mix. Scott, the foreman on site, was hard driving and temperamental. He made the project move along more than everyone else did and we were all grateful for that.

The first major thing I did when I reviewed the preliminarily plans was to change the function of the building around. The café was to be at the southern end, where the old restaurant used to be, and the new restaurant was to be in the north side of the building, where the derelict offices used to be. I did this because the kitchens were to be bigger on the south side and I felt that the café was going to have a much greater turnover of people than the restaurant. The other major thing that I needed to ensure was that there was enough production capacity in place to cater for the expected number of customers. I did not have any choice but to build three separate kitchens, something that is costly to build and extremely costly to operate. In view of the size of the building, its natural lines and the distance to travel, I created a café kitchen, a restaurant kitchen and a pastry/bakery kitchen that could change into a function kitchen in the evening.

Once our broad design was established I started to work on the fine detailing of the kitchen and of the bar. I started with a blank piece of paper and within weeks I had a complete design for all my kitchens with a budget that was eventually achieved within a couple of thousand dollars on completion of the construction. Today there is no greater compliment I can receive than my barman telling me that it is one of the best designed bars they have worked in or one of my chefs telling me that they would not change a thing in the kitchen.

We had now completed the design and the demolition had finished. It was time to finally start the rebuilding process and bring to life Victoria's ten years of planning. As soon as we started the serious construction, as opposed to the demolition of the old building, I felt we were on our way.

—

When everything seems to be working perfectly it is often then that disaster strikes, and this is precisely what happened. We had just reached our first level (the top slab had been poured the previous week) and the internal walls were taking shape. I was walking around the site as I did every day and I noticed Scott was looking pretty concerned. He kept measuring the distance between the new structural columns and was shaking his head. I asked him what was wrong and his reply had frightening consequences. 'I think we poured the columns in the wrong position!' All of the new structural columns in the southern part of the buildings were poured and set in the wrong position, with the first level slab already set on top. This was a monumental mistake, one that would put the construction behind for months. It was probably unheard of in the construction industry to make such a mistake, but it was staring us in the face.

We tried over the next month to adjust our designs, but in the end the builder took all the wrong columns out and put them back in their correct position. This happened whilst retaining the first floor slab and the roof that by then had arrived and was being assembled. The engineer had to design an incredible underground bracing system of steel to ensure the safety of the building. At least the builder owned the problem and tackled it to his credit. It made the project late, but we were able preserve our original design.

The building had been classified as a historical building a few years prior and a heritage architect was appointed to ensure the integrity of the design. The restaurant kitchen was going to be approximately in the same position as the old kitchen at Bathers'. I remember that kitchen pretty well and it was a nightmare for the staff, the waiters and for the kitchen hands. It was impossible to keep clean, as it was never designed properly in the first place. For years they were waiting for the go ahead to do a full renovation but no money could be invested until Victoria had the security of a new lease. It would have been so hard for everyone involved to live and work in a vacuum of uncertainty, but such was the reality of the Bathers' saga.

I looked at the tiny external door where all the food, produce, wine and supplies were to be received and I could see the evident problem. That door was way too narrow to handle the volume and the size of most boxes. I suggested to Scott, my foreman, that we needed to enlarge it before we got too far in the project. This request went on to Alex Popov, who was responsible for the structure, and he passed it on to Robert Moore, the Heritage Architect.

Well, it was as if I was asking to change the whole style of the building! Every modification of the original design was regarded as an assault on the integrity of the building. In the end, after much talk and remaining calm and logical and expressing my view that we needed to have some sense of practicality over a non-public, hidden service door, I was able to get it widened to a more appropriate size. Over the next six months I encountered this type of issue time and time again and each new situation needed to be negotiated and resolved amicably.

I was starting to feel a sense of control when one of the biggest problems on site when I joined was finally getting resolved. Everyone had been at each other's throats; it was a big dysfunctional team that was about to explode. In principle the unifying force on a project like this would normally be the project manager, but it seemed to me that Michael, despite his other capabilities, did not like confrontation. One of my strengths is to make people work together and I needed to achieve this more than anything else if I was to be effective in opening on time and on budget. I imposed a deadline on the final plans, I made decisions about the design to speed things up and I reinforced to all involved on the need to stay on track—after all, it was our money at stake. In this battle I was allied with Scott. He told me what he needed to know and as soon as he asked me I worked on it to provide him with an answer on the same day. We became a team; I pushed for him and he pushed for me.

Over the next few months we went from a demolition site, to a bare bone shell, to a skeleton of a building (filled with scaffolding, beams and pillars), to a building with a roof, a ground floor slab and internal walls. It was a magical transformation, and even more surprising we were catching up on time.

We were getting to a point where every small detail needed to be refined. How many phone lines did I need? What was going to be the location of each power point, data point and phone? What type of tiles was I going to use on the kitchen walls, and what about the kitchen floor? What type of dishwasher did we need, what type of taps, and how many lockers did we require for the staff change rooms? The complexity of the building, its size and the need to have an effective and efficient workplace was always at the top of my mind. It was my one chance to design my own restaurant from scratch and I was not going to miss it or make a mess of it.

Victoria was concentrating on the look and feel of the place. I could see how great she was at taking a blank concept and filling the space with her unique style. It was time to decide what settings and cutlery we were going to use. We both fell in love with amazing silver cutlery from Switzerland, and for the plates (which are critical for me to show up the food) I settled on fine bone china from Wedgwood, because of their classic lines, whiteness and the refined thinness of their plates. Victoria chose all the fabrics and came up with an ingenious system of underlay to hide the feet of the restaurant tables. Instead of purchasing serviettes she got them made out of the leftover underlay material, a great idea. She selected the cups for the restaurant and the little glass teapots and other essentials for the tables.

One of the table items that we needed to select was a table lamp. On my first date way back in Canada I had spotted something special that had never left my mind. I had taken my date to a beautiful restaurant in Provincetown, Cape Cod, USA, where they had stunning table lamps. The lamp was made from one piece of glass, with a little

242

balloon encased in a barrel of hand-blown glass. The little balloon was the recipient for the lamp oil and wicker. It was such a simple, effective and modern design that it stuck with me and I promised myself that if I ever opened my own restaurant I would have that lamp.

After I told Victoria the whole story she said, 'Wait a minute, I think I have your lamp in my garage!' After twenty minutes she came back with a box and inside it was my lamp! Apparently she had bought it ten years ago in California because she also loved the design, but she had never used it. Such was Victoria, a mad collector of beautiful things.

We had no idea where to find any more but the name 'Wolford' was written on the box. I decided to use the internet to do a search (something I'd never done before) and I typed in: 'Wolford oil lamp'. Up came the exact same lamp, which was made by a Danish designer, based in California. His design was so clever that the lamp is displayed in the Whitney Museum of American Art in New York. I emailed the company (again a first for me) and to my surprise I got an answer the next day. Not only were they happy to sell us the lamp, they were asking us if we would consider being their agent in Australia. I ordered 60 lamps and not only do we use them, we also sell them in our product room.

Often the most complex tasks of setting up a restaurant resides in the things the customers do not see, like the point-of-sale system, which allows you to place orders to the kitchen, prepare bills and keep a history of your sales. Because such a system was going to cost nearly $100,000 I needed to get this right. If you have a good system you are able to see ordinary things such as how many covers you did on any given day, how many bottles of wine you sold, how many bottles of gin you should have left and what your revenue should be for the amount of alcohol used in a week. The system should allow you to track wastage, average spend per cover and predict how much revenue you might achieve on that night.

There are two big aspects of setting up a system. The first big task is to enter all your individual items, including every single food dish, side dish and variations of coffee and tea. If that is not enough, every alcoholic beverage also needs to be entered, including the price per bottle of every single item and drink and its precise composition like Bloody Mary which have 45ml vodka, 30ml spice mix, topped with tomato juice and cracked pepper. All this amounts to an incredible task, especially if you have a huge wine list and specialise in cocktails like we do at Bathers'. The next task is to train the entire service staff in using the system. First you need to train the managers and assistant manager and in turn they have to train all the service staff.

Briefing notes were prepared for all the new dishes and drinks, forms were devised for anything needed from group bookings to requests for birthday cakes to templates for gift vouchers. Interview procedures were set and The Bathers' Pavilion Employee Manual was completed. This contained the terms and conditions of employment, the Bathers' history, the story of the partners, the description of all areas, the evacuation and fire fighting procedures, the leave and vacation rights and everything else a new employee needs to know before they start work here.

It was time to start recruiting the new team for Bathers'. There were very few candidates from the old Bathers' available to come back, so I virtually had to start from scratch. I tried to hire, as much as possible, people who I had worked with previously, people that I knew I could trust and rely on.

I firstly had to hire my Chef de Cuisines, the ones that were to run my kitchen. In the restaurant I knew I would have Xavier Mouche: he was one of my most talented chefs at Kable's with an artistic sense of presentation and a real sensitivity. For the café and the function kitchens I needed someone extremely solid, as I knew that most of my effective time was going to be spent in the restaurant kitchen. Whoever I selected needed to be a great chef and someone who understood what I expected out of my food.

I always had kept in touch with Ron, my old Executive Sous Chef from The Regent, and I thought he would be the ideal candidate for the job. Just before they reopened, after the renovations were completed, they told him that he was not going to be appointed Executive Chef in my place. He phoned me the day they told him and said he was ready to take my standing offer and help me open Bathers'.

Nichan (my Pastry Chef of 15 years) had resigned on the same day that I had left The Regent. Such was his loyalty, he was just not going to work for anyone else. He joined me, but as second-in-charge of the pastry shop, as his bad back was slowing him down and preventing him from working the extreme hours that were required. For my main Pastry Chef I hired Birk, who was born in East Germany. Birk proved to be everything I could wish for: organised, fast, clean, talented, calm and a good trainer. I could write a dessert menu with a good idea of what I wanted, but Birk would take the idea further and refine it to a perfect dessert.

Once I had my key staff in place in the kitchen I turned my attention to the front of the house and our administration. The next most important roles were those of Restaurant and Café Manager. For the café Fiona, who worked with me at The Regent, agreed to join the team. She has an easy smile, is good with the customers and staff and she always thinks of the training and other time consuming, but important, human resources aspects of running a restaurant.

My first choice for Restaurant Manager was flawed. He lasted just one day. I certainly prefer to use people that worked with me before and I was wracking my head to come up with another option when late one Sunday night I thought of Andreas. Andreas was one of my Kable's Sous Chefs, like Xavier, in fact he was Xavier's boss when Xavier was his assistant. He had left to run his own restaurant, Two Chefs on

Stanley, where he had worked on the floor as well as in the kitchen, before he sold it.

What a perfect match he was for me. He was good looking (with European grace), he understood the kitchen, the chefs and the food, but above all he was a hard worker and understood me. We were in for one of my most pleasant work partnerships, such was our mutual respect for each other and our complementary skills. He looked after the front of house for me and I ran the business and the kitchen. I relied on him to guide me through aspects of the business I either did not fully understand or did not have the time to handle. He could appease or charm customers with his calmness and quiet authority, but he also handled people who drank too much or were getting out of hand. He could relax any of the staff and get the best out of them, but he was also capable of putting his foot down to assert his authority.

For sommelier, Sally Harper joined us from bel mondo. She proved to be an incredible employee with a gift to find small wine producers and build one of the best wine lists in Sydney. Sally had a great influence over the whole business and was one of the best sommeliers in town.

In the office I assembled a team who were partially from old Bathers' and partially from The Regent. Sally looked after the functions, as she had done with me at The Regent. Kristy, my assistant, also came over from The Regent. She quickly proved to be the backbone of my office team, capable of handling all the competing demands. Nothing could phase her and it was great to have someone who I could rely on and give more and more work and responsibilities to. Jim, our calm and methodical accountant, Victoria and I choose together from a short list of candidates. I then hired Ray, my former butcher, to be my purchasing manager. The round up of the office consisted of Janine, Victoria's assistant, and Gail, the face of Bathers' to the customers. Gail became our telephonist, and was a long-term employee who was a gem with the customers.

On top of the core staff, we still needed to hire more than one hundred additional staff and the race was on to find them, train them and put them through their paces. Suppliers were selected and primed to deliver our first orders, cleaners were interviewed, as well as computer consultants and other tradespeople who needed to service the building and our materials and equipment. It was all coming together.

23

REALISATION OF A DREAM

NOW THAT WE HAD CHOSEN THE KEY STAFF AND THE BUILDING was nearly completed it was time to finish the fit out. Sydney was hit with its greatest hailstorm and the resulting damage was on a scale that was hard to comprehend. The Bathers' Pavilion was unaffected, but one of the rare bonuses for me was that the building housing the stock of one of the biggest wholesalers of kitchen equipment was destroyed. The roof had been punctured with thousands of holes and the resulting water damage was devastating. Every cardboard box was soaked, some stock was already rusting, shelves had collapsed and there was no way to render this building or stock through cleaning or patient sorting. The insurer took over the stock and had a sale.

All the stock needed to be moved, sold or destroyed quickly and here lay my opportunity to purchase all my kitchen, pastry, bar and café equipment in one place at a greatly reduced price. I was with my key chefs and we were like children in a lolly shop. There was everything one could wish to purchase to set up a full restaurant and I took advantage of this. Over two days I selected an enormous amount of kitchen material, saving me a huge amount of money and time. I could now sense that we were approaching our D-Day, seeing all the pots and chopping boards ready, even if they were slightly wet!

I felt that we had produced one of the best sets of kitchens I had ever seen or worked in. I loved walking in the building late at night, seeing the shapes taking form and the finishes being applied. I could see the beautiful blackbutt flooring being laid upstairs in the whole of the first level. I could see my kitchen tiles being applied to the walls and floors. I imagined flames in the kitchen from the grill, the pizza coming out of the wood-fired oven and I could almost smell the quince tarts and fruit jelly being made in the pastry kitchen. It was so calm and serene alone on the terrace, having finally a bit of time for myself to contemplate our progress. I felt very intimate with the hidden services in the building: it is hard to picture the sheer volume of cables, water lines, power outlets, ducting and mechanical parts that remain unseen, but are essential to run such a building.

Finally, we got power to the building. We had lights in the kitchen, hot water on tap, the computer was installed and the phone was on. There were so many trades to deal with that my head was spinning in all different directions. I needed to get the office set up quickly and soon enough I realised one of the biggest disappointments of the project. The lighting, apart from in the kitchen just did not do justice to the building. The architects did not have a lighting consultant in their office and I soon realised that we had missed a great opportunity to get this right.

In the office, which was equipped with the same lights as the restaurant, the staff struggled to read anything unless it was under the direct beam of a downlight. It was a minor disaster that everyone tried to ignore for a while. A few months in I had to change the office lights and the same applied to the function room; it is so much more costly to repair this type of problem after you open than when you build the place. My architect explained that on the last project they had done before our restaurant they had put in too many lights, and in light of this (sorry about the pun) they cut all of the Bathers' lights by half; a serious mistake.

—

My crack team were setting up the kitchen with all the brand-new equipment and there was no prouder moment for me than when I could see my kitchen actually fitted out and stocked. I had worked for months on the kitchen plan and every single little detail of it. By some magic, everything was coming together after what could have been another major disaster.

Just before we took over the café kitchen the electricians were struggling with a couple of underground lines, where some of the power cables needed to be run to service the kitchen equipment. One of the biggest warnings the builder received from my kitchen contractor was the absolute need to keep acid away from the kitchen once the stainless steel equipment was installed. Often builders use acid to clean the tiles on a building site before they hand you over the project. Acid does not mix with stainless steel, as it is extremely corrosive and will cause permanent damage. The message to avoid acid was constantly reinforced to ensure that the builder or their cleaners would not use it in my kitchen. Over half-a-million dollars of stainless steel was in these kitchens and we were not going to risk any damage.

No one could imagine that the electrician, in total frustration at not succeeding in running his cabling, decided to pour litres of acid down his conduits and, after it failed to clear his line, then set small explosive charges to blow open these lines! That rush of blood to the head could have only been caused by hours of frustration late at night to try to resolve his problem. He succeeded in getting the line cleared, but in the dark he did not realise the damage it caused to the kitchen. When all the builders arrived the next morning we saw that half of the kitchen was affected, splattered with acid all over the equipment. It was enough to make me cry.

Here was my spotless kitchen, one day before it was ready to be handed over from the builder, splashed all over by brown streaks of corrosive acid. The electrician was mortified. He was actually the boss of the outfit trying to show his workers how it was done. Luckily we were able to polish or replace most of the damage-affected pieces by opening. This project was starting to test my composure.

—

From the builder's timetable we were about six weeks behind schedule, which was not too bad considering the complexity of the project, but enough to disrupt the first function we had booked. We could not afford to not take bookings and so, in consultation with the builder, we had booked it for the month of June.

My first wedding was for a beautiful couple, who were very much involved in the planning. The bride was born in America and the groom was a laid-back Australian, not so concerned with the issue of whether we were going to make it on time. The bride was much more nervous about the whole thing as many of her friends and family were flying in from America and with no small reason she had serious concern about my ability or the builder's ability to have the building ready on time. That wedding was certainly my rallying cry to the builder to get a move on and set that week as my absolute deadline.

The Bathers' Pavilion was going to be a new place and it is amazing what type of attraction this has for the people of Sydney. The amount of bookings we were getting was amazing. From September we had several large functions booked every week, and in December practically everyday was sold for Christmas parties, weddings, corporate functions or birthdays. This wedding, however, was our first big test.

Victoria had selected beautiful fabric for the function room and the wall finish had just been completed. Because of the Heritage Listing of the building the ceiling height was quite restricting. We decided to have stunning wood floors on the first level made of blackbutt and because of this we selected the ceiling to be made of acoustic material. It was quite revolutionary at that time, yet the concept of the ceiling was quite simple. It was made of a thin sheet of vinyl, which was heated and stretched onto a small frame that was set around the perimeter of the room. Above the ceiling the void was packed with noise-absorbing material, which just soaked up any noise from the room.

The table size was also unusual. We selected a table that would sit six people. Most places that hold functions sit eight to ten people at a table, sometimes twelve. You cannot have a flowing conversation with larger groups of people, you just talk to people near you and smile at others from a distance. We selected six because it felt more intimate and because it was more like eating in a restaurant, which was what we were really trying to achieve.

The day of the wedding arrived and we were all ready. The whole evening was magical and fulfilling. Everything was perfect, even if the building was a bit sterile due to having only the first floor in operation. It is a shame that I did not spend more time taking pictures of the first few months of operation as it would have been great to look back at our achievement.

The time had now come for me to design all my menus and I started with the café menu. I wanted a very Mediterranean-based menu in the café; a clear style that the customer would understand. I did not want to do pseudo-Australian cuisine, with everything from curry to steak to fish. I knew that in our location we needed to have simple fish dishes, fresh homemade pasta, salad and wood-fired pizza. I really wanted to avoid as much as possible using meat. It was going to be very much a very fresh menu, with respect for seasonality and our harbour location.

The fact that I did not want to mix Asian and Mediterranean food was a great frustration to Victoria but I felt very clear about how I wanted to construct my menu. For the next four years she pestered me to put a curry on the menu. Firstly, I did not wish to mix styles, and secondly, to do Asian food properly it is better to have a separate team trained to do this correctly. This might happen some day, but now was not the time.

For the restaurant I had decided to have a set-price menu. I spent a lot of time thinking about what is the best way to charge and I decided that being a new restaurant on the water, with huge fixed costs like rent and wages it was better to guarantee a set price per customer. I set the price at $97 for three courses, which was at the high end of pricing in Sydney, but I figured that if people were going to spend $100 on food per person, they would want to do it in one of the most beautiful restaurants in Sydney.

I had imagined a very much produce-based menu, with the best and freshest I could find, but somehow I did not wish to fall back in the trap of just being known for my search for great producers and the support I gave to my small producers. I wanted to let my dishes speak for themselves and for this reason I avoid mentioning where the produce had come from on my menu. I was probably one of the first people in Australia to name the provenance of my vegetables, meat, snails, hare, duck, marron and other food, but of late this was very much imitated, and in some instances the line between truth and reality became blurred. I think to me it was time to move on from such a personal distinctive style.

My next big opening was the café. I could count on the stable and experienced hands of Ron and Fiona, two of my most trusted employees. With them for a couple of weeks was Xavier with a few of his top kitchen staff and Andreas. The café took shape and despite the fact that the French stone tables arrived late the place looked very inviting; its blend of beach casual with uncommercial touches really set us apart from other cafés. I was also very happy with the dishes and the way I had structured my menu. It was different, veering away from the food served in most cafés, especially on the north shore. The length of the menu provided a huge choice, offering something for everyone.

Now that we were about to open the café, all the kitchen and service staff needed to start at Bather's. It had been an incredibly hectic two months, trying to finish the building and to fill it with equipment, staff and eventually guests. There was much to finish on the restaurant side, as far as construction was concerned, but despite the difficulty in having two kitchen brigades working out of the one kitchen, we were going to be ready and the restaurant team was going to hit the ground running.

It is amazing to see how a project comes together so quickly when you are near your deadline. The streetscape and the landscaping were supposed to be ready by the time of our opening. The council had taken the opportunity to completely review the street size, direction and elevation. A substation was installed to provide enough power for Bathers', a new service road and pathway were formed and poured, and the old toilet block was demolished and removed.

Scaffolding was quickly coming down, pathways were cleaned, and the garden was being planted. The huge trees surrounding Bather's were trimmed after years and years of neglect and the place just was starting to look pretty fantastic. The final coat of paint had been applied recently, going from a brilliant white to a European white, which was closer to the original colour found under dozens of paint layers applied over the years. That colour was so much softer on the eyes and it had a tone that blended well with the beach and the surrounding landscape.

The people of Mosman could sense that the final day of construction was nearing. It had been such a long saga, with Victoria having attended over 150 council meetings in regards to Bathers' either through eventually sheer folly or with a sense that soon enough she would prevail. A lesser person or maybe a more practical person would have given up a long time ago. Still, most of the people of Mosman understood that something needed to be done and they were glad to see the day approach when the exterior and interior were to be revealed.

The café finally opened its doors with a limited menu for just breakfast and lunch for the first week. That gave the staff time to get used to the equipment, the flow of each area, and to acclimatise them to dealing again with guests. It was a deliberately slow start to give us the time to refine our skills.

From a slow evening start, the numbers built up steadily as we approached warmer weather. Families realised we were child friendly with our high chairs, welcoming attitude, pens and drawing paper. Living right above The Esplanade for the last four years I had seen the people strolling the promenade and I knew that we needed to be family friendly. I planned a pram parking area in the building and Victoria got the great idea of turning a spare disabled bathroom into a children's bathroom, filled with a tiny toilet, a very low sink and a quirky series of paintings and fittings that children were going to love.

Eventually the day arrived for Xavier and Andreas to put their team to the test. The full building was handed over in the second week of August and the restaurant was finally open. My first menu had a new focus. I wanted to have a balance between people enjoying great food, but also food that showed intelligence in the combination of produce. Two dishes became instant winners: one was my oxtail ravioli with seared scallops. I had always done oxtail ravioli, but this time I combined it with beautiful seared scallops from Hervey Bay. The sauce was made with ginger, garlic, chilli, wine and soya infusion and it became a classic. This other one was one of those 'try me if you dare dishes': it was thinly sliced abalone with Asian mushrooms, crisp fried pork ear and a master stock that blended all the ingredients together. My Chinese customers loved it and the gourmets gave that one the thumbs up.

Within a few weeks the restaurant was thriving and from that point on for the next two years I worked lunch and dinner nearly every day in the kitchen. I really had no choice; not only was I needed to call every service, but I had badly misread the amount of chefs I needed to produce the food. I did think that with nearly 40 chefs I would be okay, but the restaurant was so busy that for years I never felt that I had enough staff working in the restaurant kitchen.

My problem was that as soon as I would find a new chef, another one would leave through sheer exhaustion or realising his skills were not to the standard of the rest of the team. It was a vicious circle that never got quite better. The other problem was location. Bathers' is not in the city, and unless you have a car it is difficult to get to by public transport. Most chefs could not afford to live in Mosman or near by and consequently they needed to travel to get to work. The same problem applies to kitchen hands. They are extremely hard to come by, as again, transport is the main issue. Ron had given me nearly 18 years of loyal service, first at The Regent and then invaluably for the opening of Bathers'. For the last ten years he had lived on the Central Coast of Sydney and the travel was getting too much considering his bad back. It was very sad for me but he had given me a year to fully anchor the kitchen, as he had promised, and the time had come to let him go. We would still work together but not in the same role.

Luckily I had another fabulous Sous Chef who was ready to assume Ron's role. Phil had worked with me at The Regent for many years and he was ready to take on the challenge that Ron left him. He was a very talented chef with the experience to take on the demanding job of running both the café and function kitchen.

In our first month of opening Sydney received an unexpected visitor. A whale had entered the harbour for the first time in many years. It arrived one morning and stayed in the harbour for several weeks. It was a stroke of good luck that the whale floated, played, rested and jumped right in front of The Bathers' Pavilion for a couple of weeks. Crowds of a hundred, became a thousand and then that crowd expanded to tens of thousands of people. The promenade was full of people; the island was sinking under the weight of the masses and Bathers' was full every day from then on. People were queuing to get in, phoning to make bookings, radio stations were getting us to do commentaries. It was a whale frenzy that benefited us amazingly. It was a great omen for Bathers'.

Eventually everything became a blur. We all worked so hard it was just an amazing feat. Victoria's hope and my wishes had been answered. My sense of the business was getting very good and the same applied to the staff. We could predict how much food to order for the weekend, how many waiters we needed on a Tuesday night and how many menus we needed printed. The place was finally humming, the builders had gone and my storerooms were starting to have order. The time had arrived to focus on the little details, such as finetuning the pricing, the menus and the staff manual. I needed to search for new produces and business relationships, the function room needed to capture more weekly business.

Just when I had finally found time to do the things that I always wanted to do more work came along. Tony O'Reilly, one of the most important businessmen we had lodging at The Regent, wanted me to go and participate in a dinner in Frankfurt, Germany. Doctor O'Reilly is not someone who accepts no as an answer. He is the chairman and CEO of H.J Heinz Company, the chairman and major shareholder in Independent newspapers PIC and he is also the major shareholder of Waterford Wedgwood and Rosenthal. I firmly but politely declined his offer and thought no more about it.

A couple of months went by and then one morning I was called in my office to be told that there was a television team waiting for me in the restaurant. I went down quite puzzled and after asking what it was all about they told me that, 'It is for the dinner you are doing in Frankfurt'. 'What dinner in Frankfurt?' was my reply. 'The one that you agreed to do for Tony O'Reilly!'

I could not believe what I was hearing. I said it was all a big mistake, but the crew of four plus the producer had flown in from London to film The Bathers' Pavilion and me. I called the agency that was in charge of the dinner in London and I realised that my presence was a 'fait accomplis': there was no turning back, I had to go. I decided to take Birk, my Pastry Chef, with me as he spoke German and the trip would give him the chance to visit his parents in East Germany.

To that point I never had regular days off and the thought of leaving my team was unimaginable. I did not like the idea and I knew from past experience that these dinners were never as easy as they appear to be. The London agency told me not to worry, that they would have 100 of the best German chefs ready to work with us. It was with a lot of apprehension I prepared myself for the dinner. The others who were contributing were from the Savoy in London, Boulud in New York, The Regent in Hong Kong, a three-star Michelin Restaurant in Dublin, and myself. These chefs represented the major market of Waterford Wedgwood; at least I was going to be in good company.

My dish was to be the main course and I selected a winter dish of venison with a foie gras and liver tapenade and caramelised onion. The produce and the wine were supposed to come from your own country and since the dinner was supposed to be for 600 people I needed to find a huge amount of supplies. No money was going to be spared to produce that dinner. In attendance was supposed to be Donatella Versace and the Princess of York, Fergie. Tony O'Reilly also owned Weight Watchers in America, so I could understand the connection. The whole thing was going to be a huge event to coincide with a fair that was held in Frankfurt, which was the biggest exhibition of tabletop wares in the world.

Tony O'Reilly obviously had a vision to develop Waterford Wedgwood into a kind of Gucci of the tabletop world. He had just formed an alliance with Versace to design a new service of stunning plates, hence the Versace presence at this big gala dinner. It was supposed to be the main dinner of the fair and something to remember.

I was told to select the best wine possible to pair with my venison. This was easily said, but how do you find enough stock of any high quality wine for 600 people? I turned to Robert Hill-Smith from Yalumba and we selected the the Yalumba Signature Cabernet Shiraz of which they had a sizeable quantity cellared. It was supposed to be packed and shipped by air to Germany. Over the next couple of months I worked hard to catch up on my work, but summer was on us, I had just finished the huge month of December and I was trying to get everyone in place to cover for me while I was away. They had offered for me to take a vacation in Europe, but February is certainly not the best of months to do this and anyway I could not spare the time. I told them I would fly in to do the dinner and fly out again in the minimum amount of days possible.

I shipped my wine and my venison in the week prior to my departure, and I said goodbye to Yvette and my staff. I was a bit apprehensive about going to Germany, a country I had never visited before. I did not sleep on the flight and we had a seven-hour stopover in Hong Kong, so by the time I got to our pretty ordinary hotel situated in downtown Frankfurt I was pretty tired. We got there at 11am and I decided to just go straight to the site of the dinner. The dinner was held in at Palais Zoo, a very old building in the ground of the city zoo. It had been recently reconverted to a huge function centre of incredible quality. The outside of the building retained its époque feeling but the interior was completely new and functional.

Flowers were arriving from all over the world, and boxes and boxes of expensive high quality television sets were being unpacked so that everyone at the dinner would have a clear view of the proceedings. On the centre stage was a huge crystal ball, which was made by Waterford crystal and had been used to mark midnight 2000 in Time Square, New York. At least all these excesses augured well for the quality of the dinner we were to produce.

I walked into the kitchen with Birk and saw a perfectly clean, modern and adequate kitchen. We introduced ourselves to the chef and decided to ask a few questions about the dinner. The Executive Chef was young and professional but he told us that he was going to have six chefs with him to do the dinner, not the 100 that we were originally told. I could see big problems ahead and realised that I fairly quickly needed to get a grip of this situation. The amount of work that was required just for my venison was pretty staggering, and there was no way Birk and I could handle it ourselves. We needed them by at least Thursday morning at the latest to get ready for the Saturday dinner. The people in charge of the dinner were arriving from London that afternoon and I decided to wait for them to arrive before I developed more concern.

We met them at 6pm in the foyer of the hotel and over dinner we explained our situation with the kitchen chefs. They told me that they were going to fix it and not to worry. I had one of the absolute worst nights of my life in a hotel room on that first night. Not only was my body clock out of sync, but the bed was terrible, the pillow was foam and the automatic heater was providing me with an environment that was perfect for torture: freezing one moment and boiling hot the next.

The dryness of the room was unbearable and it just compounded my irritation.

When I got to the Palais Zoo the next morning I knew it was time to clarify our helper situation. The program was extremely tight and I could see no choice but to have six lines to dish out the food. That would require 50 chefs, if you counted the ones that needed to cook the food.

I called a meeting with the German catering company in charge of the dinner and we all assembled by lunchtime in a conference room with our famously ineffective London PR firm. My first question was how many chefs were we to be provided with for the dinner? A stunned look came across the executives when Birk relayed my question. All of my questions were going to be addressed to the owner. He checked with his subordinate, who checked with his subordinate, who checked with the chefs. I did not need translation for the eventual answer, as I knew it: six.

I pulled a piece of paper that I had received in Australia that stated that we were to be provided with 100 of the best German chefs and seeing again their stunned look I decided to pounce, to the embarrassment of my silent London PR firm. I said, 'Unless tomorrow morning I have 50 chefs in the kitchen at 9am, I will purchase my own ticket and return to my restaurant in Australia.' I was not going to put my name to a dinner that was impossible to produce and that was that. A lot of German was spoken over the next few minutes and I could see a few of the executives starting to perspire. In any case the answer came back to me, 'You will have your 50 chefs tomorrow morning.'

Now the hard part was ahead of us. I returned to the kitchen with Birk and got stuck into the production of our dish. We finished around 7pm and we ended up at a restaurant run by our catering friends and another terrible night of sleep. A least the next day at around 9am the 50 chefs were in the kitchen ready to receive instructions. I split them up into teams and paired them with the guest chefs. This was going to make things easier on everyone.

My big concern now was the Irish chef. His restaurant only sat 40 people, but he insisted on cooking for this function like he did in his restaurant. His dish was a seared scallop on a bed of squid ink risotto, topped with gold leaf. He insisted on cooking 10 scallops at a time and then serving them, then cooking 10 more and serving them, etc. This was a recipe for disaster in my eyes. I pleaded with him and implored him but he wanted to do things his way, so in the end I had to let him do his own thing. I knew the timetable was very precise in a German way as they had satellite link from around the world being programmed. I hoped for the best and feared the worst.

When Saturday came around I'd finally managed to get about three hours straight of sleep. By the afternoon everything was ready. I had organised six lines with long tables, where the food was to be plated. As guests started to arrive the first dish was served, a crab and cucumber salad with an apple jelly and cucumber sorbet. Next were fried spring rolls, Hong Kong style, with a noodle and coriander salad. We had gained 10 minutes by the time it got to the scallop dish. This was the real test.

The Irish chef was ready to go and he fired instruction to his chefs to go and then we all waited and waited for the most enormous scallops I had ever seen in my life being cooked, 10 at a time. This was not looking good. It took the chef at least 20 minutes to realise the error of his ways. Waiters were banking up in the kitchen and the food was trickling out of the kitchen. It was time for a radical change of cooking method. I told him to stick the bloody scallops in the oven. He agreed and we filled the huge convection oven with trays of scallops. Unfortunately the damage was done. I felt for him when he finished serving the scallops 45 minutes late. He was as white as the snow that was falling outside, which I could see through the huge kitchen window.

After a tomato consommé with quail and quail egg, my main course was to follow. I had made the sauce over three days having reduced it very gently until a perfect light glaze was achieved. The tricky part of the dish was the presentation and for this I wanted to have once slice of the venison loin and three quenelles of my garnish. This could be very hard to achieve in Australia, as most Australian chefs were not used to doing quenelles any more, but I knew in that in Germany they were the kings of quenelles. I have to admit my dish was flawless. It was one of the best large function meals I had ever produced and it was served in record time. The whole dinner was a huge success in the end.

Another bad night's sleep followed a bad flight and by the time I reached Hong Kong for my 12-hour stopover I had one of the sorest backs I had ever had. I never get sore backs and it was just so out of character. I put it down to the terrible bed in the hotel and this time at least the length of the stopover in Hong Kong gave me the chance to have a room at The Regent for a few hours.

My back did not get better by the time I arrived in Sydney and somehow I had lost my usual spark. I presumed it was due to lack of sleep. I arrived at 7.30am like most overseas landings do and I took a taxi home. It was great to return to summer and be home. Céleste was supposed to get her shots from the doctor at 10am so I went along too and showed the doctor my back. She had a look and could not see anything wrong with it apart from a bit of redness around my lower back. She asked me if I had anything else wrong and I said I had noticed a small rash on one of my legs. She looked at it and said I had shingles. She told me it was very serious and that I had to go straight home and to bed. She gave me a prescription and said the days of working like a madman seven days a week were over and I had reached the limit of what my body could endure.

Against her advice I went straight to work and tried frantically to catch up with all my staff, all the outstanding issues and handle everything that needed immediate attention; after all I had been away for six days, something I had never done to that point. I went home around 9pm and fell into bed exhausted, sore and concerned that I had a sickness that only rundown or older people get. It was the first time in my life that I felt truly sick. The rash on my leg went around to my back and the only description I can offer is that it is like water boiling under your skin. It was a horrendous and extremely painful condition.

Over the last three years I had pushed myself harder and harder and I learned to live on even less sleep than normal. I never had much time for any relaxation and I am sure I was stressed about many things that crept into my subconscious. I had become a prime target for something like this to happen. It took me two full weeks to start functioning like a nearly normal person and probably another couple of weeks to be back to my normal routine, except that I had promised Yvette that I would Mondays off from now on. Or at least as much as I could.

24
TESTING TIMES

ONCE I HAD RECOVERED FROM MY ILLNESS YVETTE AND I started thinking about moving homes. Céleste our beautiful little girl was only ten months old so the surprise of another baby coming was both a joyful event but also a scary proposition. Once we knew we were going to be a family of four we knew that we would have to move. We loved our apartment but it wasn't large enough for a young family. Yvette wanted a house, I wanted to live near Bathers', so we settled on something we could not afford in Chinaman's Beach.

We had organised someone to help with Céleste at the end of the pregnancy and also when we moved into our new house. I had some free time after another busy summer, so I set myself the task of renovating what I could of our new place. The house was twenty years old and nothing had been changed for all those years. The place had 'perfect bones': it was north facing, had a great pool and a spa and was walking distance to Chinaman's Beach. There was a small two bedroom flat under the house, so after changing the carpet and getting it painted, we moved in downstairs while the renovation took place upstairs.

My best friend Ray (my squash partner) is a superb carpenter and building foreman for specialised projects. I met him when he was in change of renovating The Regent, a project that took him six solid years. With his skills, we were able to work together in getting all the basic preparation done in the house. We prepared all the floors to lay the parquetry, set new ceilings and did many little jobs before the professionals come in to finish the work at hand.

Yvette gave birth in July and unfortunately our son, Sasha, was born with hydrocephalus, a condition that required immediate brain surgery. Many complications followed and many more operations. Yvette stayed in hospital for weeks and weeks at a time, sleeping mostly in a chair beside our poor little Sasha. These days he is a very happy and bubbly child, but will be left with serious problems for a long time to come. I did my best to take care of Céleste, but it was hard to suddenly lose the constant attention of her mother and for months I travelled daily between the hospital and home and then to work. There are many worse cases in hospital, so you can never feel sorry for yourself; what ever happens, happens, and you need to move on.

—

Terry Durack's first review of the new Bathers' had a huge effect on Victoria, the staff and myself. Victoria had fought for ten years to have the new Bathers', and so much effort went into the creation of a unique eating place, down to the making of our own batter, designing our own uniforms and having the best tableware possible. After just one visit, Terry wrote a very dismissive review of the whole place that equated Bathers' to a kind of Asian hotel with not much to offer. Luckily for us, we weathered this bad review and people eventually forgot it. It just goes to shows how much reviews are based on gut feeling and the personal opinion of the reviewer.

What is important to me is that we bake our own bread each day, we make our own butter and consommé, and we have the best silverware, Wedgwood plates, Riedel glasses and Swiss tableclothes. It matters to me that we train our staff with a daily briefing, that I source the best produce from all over Australia, that I offer a large menu to give a great choice to our customers and that I pride myself on having delicate vegetable dishes always on offer. Does the fact that for the first three years I was there nearly every night of the week, working in the kitchen count? I would have to say yes.

Being reviewed is a painful process that can go either way and at the end of the day one has to accept what is written. As long as we have integrity and our primary goal is to satisfy our customers that our heart is in the right place and we should be successful. I had made a decision not to make food for reviewers but food for my customers to enjoy. There is a subtle difference one makes to either get great ratings or to have a restaurant full of happy customers. At that stage I knew what I preferred.

—

By then the problems that Victoria and I were having in our relationship were getting worse. We were both Leos, with similar personalities: head-strong, driven, passionate, determined and used to doing things our own way. In retrospect, it was somehow inevitable that our relationship was going to be tested. It took many little incidents to drive us apart, despite attempts from both of us to not let issues get in the way of the big picture.

It was difficult for both of us. She was driven by a sense of style that made her contribution hard to categorise, and she needed a freedom to invest in objects, materials, fabrics, pottery, glassware and arts. My brief was to control the budget that we had all agreed on, due to the massive rent increase we suffered after being open one year. Whilst it was inevitable to me that we needed to purchase food to feed our clients, it was not so evident that we needed to constantly change the look of the place by purchasing more paintings or cushions.

It was probably annoying to Victoria that I tried to control every aspect of the business, but I was there nearly every day and worked hard with the staff at running a good operation that in its first five years of operation needed to be conservative in its spending. She probably felt restricted and confined by the ever-diminishing budget and I felt constricted by the financial pressure we operated under. There was frustration on both sides and things unfortunately got off track for no-ones fault, apart from the normal human complexities of relationships and the separate relations we had with our staff. The fact that they felt more comfortable with me had a lot to do with the fact that most of them had worked with me previously at The Regent and that I worked with them nearly every hour of their working day.

Eventually I found the situation impossible, and there were large areas of disagreement with the council looming. I was not prepared to take on any more costly battles with the council. Victoria probably rightly felt that she should have prevailed in all the outstanding issues with them, but the time and money wasted on their battles was not my way of operating. Neither of us was about to back down and the staff were getting unsettled over the differences that Victoria and I had over critical things such as the future direction of the café and the restaurant. I needed to bring back some stability.

It came to a point where I resolved to either move on or to try to fund a buy out, as our agreement gave this as an option. The fact that she chose to sell surprised me, but Bathers' is a very time-consuming business to run, with small margins. For whatever reason she chose to move on. It was sad, but Victoria has left a great legacy in the new building and it is for me to be truthful to her vision, while injecting my own style and making the business a success.

When we finally concluded our business transfer I never sat back to look at the whole place and say, 'Wow, this is finally mine'. My feelings were more one of increased responsibility. I realised that I had to make sure that I ran this thing properly, as I was now the only custodian of the business and the building. Maybe over time my attitude will change, but owning a restaurant never quite gives you the chance to relax. You need to be there working, guiding the staff, setting the right example and making the customers feel welcome, whilst providing them with a great food product.

There are not many opportunities in life that come along like the Bathers'. The location is without equal, the building is beautiful and the chance to build a viable business was all up to me. We designed a truly magnificent restaurant and this was my chance to make it a success. I was not going to miss my chance.

25

WHERE ARE WE TODAY?

THE SYDNEY FOOD SCENE IS CONSTANTLY EVOLVING AND changing. Sometimes it forges ahead in huge leaps and bounds and sometimes it retreats to gather its breath. In all the excitement of new restaurants opening what often gets forgotten are the casualties. A few people made a mark a long time ago in an age where competition was less fierce and margins of profit made more sense. The tax regime is different now, and it certainly is a huge disincentive to eat out, especially at lunchtime. It might be egalitarian to not allow restaurant meals to be deducted as fair business expenses, but it has certainly killed the lunchtime trade of most good restaurants.

When Yvette was working at the old Jean Jacques in Melbourne she saw a thriving and successful business. Jacques was passionate about his product and Susan, his wife, could ensure the numbers rolled in. Nowadays, it is no longer the case that if you serve consistently good food you are ensured the clientele and turnover to make a good profit. Most restaurateurs are just surviving and they work in this trade because they are passionate about food or have hope of a new era of prosperity that could drag them along to a better life.

As well as running on extremely tight margins, another factor that Sydney restaurants have to contend with is the trendiness factor of the Sydney food scene. Most loans for a restaurant will be taken over a five-year period, however there are very few restaurants that have five good years of trading. When anyone asks me about running a restaurant I always advise them that unless they themselves will replace or fill a key position and have the skills to do these jobs then they should forget it.

The real worry about the Sydney food scene is the incredibly high casualty rate. Many stalwarts of the industry have either closed, retired or pulled back from running their restaurants. It is not surprising that Steve Manfredi's restaurants in the Grace Bros building closed, as it was an untested market that he was brave enough to tackle, but it was very sad that he had to give up bel mondo. Steve, Franca, and the immediate family who worked around them were totally dedicated and you could not fault the food. Then when Janni Kyritsis decided he would not pursue his career at MG Garage it was a very bad indication of the chances of the inner city restaurant succeeding. After all, he was probably the most decorated and longest serving chef in Sydney. And Neil Perry and Tetsuya having to close at lunchtimes is yet another frightening indicator of the death of good lunch trade.

But one of the saddest closures was that of Banc and the great dream of the GPO held by Stan Sarris and Liam Tomlin. There was so much hard work, so much investment and at the end of the day so much sadness. And Darley Street Thai's closure is an example that not only the established restaurants are at risk; there will be other big failures and new openings, all part of the cycle of a vibrant food scene. If Oliver Shaul (the original owner of the Summit) was able to buy a Rolls Royce decades ago with the profits of his restaurant, today that could only be a dream, but maybe a dream worth aspiring to.

So where are the bright spots? Well, firstly the new divide seems to be between the haves and the have-nots. If you have a view then your chances are infinitely better to have a successful restaurant over a longer term. If you do not have a view these days then you had better invest in a good fit out. Many inner city restaurants in close proximity to the hotels will thrive, but it would be hard these days to attract people if you are near another great restaurant that has a view. A view on the harbour is so quintessentially Sydney that it is in the end a great attraction that any wise restaurant owner would wish to have.

The other bright spot is that the food in Sydney is great, the cuisine is vibrant and the choice for customers is nearly infinite. In world terms Sydney is a superb city with a quality of life truly unequalled. In comparison to the restaurant prices in London, New York, Paris, Rome and most other major cities the affordability of our restaurants encourage people to eat out quite regularly. Sydneysiders are proud of their city and will take any friends arriving from overseas to a restaurant to show off their city. Australians love their food and wine. And what they might lack in intricate food knowledge they make up in sheer enthusiasm.

The quality and availability of produce has dramatically improved in the shops. There is still a long way to get to the standards of the best that Europe has to offer, but we are a young country and will continue to improve. We have bright young chefs and obliging friendly staff. I constantly get complaints of how robotic and cold the service can be in Europe and how refreshing our waiters are here. That is a great aspect of Australia.

Despite the friendly banter of comments between Sydney and Melbourne about which city is the food city of Australia I would have to judge Sydney the winner. Firstly there are bigger dollars in Sydney. There are more head offices with their executives, more bankers, more pharmaceutical companies, a larger population and, most probably, a higher disposable income. This makes for people who are prepared or capable of paying higher restaurant prices in Sydney. In turn, that offers chefs the opportunity to have better produce on the plate and bigger, more expensive restaurant fit outs. There are also more food publications in Sydney to review, promote or publish books on chefs and their restaurants. The public, despite its tag of being fickle, is keen to support any good operator.

I love Melbourne for its realness and its traditional roots. Melbourne's personalty is more defined and easily loved. It is a place where the public support for a restaurant lasts over a much longer period of time. Where Sydney is brash, new and in your face, Melbourne offers a refreshing departure from the rat race of the Harbour City and its Italian flair is so much more omnipresent and part of the city character. They have refined the idea of local restaurants; the little places offering great food just around the corner from where you live. In Sydney that idea is only just emerging. Sydney also has nothing that comes close to the wonderful Victoria Markets of Melbourne, where there is a huge range of quality produce right in the centre of the city.

I love Sydney for its magnificent setting. It is at the crossroads of the temperature and sub-tropical zone, giving us plenty of chances to have long growing seasons and a range of great food grown around Sydney. I also love the cosmopolitan aspect of our cultural mix.

I am very happy that formula restaurants do not seem to work in Australia. Years ago Wolfgang Puck and Paul Bocuse both opened restaurants in Melbourne and they did not work because these chefs were not at the stove. Formula cafés and restaurants that have been so popular in America do not appear to survive here. I am sure we have not taken to Starbucks like Singaporeans have taken to that brand. Apart from the omnipresent fast food chains, supported by huge publicity budgets, there is not much hope for a second wave of them.

I am often asked what I think the future of Sydney dining will be? Unless you are a chef there is not much point to owning a high calibre restaurant; the economics just do not work. The need to reinforce your relevance in the market place by attending many activities can easily lead to an attitude of the chef consultant: there in spirit, but lacking the influence necessary to keep your kitchen and floor team knowledgeable and motivated. It takes a strong will to resist the temptation to constantly participate in outside promotions, dinners, guest appearances, judging contests, television spots, radio interviews, overseas travel junkets and many other activities. All of these experiences take you away from your restaurant, which diminishes the experience for your customers and short-changes your staff. The daily grind is very easy to get away from; it is much harder to dedicate yourself to be an integral part of your restaurant.

The more owner operators you have, the more personality will go in the place and the food. I think that is the trend we will see for the future. The chef is an integral element of the restaurant. That is what has changed over the last thirty years and I am proud and happy I could be part of that movement.

When I look back at all the years I have spent in the kitchen it amazes me just how far I have come from those early days in Montréal. Sasha, my young son, is so busy, full of life and headstrong, and Yvette often says, 'he is so much like you'. Maybe those shared characteristics are the reason why I have endured the rigours of working in busy kitchens, survived the many tests along the way and ended up experienced and strong enough to run my own kitchen and business.

When people say to me, 'what great things you have achieved with your life,' I always reply that I have been lucky, just in the right place at the right time, even if it does not seem to always convince them. There is certainly an element of luck in any success story. You need the right teachers to guide you, you have to possess the drive to learn, and you need the wisdom to realise what could be a great restaurant and workplace. You have to make constant sacrifices and have the physical and mental stamina to survive the demands of the job. You have to be dedicated, fast, dextrous, a quick learner, a lateral thinker, but above all, you need to have a passion for cooking. If you were blessed with talent then maybe you could make a great success for yourself in the kitchen. It all sounds terribly frightening and it is, to a certain extent.

I love what I do and I am fortunate that I live in an era where chefs are respected and even sometimes seen as celebrities. I think that it is very important to remain grounded, approachable, humble and generous, as it is a very precarious state to be at the top of your game. Complacency is your biggest treat, as it is very easy to fall into the trap of believing one's own publicity. Every day is a new start, as most of your customers will be new ones and you will need to satisfy and impress them as much as the ones two days or a week ago.

I was blessed with great parents who both in their own way moulded me to be who I am today. This puts so much responsibility on me now, as I am father myself. I am very aware of my competing demands and there is a great need to balance my working life with my family life. I will have to swim, play, camp, shop, cook and teach Céleste and Sasha as much as I am able. Even though I disappeared from Canada at 26 (but really at 19 from my parent's home) without many encounters since, they are still my precious parents who raised me and gave me the drive to learn and to commit myself to excel.

I have had the chance through cooking to travel across the world and establish myself in this incredible country. I love Australia for the chance it gave me to grow and to start a new life. The fact that I was able to contribute to the search for better produce in Australia makes me happy and proud. Educating young chefs and other young employees is my chance to give back something to this country, by showing integrity and dedication and leading by example.

The past has been extremely fulfilling for me but there is still a need for me to continue striving to create one of the better eating places in Sydney. I do not wish to be elitist; I just wish to make people happy and proud to see what we can offer in Australia. I receive as much enjoyment seeing families in the café coming again and again as I derive from seeing a full restaurant. I will always remember my first meals in some of the great restaurants in California, France and Italy and if I can reproduce any of the magic of these amazing places I would be more than fulfilled.

One of the great advantages I have is that I have a business large enough to occupy me and I do not have to search for other projects. There is enough work to keep me and my team focused and busy as there is always plenty more to do to ensure you can survive for another year by making your customers return. A restaurant is a very complex business to operate: the margins are very low and the seasonality of the turnover is often crippling. Only by being there and finetuning your operation can you achieve consistent returns. It is a very labour-intensive business that operates seven days a week, nearly 24 hours a day (if you count the late cleaners and the early baking shift). To understand and manage this complex business as well as being creative, motivated, happy and fresh looking requires a healthy and positive disposition. Your staff look up to you to motivate them and your customers will always glance to see if you are there, even if it is Sunday night or Monday lunch.

These days your revenue mostly comes from the pockets of food lovers, rather than from corporate generosity. In order to survive you need to constantly adjust your prices, products, menus and offerings. You need to create wine dinners, classes, book launches, lectures, special menus and search for any business you can find. It is important to remain dynamic and focused and never lose sight of the reason people come to our restaurants: for the good food.

I am not only blessed to have made my home in Australia, but I am also blessed to have had the chance to design a great restaurant in one of the most stunning locations in Sydney. I love the vibrancy of the café, I love the complexity of the restaurant, I love talking to my customers and I feel duly bound by my staff. It would by easy to get complacent and hope for the best, but in reality I know that for all the glamour side of being a owner-chef there is a very real side of performing for a public who seek great food, staff who need guidance and the business aspect that needs to be carefully nurtured.

Tomorrow will bring new challenges, more planning, guiding, working and satisfying our clientele, but I will do this in the sure knowledge that I have the support of my family, my staff and my customers. My role is to ensure we are truthful to them and their needs and maybe along the way we can create some magic for them all.

INDEX